Towards
The
Third
Modernity

How ordinary people are transforming the world

Alain de Vulpian
Translated by Matthew Carey

Foreword by Arie de Geus

Published by:
Triarchy Press
Station Offices
Axminster
Devon. EX13 5PF
United Kingdom

+44 (0)1297 631456
info@triarchypress.com
www.triarchypress.com

A catalogue record for this book is available from the British Library.

Translated by Matthew Carey -
matthew@westhay.com

Cover design and image by Heather Fallows -
www.whitespacegallery.org.uk

ISBN: 978-0-9550081-9-1

Contents

Preface
By Arie de Geus

v

Foreword
By Rosie Beckham

xi

Chapter 1
Understanding the evolving modernity

1

Chapter 2
The 20th Century's First Modernity

12

Chapter 3
A crucial decade: the threshold between the First and Second
Modernities (1965-1975)

40

Chapter 4
People in touch with their vitality

65

Chapter 5
Smart people looking for meaning

85

Chapter 6
An organic social fabric emerges

108

Chapter 7
Dreams of peace and the threat of violence

142

Chapter 8
Business faces up to mutations in society

175

Chapter 9
Hopes for smarter societal governance

198

Chapter 10
Planetary governance tries to find its way

221

people, nurturing us with a re-empowering and re-politicising potential. Moreover, he has the authority to assert this through the encyclopaedic Cofremca/Sociovision archive of information – which allows him, perhaps more than most, to identify patterns of change that have emerged over their nearly 60 years of research. In short, Vulpian's is a monumental labour undertaken with wisdom, compassion, humour and abundant enthusiasm by a modern-day sociological Hercules.

Rosie Beckham
April 2008

Chapter 1
Understanding the evolving modernity

For our clients in 1954, the world was changing fast and we needed to help them make sense of it. Most of those who came to us had, like us, the sense that a spectacular kind of modernisation was under way. We had to try and uncover and help them understand the trends that could make a new product a success, that could reawaken a dormant market or lead to the collapse of a flourishing one, that could see the rapid growth or sudden decline of a particular brand, and that could see new forms of organisation take off or be ignored. Likewise, we had to uncover the hidden strengths that a region could draw on in the quest for modernisation and the trump cards that a politician could play in order to get elected.

To do this we had to develop and use new investigative and analytical tools. Ones which would enable us to understand what was going on and allow our clients to act in ways that would help to steer things towards a more desirable outcome.

In the middle of the 20ᵗʰ century the social sciences in France were of little help to us. We drew our inspiration from Alexis de Tocqueville and Max Weber, but their methodological individualism was not much in favour in Paris at the time and systems thinking was not yet fashionable. Economics and sociology were supposed to develop general laws based on fixed correlations and supposed relationships of cause and effect between macro variables. With Marxism and psychoanalysis all the rage, ideas like the class struggle and the Oedipus complex were used to try and explain history, economics and society as a whole. But we didn't find anything there to help us answer our clients' questions.

Naturally enough, then, we turned to anthropology and, particularly, to ethnology, which was then in the ascendant in France. But its field research tools were of little help. At the time, ethnologists saw the 'primitive' societies that they were studying in Africa, Asia and South America as societies without a history. They wanted to understand the structure and identity of a people or a culture – not the ways in which they were changing (especially when change was so often caused by contact with the West and was therefore seen as synonymous with destruction). But, for us, it was precisely the question of change that was most interesting.

Then we came across David Riesman[1]. He confirmed much of our thinking and opened up new avenues for us. In *The Lonely Crowd* he analysed the changes that were taking place in American society and the ways in which these changes emerged from changes in people's daily life. Most notably, he demonstrated the very strong links between individual characteristics (drives, shared values, etc.) and broader forms of society and social control. He also showed how these two phenomena mutually shaped each other.

In *Faces in the Crowd*, Riesman published a number of the interviews which had led him to build his model and which illustrated the main socio-cultural types that he had identified in the US population.

Riesman confirmed our convictions and intuitions: to understand social and cultural change, we had to go 'into the field' to observe and interview people. Many individuals, all acting for themselves alone, driven by personal motivations which might be clear or hidden, rational or irrational, produce, both cumulatively and by their interaction, kinds of social, cultural, economic, political and organisational phenomena that interested us. But these individual actions form part of a larger web of interactions in the physical, social and economic environment and cannot be understood except as a part of this web. The whole influences the parts and vice versa. So, in our turn, we had to go and investigate not only *individuals* but also the *sociosystems* in which they were imbricated, in order to build for ourselves an ethnology of change in modern societies.

In many respects, these societies are organisms or living tissues and, therefore, extremely complex. To understand the trends and currents at work in these complex, living societies we would have to develop a kind of microsystemic social biology.

So it was that we began to talk of a sociological microscope, by which we meant a new tool that would give us a more focused and accurate view and allow us to uncover aspects of people's reality not previously seen.

However, in the 1950s and '60s it was difficult to uncover the real sensations, emotions and intentions which lead us to take a particular course of action. To underline their semi-conscious but decisive nature, and to encompass the distinct notions of motivations, drives, needs, stances, values and desires, we

---

1   Riesman D, Denney R & Glazer N. *The Lonely Crowd: A Study of the Changing American Character.* New Haven, CT: Yale Univ. Press, 1950. And Riesman D. *Faces in the Crowd: Individual Studies in Character and Politics.* New Haven: Yale Univ. Press, 1952.

called them 'tropisms', using a term that is generally applied to those forces that govern the movement of plants: that which tends to encourage a living organism to move in a certain direction.

For example, asking the question 'Why did you do that?' seldom elicits any useful information. The answer tends to sound like an *a posteriori* justification and to make reference to particular social stereotypes. In many interviews, we saw exactly these rationalisations and justifications that say little about real motives. In 1954, for example, Air France believed that people's fear of being involved in a plane crash was a major obstacle to the growth of air travel. They asked us to do some research to help them understand how to overcome this obstacle. The sociological microscope showed that the company was mistaken. Travellers did indeed use their fear of being in a plane crash to justify their use of other forms of transport but, when pushed, the real emotion that held them back proved to be nervousness in the face of something too new, too modern; a form of transport reserved for film stars and politicians; a form of transport that they were afraid they didn't know how to use properly.

In the vast majority of cases, the real motor force was this timidity in the face of the technical, social and cultural strangeness of air travel. And, of course, the actions that Air France needed to take to counteract this sort of nervousness were entirely different from those they would have need to take to reassure customers afraid of dying in a plane crash.

Discoveries of this sort were not unusual. In the 1950s and '60s, most of the people we interviewed were scarcely aware of the underlying feelings and motivations that led them to act in a certain way. After the event, they would tend to construct a rational explanation that paid little regard to these underlying motivations. Not that these tropisms were 'unconscious' in a psychoanalytical sense: rather, people simply didn't bother to notice or describe them unless encouraged to do so by the new interviewing techniques that we had developed. And the ability to decode, or help to decode, these intentions and motivations is a natural human capacity. Some people are naturally more closely attuned to others and have a sharper empathy in such matters and it is this capacity that the sociological microscope has to try and replicate in the artificial situation of an interview.

In this respect, David Riesman's approach seemed a little too directive and a little too close to 'closed questioning' for us. But we were helped by our awareness of the work of Kurt Lewin, Robert K. Merton and Carl Rogers.

One of Lewin's major contributions as a Gestalt psychologist and sociologist was that of the in-depth interview used to support and complement the empathy of the interviewer.

For Rogers[2], the father of non-directive, client-centred therapy, the crucial thing was to understand the whole person and help clients to the same awareness and understanding of themselves, independently of any psychological theory and independently of any interpretation by the therapist. From him we learnt the need for our interviewers to assume the role of neutral, welcoming, accepting confidant and to reflect back what they heard, understood and experienced in the interview. The interviewer should attempt neither to interrogate, interpret nor judge. Interviewees would, in this way, be encouraged to explore their feelings and mental processes more deeply.

From Merton we learnt a skill that could be called 'retrospection'. We had found that, even when someone had not been fully conscious at the time of what had motivated a change in their characteristic behaviour or way of life, those motivations still left traces in the individual memory. While those traces were not normally accessible in normal life, it was possible to reawaken them. In this respect, Merton gave us the idea of developing an approach to interviewing that he called 'retrospective'. So, we found that we could help interviewees to relive a situation or moment and in that way to recall images, dreams and ideas that had been present for them at the time.

Projective methods of personality assessment were also an important source of inspiration for us. Here the researcher would show the subject pictures of confusing or ambiguous scenes and invite the subject to say what was going on and to speculate about what had been happening immediately before and what might be going to happen next.

Drawing on ideas like these, the sociological microscope gradually emerged during 1954 and 1955. Using a tape-recorder was an important step forwards for us, as it gave interviewers the chance to listen again, sometimes with the interviewee present, to explore the significance of what was said in more depth and to improve their interviewing skills and technique.

We were on the right road. The sociological microscope gave us a way of understanding people and their sociosystems. Take the example of air travel already mentioned. In our research for Air France we interviewed Mr X, one of the company's many potential customers who was reluctant to fly not because he was afraid of an accident but because of a general anxiety about

---

2   Rogers C. R. *Client-Centered Therapy*. Boston, MA: Houghton-Mifflin, 1951.

what it would be like, how he should behave and so on. Mr Z, however, flew regularly and enjoyed the sense of belonging to the happy elite that took the plane regularly. In French society at the time, we saw men like these often enough to be able to discern two distinct social types. Each type shared motivations and a picture of travel and society as a whole that were self-sustaining. The more Mr Z flew, the more his experience of air travel and his sense of belonging to a special elite was reinforced. The more Mr X *did not* fly, the more he felt excluded from that special elite. Air France further reinforced both these positions, giving its passengers champagne and caviar and constantly building an elitist impression of air travel in the way it communicated with customers and potential customers. Furthermore, Air France pilots and cabin crew enjoyed the glamorous lifestyle and enjoyed being seen to be part of this new elite. Apparently, then, the stability and equilibrium of this system was guaranteed by Air France's approach to air travel and to its passengers.

Looking more closely, however, we could also see that this system was not so stable and fixed after all. It was susceptible to change: change that would happen anyway 'naturally' and that would move things in a particular direction. For example, if one day Mr X was forced to go to New York urgently on business and didn't have time to go by sea, then he would fly. He would be charmed and flattered by the experience and would want to repeat it. Thus, Mr Z's type grew in number. And by interviewing Mr X it became clear how this kind of change could be accelerated and what Air France could do to encourage this change.

This example shows how the process of change operates at three levels of social reality. First, at a micro level, we can see what affects the choices and decisions made by Mr X and Mr Z and what might lead them to act differently. At a macro level, we can see how Air France's advertising and the behaviour of its staff have an influence on the development of air transport. Finally, at a mega level, we can see that business life is changing, that people are more often in more of a hurry and that this will affect decisions about many things, including air travel. We train our microscope on individuals, but it gives us information about social interactions, about social groupings, about organisations and about society at large.

In this same example, we can also see that the approach can be looked at in terms of *systems*, *scenarios* and *strategy*. It describes society and social developments in terms of systems and processes. It allows us to consider different possible future scenarios for the future of the system. And it allows social actors (businesses, governments and others) to evaluate strategic options open to them for shaping change.

Detection and analysis of socio-cultural currents

During the 1950s and '60s it became increasingly clear that at the heart of the changes we were seeing (for example in the take-up of air travel) lay a transformative change in the motor forces that led people to act or behave in a particular way (their tropisms). Thus, in the process that was leading towards increased air travel, one decisive change was that a sense of timidity in the face of modernity was being replaced by a desire for modernity and a desire for the prestige that came with being seen to be modern. We saw new tropisms like this emerging in many areas. And they affected different age groups and different social groups in different ways.

We saw the same kind of phenomenon in Sweden and David Riesman and his collaborators made similar observations in North America. Drives, desires, emotions, ways of thinking, attitudes and personality traits were all changing in similar ways and in similar directions. These changes I call 'socio-cultural currents'. They don't necessarily include changes of opinion nor even some changes in values. Rather, socio-cultural currents refer to lasting changes in ways of thinking and mental models which lead people to act differently and lead whole populations to change their behaviour. They aren't fluctuations or fashions but slow and steady currents, representing the diffusion of a particular tropism through a population. Our observations showed that many of them would affect an additional 1-3% of the population each year (and so, around a quarter of the population over a period of ten to fifteen years).

During the 1950s, we tended to come across these socio-cultural currents without particularly looking for them and we didn't always try to describe them systematically. But after several years, and after seeing how useful the information could be to our clients, we began to research and record them systematically. Between 1968 and 1972 we conducted an in-depth analysis of most of the data from our sociological microscope over the previous 25 years. This analysis highlighted the main changes to the tropisms that we observed operating in the French population. By 1972 we had, accordingly, identified and analysed 28 socio-cultural currents. By combining the data from our sociological microscope and systematic observation of changes in people's behaviour and way of life (weak signals of changes that were under way), we could shed light on the upstream and downstream systems at work in each case. By upstream system I mean the whole web of entangled connections that lead to the spread of a given tropism: exploring this upstream system helps us to back up our intuitions about how this socio-cultural current is likely to develop. The downstream system relates to the cascade of changes that this new tropism is bringing about in social structures and in people's ways of life and ways of thinking; understanding these changes brings with it the seeds of many timely innovations.

At the same time we set about the laborious task of creating a battery of questions and tests which we put to a representative sample of the population each year. This allowed us to score each interviewee on each separate socio-cultural current and to undertake a whole range of statistical analyses.

By combining the sociological microscope, our observations of weak signals and the results of quantitative surveys using polls, we were able to develop a system of (upstream) observation and diagnosis and (downstream) anticipation and prognosis. Using this system, we were able to advise our clients on the wisest course of action at times of rapid change. We presented this new system to the business community in 1972 and 1973 under the name 3SC (Système Cofremca de Suivi des Courants Socio-Culturels). Among the first subscribers to this service were L'Oréal, Royal Dutch Shell, Nestlé, Carrefour, Electricité de France, l'ORTF (national radio et television), Renault and Fiat.

A service monitoring socio-cultural change, using more quantitative measures but with similar roots, was begun at the same time in the USA by another pioneer, Daniel Yankelovich. Other observatories of change, inspired by 3SC or the Yankelovich Monitor, were established in the main countries of Western and Northern Europe, Canada, Brazil, Argentina and Japan during the 1970s. Most of these groups would meet at an annual seminar to share and compare their discoveries. The results of all this research provide the raw material on which the analysis and conclusions of this book are based.

Understanding the modernising process

Since 1996 I have been able to stand back and take a broader view of our research, as well as re-examining many of its components in detail and comparing our results with those of our international collaborators. My conclusion is that we are being carried along by a 'civilising process' about which our research can tell us a great deal.

I have borrowed the term from the German sociologist Norbert Elias[3]. Plotting the path that has led Europe from feudalism to the sovereign state, unravelling the complex interactions between institutions, individuals, customary ways, the church, the market, different social classes and much

---

[3]   Elias N. *Über den Prozess der Zivilisation.* Basel: Haus zum Falken, 1939.

more besides, he shows us that the resulting transformations have emerged out of an extraordinarily complex process that nobody actively sought or guided.

A similar process has been at work throughout the 20th century in the West. A living system of connections and interconnections is transforming Western people, their society, economy, culture and institutions. Our observations help us to understand how changes in people's individual tropisms combine to bring about changes in the social fabric (and how these larger changes in turn reinforce changes at an individual level). They help us to understand how individual and social-level changes have led us to choose particular technical and technological innovations and how they, in turn, have reinforced changes at an individual and a social level. They help us understand how some powerful social actors (states, political parties, businesses) resist change, whilst others embrace it.

No-one is directing this system of connections and interconnections. Those who are involved have no clear idea of the effect of their actions on the system as a whole and even the most powerful social actors can at most only temporarily deflect a process which will eventually bypass them or carry them with it.

Our observations reveal dynamics: that is to say systems that are moving in a particular direction. These dynamics are powerful and impose themselves upon us, but they are also fragile and can change direction or even go into reverse. So the civilising process is not predetermined and its direction can easily change. It is not impossible, if we understand the process and its mechanisms well enough, to influence its course and direction, and we can use our understanding of it to anticipate possible future scenarios.

What we found conformed very precisely to the model that emerged from the work of Nobel Prize winner Ilya Prigogine on dissipative systems. This model showed that, unlike relatively stable systems (for example, a solar system), dissipative systems do not follow a predictable course as they develop. Their process of development is characterised by:

- Shaping trends whose course it is extremely difficult to alter, even by applying enormous force.

- Sharp changes of direction: when one of these systems has reached a certain point, an apparently minor fluctuation, a microscopic force or action (Edwards Lorenz gives the example of a butterfly flapping its wings) can have a macroscopic effect as it steers the system in a new direction'

The First and Second Modernities

The civilising process that has stretched from the early 20th century to the present day, serves to modernise us. So let us call it a modernising process.

We often use the terms modern and post-modern to describe the periods before and after the 1960s and to indicate that a radical break with the past took place then. But, as I argue in this book, rather than a radical break with the past there was a change of direction characterised by an underlying continuity. So it seems to me more helpful to use different terms. For that reason, I call the first phase of the process of modernisation (which had its beginnings in the late 19th century and blossomed after the Second World War into the society of mass consumption), the First Modernity. The next stage, whose first signs were visible in the late 1960s and which we are still immersed in, I call the Second Modernity. And we will leave room for a Third Modernity yet to come.

Slowly and steadily, over the course of the last hundred years or so – and not without set-backs – ordinary people in search of happiness and personal pleasure have emancipated themselves and looked for self-fulfillment. It has been an irresistible process: emancipation from authority, traditional morality and social norms; the loss of the authority of the father over his child, of the husband over his wife, of the boss over his employees, of men over women, of the old over the young. These tropisms – happiness, emancipation and achieving better conditions – which had already begun before the opening of the 20th century in certain precursor sectors, then imposed themselves on a growing proportion of the population, which became the majority after the Second World War.

For the first seventy years or so of the 20th century (the First Modernity), more and more men and women in the West fought to free themselves from a morality of duty and sacrifice, to escape suffering of the worst sort and the heavy hand of traditional authority, and to move upwards in society. They were encouraged to exercise self-regulation and self-control so that they would remain pliable. And the kind of individuals they turned into tended to be rational, intellectualising and cold. In this way, they achieved a certain freedom. But cut loose from their roots and their ancestral ties and wisdom, better able to read than to navigate their lives effectively, these individuals remained strangers to themselves and looked for buoys to moor against. They were still far from autonomous and readily manipulated. These were the members of the First Modernity who would be taken in hand by governments, political parties and big business and who would play their part in the establishment of a mass society into which they would be completely absorbed.

Nevertheless, they would push their quest still further over the next thirty or forty years (the period of the Second Modernity). They freed themselves from repression and shame. They got more closely in touch with their physical sensations, with their emotions and drives and with their empathy whilst, at the same time, developing their capacity for rational thinking and analysis. But their rational selves were no longer in conversation with other rational beings, nor with books and ideas. Instead, they were in conversation with their intimate selves and with those of other, like-minded people. Thus, groping their way blindly and often painfully, many of them would have their first experience of autonomy and would manage to fashion for themselves the kinds of pleasure and forms of happiness that really suited them. They would become more complete people, full of vitality and much more capable than their predecessors of navigating their lives wisely and giving them meaning.

Contrary to a belief widely-held at the time, society was not falling apart. Using new communication technologies, these people would build the relationships that they wanted with one another, and would create a flourishing mass of informal, non-hierarchical networks and sociosystems which would come to life, self-organise and transform the very fabric of society. And so, an extremely convoluted and complex organic society took the place of mass society.

These more complete people, these smart and pragmatic strategists lost their susceptibility to the old order and could no longer be easily manipulated. This living and largely self-regulating social fabric was very resistant to the old order's coercive power. New ways of running things have emerged in families, in start-up businesses, in some associations and networks, in some local authorities and in some areas of big business. But most old-style corporations, states and institutions have found it difficult to shed their hierarchical, bureaucratic and technocratic tendencies. As a result, a deep divide has opened up between the leaders of society on the one hand and the society of ordinary people on the other. This divide is, without doubt, one of the principal characteristics of the Second Modernity.

Stresses, discomforts and dysfunctions appear as a result. But these are not the signs of an inevitable decline and fall. Rather, they are the symptoms of a society painfully and dangerously in labour. We will see that the civilising process currently under way could give birth, in the next few decades, to a Western – and perhaps global – society, a Third Modernity characterised by hedonism, humanism and harmony. This is the optimistic scenario. But if a wiser system of governance does not manage to emerge at the level of big business, the state and across the whole planet, we run the risk of wasting this opportunity for progress, falling back into our old warlike ways and becoming once again a tense, divided and violent society. In short, the modernising process puts at our disposal levers of change that mean our dream of avoiding this catastrophic scenario is not wholly unrealistic.

In a small number of 'precursor' countries (the USA, Sweden, France and the UK), the progression from First to Second Modernity was very clear. They clearly entered the Second Modernity from the mid-1960s onwards. Elsewhere, things were less clear. Others, like Canada, began late but caught up fast[4]. In Germany, Italy and Spain (countries emerging from post-war reconstruction or fascism), a process of change that had taken forty years in the precursor countries was completed in half the time. And in countries like Russia, China, Taiwan, South Korea and India, which came only in the 1990s to the First and Second Modernities, the two are intricately intertwined.

---

4   See Adams M. *Sex in the Snow - Canadian Social Values at the end of the Millennium.* Toronto: Viking, 1997.

Chapter 2
The 20th Century's First Modernity

The earliest sightings of what we think of as the 'modern world' came in the late 19th and early 20th century. It was to be seen in Vienna. It was there in Paris, with its avant-garde artists, its dressy shop windows, posters, cinema and new fashions that were beginning to transform the lives of French women. London had its sport, suffragettes and international finance. In the USA, Taylorism, Fordism and the new, rational approach to the organisation of business and marketing heralded the arrival of modernity. Here, too, it was characterised by the growth of advertising, political propaganda and organised party politics. It was to be seen in Moscow, with the October Revolution, and in Rome, with the rise of fascism. Later, Sweden and the United States were the first to create a welfare state, followed, after the Second World War, by Great Britain and France.

So the United States, France, Great Britain and Sweden were in the vanguard of this First Modernity. That France got there so early, and modernised with such verve, is doubtless the result of particular historical circumstances. It was the first Western country to experience in the late 18th century that gradual loss of Christian faith, which would later sweep across the whole of Europe. A hundred years before any other country, birth control was widely used in France and with it came the 'discovery' that sex can be for pleasure and not just for reproduction. France and the United States both promulgated the concept of human rights. Then, with its talent for innovation and its industrial clout, the United States led the move towards a society based on mass production and mass consumption. Sweden, though late, was completely de-Christianised by 1900 and, as early as 1930, had managed to eliminate the twin spectres of poverty and insecurity as the Social Democrats rose to power. As its population found itself free to think of other things besides God and day-to-day survival, they became the first people in Europe to banish sexual taboos from their everyday life. After the Second World War, the Swedes and then the French followed the Americans in their relentless pursuit of well-being and bulimic consumption, while Britain and Germany languished in post-war economic deprivation and the Latin countries found themselves neither culturally nor politically ready to join the modern world.

The West hesitated in the face of several different scenarios. For a start, should the state be democratic or dictatorial? The idea of a mass society that was not only hierarchical, but also dictatorial and totalitarian, gave rise to two distinct political approaches: communism and fascism. The struggles between and within these two ideologies led to purges, the gulags, the Holocaust and the Second World War. Ultimately, both ideologies failed. The other great choice lay between two different economic systems: should the economy be regulated by the market or planned and centrally controlled by the state? The advocates of the latter were eventually to be confined to various national communist parties and progressively lost the influence they once had.

Overall, if we leave aside the question of the West's handling of its colonial legacy, these developments brought us thirty years of peace and democracy after the Second World War. Economic growth was truly remarkable: the spectacular rise in living standards was both a product of the process of modernisation and one of its driving forces. The achievement of any kind of social balance was in some ways surprising, as societies composed of previously mistrustful and hostile social groups gave way to a vast middle class, stratified only by different levels of wealth. These social shifts brought with them some astonishing changes in outlook. Western Europe and North America saw the emergence of mass, hierarchical societies which, unlike in communist and fascist states, were individualistic, democratic and regulated by the market and consumption. Paradoxically, this sort of society increased individual freedom, whilst at the same time strengthening the power of the state and of big business.

But this form of society could not last and was to be superseded by a Second Modernity.

The Slow and Painful Struggle for Emancipation

After the Second World War, freedom really began to flourish, with two motivators being particularly prominent: the search for personal happiness and the tropism of social advancement.

The search for personal happiness

At the start of the 20th century, a few groups of precursors broke with the prevailing morality (which can be summed up as one of suffering and sacrifice), and instead sought to place freedom and happiness above social and moral strictures. They rejected authority, the constraints of convention and the most restrictive taboos, and lived out the underlying current of *hedonism*. Initially, this current made only a few waves in wider society, but from 1945 it exploded onto the scene in North America and the more privileged European countries, and from the 1960s swept the rest of modern Europe. Most people were affected. This new hedonism constituted a kind of cultural revolution that transformed people's attitudes, habits and the whole way that society worked. This was particularly apparent in people's family life and in their sexual behaviour, as well as in their approach to work and consumption; it also made room for mass leisure activities.

As the prevailing ideology of duty began to fade, so suffering and sacrifice, once thought to be positive attributes, lost their primacy. People struggled to free themselves from the authority figures they found most restrictive: fathers, husbands, bosses and so on. They did so, however, without fundamentally calling them into question.

Most of the interviews conducted by Cofremca during the 1950s and '60s showed that people were less concerned with where they were heading than with what they were breaking away from. When they felt a positive sense of direction, this often boiled down to little more than abstract, impossible dreams. Later on, however, in the Second Modernity, they took on a more positive and concrete form.

A more open sexuality. The calling into question of sexual taboos characterised the whole of the First Modernity. There was, very obviously, a strong current of early sexual liberalism, which spread at different speeds in different countries. More than anything else, it acted as a barometer of social trends in general. Being, or at least trying to be, sexually liberated was the surest sign of one's modernity.

Debate about sex and sexuality was increasingly present in conversation, the cinema, in magazines and literature, but also in the daily lives of those we interviewed. Enforced chastity became a source of increasing resentment as people began to feel that it was solely based on outmoded social conventions. But guilt didn't feel good either. Whether to take the plunge became an important question. 'Should I be open about it?' 'What will my parents think?' In France, the confessional, which allows for absolution of one's sexual peccadilloes, was often the starting point for a process of soul-searching that sometimes led to a definitive break with the church. Young French girls, who tended to be more influenced by the church and by wider social norms than their Swedish peers, generally lost their virginity later.

However, although Love became an important and valued concept, and a love marriage something one would wish for one's children, until the 1960s, sex outside marriage was still frowned upon in most countries. Advances in sexual freedom were largely covert.

During the 1950s, girls' virginity and wives' fidelity remained important values for most social groups in Great Britain, Italy and America. For the urban working class in France – already somewhat distanced from traditional morality – having a child outside marriage was just one of those unfortunate things. Cohabitation, which did occasionally happen, was generally forgiven: 'so long as they love each other'.

The two countries that led the way in sexual matters were France, with its open discussion of sexuality, and Sweden, with its open practice. From the 1920s and '30s onwards, the French began to feel that they could talk about sexuality in books, images, films and general conversation. France welcomed a wave of explicit Anglo-Saxon literature – decried at the time as pornographic – from the likes of James Joyce, D.H. Lawrence and Gertrude Stein. In the 1950s, the Anglo-Saxon world was still in thrall to official prudishness, whereas France remained an exception, a haven that defied the prevailing morality. Henry Miller, for example, who was censured and censored in his own country, was welcomed in France, where he achieved international fame. At the same time, a growing number of ordinary French people learnt to appreciate or tolerate writing or images that referred to sexuality. Attempts to censor or suppress them came to seem more and more ridiculous.

In Sweden, more than anywhere else, sexual freedom swiftly became a practical reality. The general population's ideas of sexual morality changed radically. As early as 1932, surveys showed that a majority of the population thought it was unreasonable to expect a girl to be a virgin when she married, though this tendency was more marked among the young and among city-dwellers. Elsewhere in the West, it wasn't until the 1960s that demographic statistics showed a similar change in sexual mores.

It seems very likely that sexual behaviour grew richer and more varied throughout the period of the First Modernity. Guilt and the fear of hell and damnation slowly faded. Better contraception meant less recourse to coitus interruptus and sexual practice could relax and flourish. Sexual partners could turn their attention to each other's bodily sensations, feelings and emotions during sex. Perhaps women also began to make their presence felt. For instance, in 1972 Marvin Sussman[5] observed that increased sexual refinement within relationships was linked to improvements in the status of women, to a decline in male dominance and to a decreasing tendency for the woman to sacrifice herself.

At the same time, in the 1960s, contemporary magazines sought to teach their female readers to expect to have an orgasm during sex. In France, interviews showed how the old relationship between people's professed values and their behaviour in practice had been up-ended. In the traditional model, when people got up to more than was thought to be normal or acceptable, they felt guilty for being over-sexualised. Now, a countervailing model took root: to some extent, people felt anxious or guilty because they weren't doing enough to be normal. Young girls felt bad about still being virgins. For young and supposedly liberated 1960s women (readers of *Elle*, for instance), sexual pleasure had become the norm. Orgasms were a must. Women who couldn't have one were thought to be deficient in some way.

A warm and loving household. One myth to emerge during the First Modernity, and one which soon took hold amongst the population at large, was that of the ideal relationship where one's partner simultaneously meets one's emotional, erotic and companionship needs. The love marriage in this sense soon became a central myth in societies that were still fairly prudish, both in public and in private. It offered a kind of compromise with conventional morality, one that allowed the modern approach to hedonism to enter people's sex lives – even in the most apparently inflexible countries and social circles.

The mass media also held up to young people the idea of the love marriage as an ideal arrangement: love one another, set up a happy and long-lasting household and work on your love life – but be sure to do all that within the bounds of marriage for life.

In 1959, the American sociologist, Jesse R. Pitts, noted that the French – even the aristocracy and the haute bourgeoisie – had caught up with the Americans insofar as love marriages were concerned. Even if the young lovers' parents did *not* approve, there was little they could do now that young women could go and find work in an advertising agency and get by without financial support from their parents.

Our research showed, however, that parents had another good reason to give way. They had begun to care deeply about maintaining the warm and loving

---

5   Sussman M.B. 'Family, Kinship and Bureaucracy' in *The Human Meaning of Social Change*, eds. Campbell A. & Converse P.E., New York: Russell Sage Foundation, 1972.

relationships that they had developed with their children. Hedonism had also spread into the parent-child relationship. Children discovered that they could derive pleasure and happiness from this relationship and from the warmth and affection that came with it. They too sought to maintain it. Patterns of authority in families were thus challenged – and only gently enforced so as not to jeopardise the newly established emotional warmth. The most contested form of authority was that of the father over his daughter, and the most common battleground was over 'loose behaviour' – girls wanted to go out when and with whom they pleased. Between the wars, many girls did indeed carve out a certain room for manoeuvre. Young middle and upper-middle class girls could go out in the evening without being chaperoned and if they did overstep the mark, sexually speaking, then what mattered was to keep it quiet.

And so the household became one filled with emotional warmth: affection, tenderness and erotic feelings. It was a household whose cohesion grew out of (hopefully) lasting emotional ties, and whose stability was ensured by social and moral conventions (although only with difficulty and only until the late 1960s).

This household was also becoming a centre for consumption. Relationships ran more smoothly if the family was well off and able to ensure a good level of material comfort for its members. Ideally, the husband brought home an ever-larger salary and the wife took care of everyday household matters. Together they decided what to buy and managed emotional affairs. The better-off sections of the population had discovered domestic appliances in the 1920s and '30s and, as the use of domestic servants decreased, the advent of modern conveniences made housework easier to manage.

In both middle-class and working-class families, the woman often assumed many different roles. As both a mother and a wife, she gave love and affection and received it in return. She wanted to be both a good housewife and a modern pleasure-seeker. This gave rise to inevitable conflicts. For most women, these continued until the late 1960s, although the burden tended to ease as resistance to pre-packaged food and labour-saving household appliances gradually weakened across the West.

Shopping becomes a matter of taste and personal choice. The explosion of consumer demand and its systematic stimulation were among the key innovations of the First Modernity. The new Hedonists were driven to consume, as personal preferences, tastes and desires replaced tradition and habit in determining their choices.

In the late 19th century, Paris had effectively invented the shop-window display and window-shopping. But few people were sufficiently aware or affluent enough to follow through on their budding consumer desires. By the late 1940s and early '50s, however, even the working classes were developing a sense of security and confidence about the future. Most European and North American employees interviewed in the 1950s had lost their visceral anxiety about the future. They felt their jobs were pretty much guaranteed, that their salaries would rise and that their children would have a better life than they had had.

As long-standing suffering and insecurity began to fade, people could now pursue pleasure and happiness. Once post-war restrictions were lifted and the reconstruction effort had eased off, shop-windows and advertising began to tickle people's desire to consume. The United States, France, Sweden and Switzerland led the way. More and more people felt that they had the right to hanker after good fruit and vegetables, ready-made meals, a refrigerator and a car, and they were prepared to work longer hours to pay for them.

Alongside this growing consumer demand came a new desire to indulge personal tastes and preferences. From the 1950s onwards, many interviewees mentioned their personal tastes: 'I like this, but not that' food, decorative object, item of clothing or car. In fact, preferences were often negative. They didn't like such and such a car or style of clothing. The problem was often one of how (in the face of parental opinion, convention, habits and logic) to avoid doing things one didn't want to do. Where preferences were positive – 'I like this and I want it' – tastes were often still conventional and collective. In France, for instance, a growing proportion of housewives said they wanted to cook varied and innovative meals using magazine recipes. But they complained that their husbands and children were unreceptive to innovation. They only wanted steak and chips.

Less work and more security. Harsh working conditions and fear of what the future might bring were not new problems, but in the 1920s and '30s they were still the main ones for most agricultural labourers and manual workers.

Fear of losing your job (and your daily bread), especially when there is no welfare safety net, can provoke intense and overwhelming anxiety. This anxiety was still apparent in many of the interviews we conducted in the 1950s, even though a more optimistic attitude had begun to prevail. In such a context, it is not surprising that improvements in job security (along with a better quality of life) became one of the principal demands of the working classes.

And work really did remain stressful and physically demanding: for agricultural labourers; for working-class women who, as well as holding down a full-time job, had to keep house, cook on wood-fired stoves and lift heavy loads. In 1930, working class jobs were back-breaking, with long days and working weeks, no paid holidays, often hellish working conditions and new 'scientific' production lines, which frequently led to boredom, fatigue and mental problems. In the run up to the Second World War, the working classes in many countries fought for and won substantial improvements: a shorter working week and paid holidays.

Amongst the working class, the growing hedonist appetite for happiness, leisure and luxury goods was a major factor in the transformation of their lives. But it was often concealed behind the overall push for workers' rights. Workers interviewed in the 1950s often mentioned the achievement of a 40-hour working week, paid holidays and the creation of social security as major victories in their own right. Their behaviour often seemed more militant than hedonistic. It was only if the interview was drawn out and tackled issues in greater depth, that the researcher could see the massive improvements in well-being that such advances brought.

It is important to emphasise that in most of Europe and North America, this well-being didn't come from changes in the actual work performed, but from better job security and from having more free time. For a few decades longer, work and well-being would still belong to different, ideologically separate worlds. Once again a precursor, Sweden was the only country in which as early as the 1950s our researchers found explicit, widespread worker demands for improvements in the quality of working life (rather than a simple focus on pay and hours), as well as considerable thought given to the matter by companies, consultants and academics.

For most European and North American agricultural and manual workers, work still had an almost sacred quality to it and the old ideology of hard physical labour remained so firmly entrenched that it hid the growth of hedonism from view. Some individuals even vaunted their poor working conditions. This ideology of hard work (no pain, no gain) was particularly tenacious in North American culture where, at the end of the 20th century, the work ethic was still in the ascendant, even though it was moribund in the rest of the Western world.

Leisure. Even before 1914, English gentlemen had discovered sport and the attractions of the Côte d'Azur. A small group of free-thinking artists and intellectuals were pioneers here. The Années Folles invented future mass leisure activities like jazz, fast cars and the cinema. Well-heeled Parisians went to Deauville. Seaside holidays replaced long summer holidays in the country. The upper-middle classes discovered the summer sun.

During the 1930s, popular culture took root in the United States, France, Germany and England. It spread to the middle and working classes, who developed a taste for pleasure, travel and entertainment that was already to be seen in the upper-middle classes. Magazines appeared with a mass, often female, readership, advertisements sold cheap dreams, the cinema, the music-hall, radio, gramophone records, detective and romance novels... Sport spread beyond the upper-middle classes and became a sort of spectacle (boxing and football matches, the Tour de France) perfectly suited to this new, popular culture.

After the Second World War, the demand for entertainment and leisure activities grew further, stimulated by the development of three pre-war inventions: the car, television and holidays. The state didn't have to make great efforts to fill people's leisure time. As more people had more leisure time, so they acquired a private life. In their free time, people tried new leisure activities and it became increasingly clear that there wasn't enough free time to do everything one would like to do.

The tropism of social advancement

In their quest for emancipation, many people sought to escape from conditions and situations judged to be inferior and tried to imitate their supposedly happier 'superiors'.

During the first two thirds of the 20th century, a tropism of social advancement spread through the upper-middle and middle classes, before encompassing society as a whole. To look and feel more modern, people adopted new habits and dreamed of particular material possessions, which would be symbols of their advancement. As it spread, this tropism, alongside hedonism, became the other great vector of social change and of the extraordinary economic growth that accompanied it.

The precursors came once again from the upper-middle classes. During the 1920s and 1930s, the way of life of the upper-middle classes (and that of other people who imitated them) was transformed. Not all in the same way, though. The more adventurous welcomed domestic appliances into their homes: electrical goods, hot running water, bathrooms, telephones, radios, cars and the wealthy often acquired second homes. Beach holidays became a must. Hunting too. Winter sports began to develop. The rest of the middle classes followed, even if their more limited financial means prevented them, at least in Europe, from following too closely.

These new comforts and values were not driven by any single motivating force:

- Some wanted, above all, just to be part of the changes that were taking place. They wanted to keep up with new developments in science, technology and everyday life, to make their homes more comfortable and to improve their general standards of hygiene. Sometimes this took the form of a freer lifestyle, especially for young girls.

- Often, the pursuit of prestige was the key factor. It was less about living one's life than of parading one's wealth and success in front of others. D.H. Lawrence, like other contemporary novelists, examined this quest for prestige. In *The First Lady Chatterley*, he wrote:

She was on the stage of social events. She held her own in conversation and repartee. She dressed in her own way to please herself. And by exerting the peculiar heavy sort of power that was in her she held her own and gained ground in the shifting company. She enhanced her own prestige in the temporary crowd... In a world which fights solely and simply for that unpleasant substitute called prestige, a sort of shoddy superiority that is the margarine which butters the social bread since the war as a substitute for the old superiority of rank and talent, she knew how to hold her own.

The masses follow suit. It wasn't until the 1930s in the United States, and the post-war period in the most advanced European countries, that this tropism of social advancement spread to the wider population. When it did so, it fed into the drive towards consumerism. By around 1970, it became clear that the desire for personal social betterment now played the determining role in the social and economic life of the whole of North-West Europe. As in earlier years with the upper middle classes, it took two principal forms: prestige and modernity.

The pursuit of prestige. People sought to impress their peers by demonstrating their wealth and, in so doing, they reinforced their own self-respect. They bought a fridge, a bigger car, a better tractor than their neighbours, owned a smarter flat, travelled by aeroplane, holidayed ever further afield, and so on. This drive was often experienced as an irrepressible longing to possess something that others already had. The longing was less a desire for the thing in itself than a desire to *show* that one had it and that one *was* somebody. (Though this underlying motivation was often disavowed.)

The fascination with modernity. Since the 18th century, certain elite groups had been promoting an ideology of progress. Gradually, the masses had acquired a taste for modernity. People who, up to this time, had been happy with their place in society and with their way of life opened up to the idea of change. They wanted to feel modern and to be seen as modern.

Interviews conducted after the Second World War, allowed us to identify the overlapping sets of values and beliefs that formed ordinary people's idea of modernity. The idea of progress was crucial: the idea that we were heading for a brighter future. Progress, in this sense, was first and foremost technical – electrical and mechanical and rooted in science. It included humanity's growing mastery of nature and the systematic and rational development of industrial production. Science was discovering new technologies for improving our quality of life. It promised limitless sources of energy and complete control over nature. Medical advances and the miracle of antibiotics would eliminate disease and lengthen our lives. But progress was also seen to be economic and social. Salaries rose, social and job security improved and advances in our general well-being continued apace. What's more, since the Enlightenment, the idea of progress had also included an idea of emancipation (for men and women) and the individual's right to seek out freedom, to think freely and to pursue happiness.

The myth of modernity as a lever of change. This notion of modernity was often a way of rationalising or hiding other, less palatable, motivations. Using the idea of modernity to explain particular forms of behaviour was also a way of justifying them, of avoiding admitting to oneself or to the interviewer that they also make one's life easier or confer prestige. In the post-war years, many women, for instance, wanted a washing machine. In-depth interviews showed that their primary motivation was a desire to avoid the drudgery of washing by hand, but they refused to admit this, even to themselves, and instead claimed that as it was modern, they shouldn't be ashamed for wanting one.

The myth of modernity didn't just allow people to get on in life, to hanker after things and to keep up with the Joneses. It also set the tone for society. In the pre-war years, being modern was a way of standing out from the crowd. Afterwards, it was being old-fashioned that made you stand out in most social circles. In Europe and North America, being (even just a little) modern became the norm. You had to show your modernity to others and, if not *feel* modern, then at least *act* it. To reject modernity was to cut oneself off from others. For instance, in our 1955 survey of city-dwellers' attitudes to household appliances, we didn't find a single interviewee who said, 'I don't want modern appliances'. Even the old wanted to modernise a little, to take advantage of the trend. The nearest we came to a negative reaction was one like this to a particularly sophisticated appliance, 'That's great. It's modern. But it's a bit *too* modern for me.'

In France, the myth of modernity was a particularly powerful lever of change. The French were typically afraid of novelty or change and were profoundly conservative. But with the arrival of the myth of modernity, they were forced to change. Most of our interviewees mentioned the idea of a break or rupture. Before, we weren't modern; now we are or will become so. Nor were our interviewees proud of their former selves. They rejected pre-war French society and lauded America, the Resistance and the young. This was the dawn of a profound revolution: the old aped the young and children began to teach their parents. This was not an entirely new phenomenon, but throughout the 1950s and '60s it became so powerful that it transformed a central aspect of our society – we went from one where it was obviously parents who were meant to educate their children to one in which the educational process worked both ways.

Many French people, but surely also Americans, English and Italians, lurched headlong towards modernity. They forced themselves to abandon their old, comfortable habits for new and sometimes unsettling ones, just 'because they are modern'. So businessmen, even if they preferred to go by sea and were not really short of time, forced themselves to fly to the United States. People wolfed down mass-produced food, even if it didn't taste of much. Similarly, many of the rich inhabitants of Bordeaux who built themselves a new house, deliberately chose large bay windows even though they made them feel uncomfortable. This contradiction was explored in a regional study carried out in 1960. One of our interviewees explained to us: 'I'm all for modern things. They help your wife. In fact there's hardly any work left to do in the house. It's much better than before: running water, water-heaters, bathrooms and big windows. I'm for everything modern.'

But most people we interviewed in the region had clung on to another basic French personality trait. They liked their privacy and liked to shut themselves away from prying eyes. To cope with the discomfort they felt about installing large windows, many of them bought blinds and curtains. Others, meanwhile, slowly grew to like this new lifestyle, becoming more open to the outside world.

This touches upon one of the fundamental functions of the myth of modernity – it taught people to discover the benefits of these new ways of living. They acquired new habits and appliances, not because they wanted them per se, but primarily so as to be modern. But as they used the refrigerator, say, they discovered its advantages and this reinforced their desire to make their life that bit easier. With the acquisition of a bathroom, they learnt to enjoy washing and pampering themselves and this fed their burgeoning sensuality. And life in large-windowed houses helped them to change their approach to the relationship between public and private space. Thus the myth of modernity acted as a formidable social lever, forcing people to change their ways of life and ways of thinking. Its influence continued throughout the 1960s.

The Deep Roots of Emancipation

This movement towards personal freedom, happiness and social advancement was rooted in several centuries of history.

Reason, democracy and human rights

Reason and democracy in Europe have a venerable history. 13th century England witnessed the birth of a form of parliamentarianism that set limits to the monarch's power. The Renaissance offered up the open-minded quest for truth and understanding as an alternative to dogmatic belief in absolutes. The Reformation called for individuals to read the Bible and to interpret it using their own powers of reasoning. In the 19th century, the supremacy of reason and the intellect, bolstered by widespread literacy and the triumph of science, penetrated even profoundly Catholic circles. The Reformation also chipped away at the sacred character of ecclesiastical authority. The free development of ideas undermined the absolute power of kings and patriarchs. The French and American revolutions enshrined human rights. And so a process begun in the 13th century came to fruition in the 20th century and ultimately allowed for remarkable progress in terms of ordinary people's emancipation.

De-Christianisation

The movement towards de-Christianisation was both a precursor, and a symptom, of the new wave of liberalism and hedonism. De-Christianisation and secularisation enabled people to escape God's gaze and a moral system based on suffering, duty and sin. Massive urbanisation cut millions of young people off from the main bastions of traditional morality: parents, grandparents, village life and the local priest or pastor.

The rupture was sudden and very evident from the 18th century onwards in parts of Catholic Europe. It was particularly powerful in France, where the practice of contraception had a hundred year head start over the rest of Europe. Thanks to the "dark lore" of contraception, birth rates began to fall from the late 18th century onwards. The second wave of de-Christianisation, stretching throughout the 19th century and spilling over into the early 1930s, destroyed the grip of Protestantism. From 1965 onwards, a third wave struck the rest of Catholic Europe, both in France and elsewhere.

As Christianity's foundations gave way and God and sin were cast out of the daily life of most European people, a whole moral system was threatened. But the relics of Christianity continued to influence society for a while yet. Traditional morality, with its duties, taboos and ideology of shame, was still enforced into the latter half of the 20th century. Breaking away from these morals and wider social norms was a slow and painful affair for people on the path towards personal freedom.

The strength of the link between de-Christianisation and the later wave of emancipation and hedonism is confirmed by statistical analysis that Cofremca carried out in France in 1974. This showed that the different social currents of Hedonism, Sexual Liberalism and Polysensuality (which are defined later) were particularly strong in those regions that had de-Christianised earliest: the Paris basin and the southeast of the country. Western France, on the other hand, resisted such pressures.

Meanwhile, in the hundred years to 1950, Sweden had gone from being a country of die-hard Protestants to an almost completely de-Christianised pioneer of hedonism and polysensuality. It may well be that Lutheran Christianity, which prevailed from the 16th to the 19th century, was simply superimposed on an ancient and underlying substrate of paganism that finally awoke from its slumber. This would explain the speed and ease with which the change occurred.

The situation was completely different in the United States, where Puritanism and the Protestant ethic were better able to resist hedonism and freethinking than in Europe. God and sin remained important elements in many people's daily lives. Not only did the religious question split the USA into two opposing camps, but many Americans found themselves torn between guilt and desire. They pursued happiness, pleasure and sexual satisfaction, but they did so hesitantly and were easily and often filled with remorse. Writing just after the Second World War, André Siegfried[6] noted that in many states there were

---

6   Siegfried A. *Les États-Unis d'Aujourd'hui*. Paris: Armand Colin, 1948.

still numerous laws defending religion: it might be illegal to work on Sundays, teach evolution, blaspheme or deny the existence of God. He showed that for many people, sex outside marriage was the ultimate abomination. This position is still in evidence today.

An Individualist, Uniform and Hierarchical Social Fabric

After fifty years of feeling its way forward in the dark, a new social fabric had emerged. It allowed semi-emancipated individuals and socially adept leaders who could understand and manage them to establish a temporary and more or less harmonious *entente cordiale*. This social fabric was individualist in that, cut off from their roots and traditional support networks and obligations, people had won themselves a good deal of freedom of choice. It was hierarchical in that people took their models from above and were susceptible to being influenced by the powerful. It was uniform in that people gathered themselves into one relatively homogenous whole to whose standards they conformed: society was moving towards a situation in which everybody was middle class and traditional class boundaries were blurred.

Fashion as a reflection of this new social fabric

Changes in the role of fashion from 1900 to 1970 reflect changes in the wider social fabric. Around 1900, few people had ideas above their station. On Sundays, workers dressed like workers – the husband in a flat cap and his wife bareheaded. A Bavarian peasant dressed like a Bavarian peasant and a member of the upper-middle class dressed like a member of the upper-middle class. The latter vaguely followed changing fashions and were imitated by a few members of the emerging middle class.

In the 1920s and 1930s, however, everything changed. Many white-collar, and even some blue-collar, workers began to adopt certain items of upper-middle class dress. After the Second World War, the rest followed suit. Indeed, from the early 20th century onwards a system had begun to emerge that would dictate the way people dressed until the early 1970s. This self-organising system, created by changing lifestyles and with the help of all those involved, owed nothing to the formal dictates of an overarching body, which in any case didn't really exist. It was a sort of gradated pyramid. At the top were a few Parisian fashion houses that together, and in tune with the spirit of the times, launched new fashions every six months. Just below, was a small armada of women from the Paris jet-set, accompanied by a few wealthy Americans,

English ladies and so on. A few women's magazines kept the lower echelons of the pyramid informed of the goings on above them. The further one was from the summit, the more widely acceptable it was to wear last year's fashions. Tailors and dressmakers copied them. Shops sold dress patterns that allowed some women lower down the pyramid to make themselves fetching and fashionable little frocks. Prêt-à-porter establishments sprang up too. Women, and especially young women, lengthened or shortened their skirts as they saw fit and dreamt of a different colour blouse. And so, with everybody convinced they were doing as they pleased and following their own personal tastes and preferences, they nonetheless bowed to the sovereign dictates of a higher power, one with the latest advertising and media tools at its disposal. Later, with the help of television, fashion quickly spread into the furthest corners of rural life.

This system produced uniformity. In 1900, an observer could, even on a Sunday, spot a member of the urban or rural working class or bourgeoisie at fifty paces. By 1970, it was harder to tell the difference. But fashion now also produced variation and change. With hindsight, major trends can be seen. With the help of Paul Poiret (1903), Coco Chanel (1920) and Christian Dior (1950), women freed themselves, moving from corsets to stockings and suspenders, and then to tights. Men similarly progressed from the formal jacket to the pullover. It became less and less necessary to wear particular outfits for particular occasions. Fashion reached further and further into all walks of life, both liberating and constraining people as it went. Fashion houses, prêt-à-porter establishments, tailors and others helped women to free themselves from the tighter constraints of tradition, but they also kept them locked into a system, which they nevertheless freely and happily followed. It kept things in order and massively increased uniformity. Individualisation and homogenisation not only coexisted but also were mutually reinforcing.

The powerful keep society under control by meeting the people halfway

Innovative elites from the public and private sectors (engineers, entrepreneurs, the media, politicians, designers and the like) discovered how to make the most of this situation. Using advances in manufacturing and communication technology, they found ways of self-organising, as well as new management strategies, which allowed them to meet and satisfy the needs of individuals already on the road to emancipation and at the same time turn them into docile subjects. Bewitched by ideology or the race to consume, individuals melted easily into homogeneous masses: aggressive, nationalist masses; revolutionary, proletarian masses; middle class masses racing to consume. They worked hard and consumed harder. The people at the top amassed enormous power.

Between the wars, the political, economic and cultural elites who took the initiative and innovated were driven by an idea of progress. The carnage of war, the stock-market crash of 1929 and the apparent failure of liberal economics and even capitalism all argued in favour of a rational, technical approach. The elites appointed themselves leaders of the masses. Breaking with pre-war liberal thought, an elitist and technocratic mentality grew up on both sides of the right/left political divide. The idea of progress, whether in terms of science and technology, history or human development, underlay this shift. No more *laissez-faire*! Rational intelligence and intervention by experts, states or political parties could do better. Parliamentary systems seemed incapable of coping with crisis.

States get involved and take control. After 1945, there was a spectacular expansion of state power. Throughout the 19th and early 20th centuries, nation-states in Europe and North America were sovereign but lightweight. Each had an internal monopoly of violence and the power to lead its people to war or off on colonial adventures. Propaganda helped to maintain a virulent form of nationalism. The peoples of Europe were ready to kill one another. But in a context of rapid democratisation and economic globalisation, the state had rarely intervened. Then, after 1945, welfare states were set up and the number of civil servants and level of public expenditure increased massively. These democratic, but also interventionist and bureaucratic, states, trying to protect the poor, acquired enormous power over their citizens and contributed to the transformation of the whole fabric of society.

After the First World War, Swedish socialist civil servants, just like their English Labour and French Gaullist, socialist and communist equivalents, thought they could identify what was in the public's interest and thought that they embodied it. Even federalist civil servants in the United States shared this perspective. They felt that only they could speak on the public's behalf. They also believed that strong and intelligent individuals could shape people and society as they wished. When it came to advertising and propaganda, they believed in the power of slogans and of repetition. They liked to equate their ability to influence the masses with the relationship between hammer and anvil, whereby the blacksmith forges a piece of metal into the desired form. In Europe, civil servants were convinced of the need to reform and modernise society and to bring the economy under control. Though they weren't entirely conscious of the fact, they liked mass society. It called for uniformity, rational explanation, standardisation, codification and planning – all of which suited their particular intellectual style and which encouraged the development of bureaucracy and rule by technocrats.

These civil servants happily applied the mechanistic rationalism of engineering to society and the economy. Marxist ideas of authoritarian or bureaucratic planning as a means of achieving social and economic progress appealed to them. But they were even more easily seduced by Keynesian theories, which established an almost mechanical relationship between the distribution of surplus revenue to poorer sections of society and the goal of full employment.

Immediately after the First World War, the economic dilemma of whether to opt for a market-led or a planned economy had still not been resolved. Early on, the United States had clearly chosen the former option, but Russia continued down the opposite path and Europe remained undecided. There were strong communist parties in Italy and France. Either as a response to changing circumstances or because of the long tail of outdated political ideologies, France, Great Britain and Austria nationalised large swathes of the economy in 1945 and 1946. Nevertheless, Western European public opinion was impressed by the performance of US business, which continued to grow in prestige. And so the masses tended to align themselves with the market rather than with a planned economy. From 1946 onwards, surveys showed that French and British public opinion had swung against nationalisation. People saw it as a sort of state intervention, which had begun to fall out of favour.[7] Much of the elite fell into line. According to many surveys, by the early 1950s, the French saw the state as musty and bureaucratic. People contrasted it unfavourably with what they saw as the dynamic and modern world of big business.

Yet the state remained interventionist and welfare-oriented and still had enormous power over society and the economy. In Western Europe and North America the state didn't aim to plan the economy as a whole, but only certain parts of it. It left room for the market, for unfettered interaction between individual consumers, for competition between businesses and for trade unions. But it intervened and tried to influence them with its bureaucracy, its plans, its subsidies, its taxes and its national targets. The welfare state combined the organisation of a social security system with a full employment policy, labour legislation that protected workers from ruthless bosses and

---

7   Andrieu C. 'Nationalizations Comparées en Europe après 1945'. XXème *Siècle*, No.8, p.133, 1985

state support for trades unions, especially in their struggle for higher wages. For both social and (Keynesian) economic reasons, it allotted itself the task of redistributing income in favour of the poor.

The welfare state was a joint creation of Europe and the United States. Indeed, the term 'social security' first appeared in the United States, with the adoption, in 1935, of the *Social Security Act*. But it was Sweden that really set the tone for what was to follow. The Socialist Party first came to power in Sweden in 1920, and firmly established itself as the dominant party from 1932 onwards. It favoured increasing the lowest tier of salaries as a means of stimulating consumption and economic growth and it encouraged direct negotiations between the national employers' confederation and the trades unions. The policy was successful. Social conflict abated and working-class living standards swiftly became the highest in the world. Sweden created a welfare state inspired by its own national culture and held it up as a model to the rest of the world. This model was a gentle form of social organisation where everything is managed from above to make people's lives easier; where the state takes care of people, especially the underprivileged. Not only did it look after the living standards, health and freedoms of the Swedish people, but also their happiness and personal development. From the cradle to the grave, society intervened to defend and protect individuals from themselves (alcohol abuse) and from others (exploitation or restrictive social customs). It aimed to help its citizens to become harmonious, healthy and well-rounded individuals. Those who didn't want to marry shouldn't be made to. Children should be given sex education from an early age to help rid them of their complexes and uncertainties.

Businesses were the champions of the First Modernity. They played an essential role in its development and blossoming. They also derived power and prosperity from their involvement.

In the main, the scientific and technical innovations that businesses used to build the First Modernity had been invented or discovered in the late 19th and early 20th centuries, and had been waiting for somebody to take them up: chemistry, mechanics, electricity, cinema, radio waves, scientific organisation... Well-informed innovators saw them being deployed in four main directions: to improve industrial and agricultural productivity, to build new consumer goods, as a means of mass communication and finally for military purposes.

There were two crucial forms of interdependence between business and ordinary people, which allowed the First Modernity to flourish. The first saw companies invent modes of production, management and work-relations that brought their employees job security and pay rises, encouraged them to work, maintained competition over living standards and spurred on the race to consume. The other form saw innovative companies devise products, marketing tools and mass communication techniques that reinforced and standardised people's desires and helped to establish clear hierarchies of modernity and social status, which encompassed and encouraged the race to consume. The past masters of these techniques shaped and directed people's way of life whilst simultaneously expanding and increasing profits. Let's look at these two systems in more detail.

The salaried labour model. Those innovations that survived, prospered and made truly significant contributions to the development of this model of social organisation were: mass production, Taylorism, Fordism and the idea of a career structure.

Mass production. The United States sparked the revolution in productivity. Businesses set out to organise labour so as to maximise the number of units produced and reduce the unit cost. In other words, they invented a form of mass production based on rational, hierarchical organisation. Of all European countries it was Germany that, throughout the 1920s and '30s, most closely followed the American model.

Taylorism. Also born in the USA, this was a major innovation, though it took 50 years for it to spread to the whole of Western industrial production. F W Taylor was working as an industrial engineer in Pennsylvania at the turn of the 20th century when he came up with the idea of introducing mechanisation into all labour processes. He carried out his first experiment in the Bethlehem steelworks, where he set up a radically different organisational model, one that was mechanised and hierarchical. Through close observation and by carefully timing different activities, a process could be broken down into elementary tasks. Individual workers now no longer needed any special skills; they just had to learn how to perform their allotted task. Their wages were individualised: the faster they worked, the more they earned. And so they accepted the implicit Taylorist contract: the labour process was broken up, and in return they worked fewer hours and earned more. This, in turn, brought with it the opportunity to become more involved in the race to consume.

The downside was that manual labourers' work became more and more disconnected from its productive end-point. A man's work was no longer a trade nor a source of fulfilment. It was only outside the factory gates and far away from their co-workers, that people could look for fulfilment. Work was only a good thing in that it brought financial security. It was wages, not work, that mattered.

Fordism. Henry Ford invented a new economic model that has been widely imitated and played a determining role in 20th century industrial history. The rational organisation of the production of automobile components allowed for the transition, in 1914, from stationary assembly to production line assembly. The time it took to assemble the chassis of a car fell from 12½ hours to 1½. The price of a Model T Ford fell from $950 to $290.[8] Sales soared and this allowed Ford to pay his workers higher wages and so transform them into potential customers. Higher salaries created the consumers that the company needed and integrated workers into consumer society. It was one way in which society could buy social peace and ward off revolution.

After the Second World War, Taylorism and Fordism rapidly conquered Europe. Company directors, like everyone else in France and England, were fascinated by the myth of modernity and by US prestige.

Career structures and ambition. The number of managerial positions on offer increased and hierarchies grew more complex. The pursuit of happiness, modernity and conspicuous consumption led employees and managers to compete for jobs with more status and higher pay. This competition emerged spontaneously but it was increasingly stoked by senior management and sometimes formally organised. In turn, this reinforced the race to consume.

The 'race to consume' model. Haphazardly, and in competition with one another, companies sought to appeal to the market. With each new innovation, short-term relationships were established between new products and consumers, whose habits began to change. This new system, born of the interaction between innovators, companies and consumers, worked so that companies grew in strength while consumers' desires were encouraged and met and they emerged relatively satisfied.

Of course, not all companies prospered. The major firms of the 1950s and 1960s had all started out as small or middling companies which had made the most of the opportunities provided by modernity. Others faded away or disappeared. This was corporate natural selection in action.

Mass marketing emerged in the United States and gradually developed on both sides of the Atlantic. Companies learnt how to choose the right products: ones that could be mass-produced and were likely to appeal to the masses

---

8   Freidel F. *America in the Twentieth Century.* New York: Alfred A. Knopf, 1970.

of financially solvent consumers. They learnt to create and tailor their product and brand images, to choose where and how to advertise and how to distribute their goods so that they could best meet the needs of potential consumers.

But marketing was often a hit-and-miss-process, sticking with what worked and dispensing with the rest. It believed in endless repetition, but it also believed in information, intuition and manipulation. And so, soon after the Second World War, we see a boom in motivation research. Advertising agencies tried to find out what made consumers tick, what they responded to or resisted, so that companies could adapt their new products and present their new ideas in a favourable light. [9]

Those companies that prospered in the marketplace were often the ones that encouraged consumers to compete for their products by playing on the obsolescence of older models and developing a clear hierarchy of different brands and ranges. Modern products were rapidly replaced by newer, yet more modern models.

The mass media were also composed of more or less free and independent companies. They began competing with one another at the beginning of the century, imitated one another, and closely observed their audiences' sensibilities, trying to adapt themselves as they went. Advertisements blended in with the factual or editorial messages diffused by magazines, the popular press, cinema, radio and soon television in a huge free-for-all that fed people's desires and dissipated their feelings of guilt. They helped to homogenise people's dreams and habits, such as building a career, finding the love of one's life, raising wonderful children, going on holiday, leading a comfortable life... In particular, the media helped to popularise the idea of love marriage and of life-long, sexually fulfilling, monogamous relationships. But the media also laid the foundations for the next stage of modernisation, by helping consumers to think about life, about themselves and about others.

A homogeneous and pyramidical social fabric

In a society whose hierarchies were still strong, but losing their sharp contours, people were all of a sudden allowed, and even encouraged, to shake things up. This was a society where people paid the old hierarchs less and less heed, but where hierarchical mimesis (imitating one's social 'superiors')

---

9   See, for example, Packard V. *The Hidden Persuaders* New York: David McKay, 1957.

was still going strong. This society responded well to companies' attempts to locate their products and brands at particular points in a more or less clear-cut value hierarchy.

The clearest signs of modernity were appliances, household fittings, cars, holidays, clothes, prestigious brands... all of which cost money. To improve one's 'modernity quotient', one had to live a more materially comfortable life. The hierarchical scales of value by which modernity and status were measured were thus intertwined. Modernising households were also happy households. The whole current of social advancement flowed into that of hedonism. The equation 'progress = modernity + status = happiness' became not only credible, but also motivational. The most modern, materially comfortable and happiest lifestyle was that of the upper-middle classes and senior managers. In the 1950s and '60s, their lifestyle choices inspired the masses.

In our interviews with people from across the social spectrum, the longing to consume emerged time and again. Such longing, however, was extremely measured. People didn't dream of the unattainable, they only wanted things that were that little bit bigger, more modern and more expensive than those they or their neighbours already had.

And so a coherent group of informal and discrete, but extremely powerful, sociosystems emerged, and together formed a gradated pyramid. In such a system, everybody looks over their shoulder at the person who is hot on their heels or the one they're overtaking. And everybody looks ahead to the next person, who does the same, and so on until you reach the top of the lifestyle hierarchy. Thus it is very much the summit of the pyramid that sets the overall tone.

Much of the population gradually becomes middle class. Improvements in living standards and regular salary increases, combined with the efficacy of the consumption pyramid, gradually turned the working classes away from revolution and towards consumption. A growing number of working class households owned, or dreamt of owning, their own house, bought a car, or saved for one, listened to the same radio stations, watched the same television channels and read the same magazines as white-collar workers or even the upper-middle classes. These possessions, connections and cross-overs increased individualism, reinforced the importance of the household and broke up old forms of class and neighbourhood solidarity. They integrated workers into wider society, which meant into the expanding middle class.

In France, Italy and especially in England, this integration didn't go uncontested, but it went ahead nonetheless. In the 1960s, we still came across workers with a strong class-consciousness, manifest in their lifestyle. We also met some people who struggled to improve their living standards and tried to imitate upper-middle class lifestyles, but who simultaneously propounded a revolutionary ideology that was completely at odds with the reality of their motivations and their everyday lives. Between 1950 and 1970, both groups went into strong decline. Integration was well under way.

Agricultural modernisation reduced the need for rural manpower. Consequently, the countryside population poured into the cities, swelling the urban working classes. However, productivity gains allowed industry to increase production without employing more manual labourers. Instead, white-collar workers, bureaucrats, technicians, sales personnel and managers (in other words, the tertiary sector) became the dominant group, though to different degrees in different countries. This too served to increase the size of the middle class.

On top of all this, growing numbers of agricultural workers and members of the upper-middle classes were gradually assimilated into the middle classes. Even for those farmers who continued to work the land, life had changed immeasurably. Farming was becoming a solitary business, just a man with a machine. Once they had household appliances, comfortable houses, cars, telephones and televisions, farmers' lifestyles and quality of life weren't so very different from those of the urban middle classes. The upper-middle classes were also drawn into the middle class sphere of influence. Inheritance and dowries were no longer enough; they also needed qualifications. They had to work. Marrying for love undermined attempts to consolidate family wealth and status through alliance. Many upper-middle class women, as we have seen, were tempted to work as a means of ensuring their independence and financial security.

Thus, little by little, there emerged an enormous middle class. Although consumers weren't all of a piece, they all had similar aspirations. They could easily be grouped into a small number of fairly large, hierarchically arranged segments, each with a distinct lifestyle. Marketing experts defined a series of groups, ranging from the richest to the least well off, which are internationally known on a scale from A to D or E. These groups are defined by a combination of socio-demographic indicators, which companies can easily identify and whose evolution is closely followed by statistical tools, surveys and panels.

Creative interdependence

Life has its own logic

In this chapter, I have tried to tease out several key aspects of the complex process that led to the emergence, in the 1950s and '60s, of an individualist and hierarchical society predicated upon mass-consumption and stable in the short term. There is an apparent logic to the different steps discussed. Each seems to carry within itself the germ of the next, as if the whole thing were pre-determined. People's desires and commercial innovations dovetail seamlessly, as if it had to be like that. Sequences interlock with other sequences, symbioses and synergies flare up, flourish and clear the path that society took, whilst other possible paths seem with hindsight to have been dead-ends. Retrospective description can make things seem logical, somehow necessary and perhaps pre-determined.

This is an optical illusion. Think what would have happened if all forms of mass communication and mass media in Europe had fallen into the hands of a strong and determined state. Or if German nuclear research had outpaced the Manhattan project and the Axis powers had won the war. Or if Stalin and Hitler's alliance had lasted? Is it unthinkable that Europe might have become a mass totalitarian society and that this might have stretched far into the 21st century? Perhaps not. Although, it's fair to wonder whether it's possible to hold back a flood of men and women who have once tasted freedom.

If some overarching Hand of History did not drive this historical process, perhaps it was directed by elites and by key social actors possessed of remarkable intuition and Machiavellianism...? No! Seen from above, innovators, companies and states seem to have done just what was needed to develop mass markets, to create docile and hard-working citizens and finally to create a social model that perfectly suited them. But if we look more closely, this argument doesn't stand up. We only reached an individualist and hierarchical society based on mass-consumption after fifty years of trial and error. It took decades for the innovations that now seem decisive to become widespread. Though history has hung on to the names Taylor, Ford and Beveridge, thousands of others (whose innovations didn't succeed) have been forgotten.

It is fairer, and more useful, to represent all this as a spontaneous and self-organising process that develops according to life's own logic. Innovators often have a keen awareness of the social system within which they innovate. But the success or failure of a given innovation often owes much to coincidence.

It is fairly common for innovations to come about by chance or to succeed for reasons largely unconnected to the innovator's intentions. Sooner or later, those who copy an innovation tailor it to suit their situation and the copy is often better than the original. It too will be copied.

A breeding ground for emancipation

There is a paradoxical element to the form the First Modernity took as it grew and flourished. People freed themselves, but at the same time they huddled into conformist masses directed by states and companies. This was a society both free and in chains.

The emancipation of ordinary Europeans and Americans in the 1950s and '60s was very real. The withering away of social conventions, the sense of duty and moral taboos, along with the explosion of individual desire for pleasure, happiness and advancement were mutually reinforcing. They undermined a static social and economic order. But these individuals displayed an astonishing conformism and unconsciously allowed themselves to be manipulated. They gorged themselves on hedonist, modernist and status-related fripperies, which experts and those in power encouraged them to buy into. They didn't see the trap.

People looked for individual pleasure, but this pleasure was socially conditioned. At Cofremca, we began to understand better this conformism when we interviewed Europeans who were gradually coming to realise how they were being manipulated and the ideological and consumption traps they had fallen into.

Most people who came of age in the first half of the 20th century had only received a primary education. In most Western countries, they were among the first generations to benefit from mass education. It was this, coupled with a gradual distancing from family and village life, that severed their intimate ties with the wisdom of their rural, ancestral culture. Cut off from their roots and traditions, they were individuals, but not yet independent ones. They were expelled from a culture, based on intuition, emotion, human relations and the spoken word, and thrown into an impersonal and still embryonic culture based on the written word.

People now attached great importance to reading, writing and the clear expression of simple reasoning, but they hadn't properly learnt to challenge received ideas in the light of their lived experience or to develop a critical perspective. They were ready to take on board any idea that was somehow in sync with their feelings or with their inner emotional worlds, of which they were only partly aware.

In the 1920s and '30s, and even as late as the 1950s, most people were, to use David Riesman's typology, 'inner-directed'. They tended to look at the world in very clear-cut, black and white ways and to adopt one particular world-view to the exclusion of all others. When it came to political currents or ideas, most people either bought into them wholesale or rejected them outright, and only rarely sought to mould them to the reality of their own situation. This tendency laid the ground for mass ideologies.

The other factor, mentioned above, which helped make people a fertile breeding ground for mass ideologies, as well as the pliant subjects of top-down models of work and consumption, was the continued existence of a hierarchical moral world. The Enlightenment, de-Christianisation and the spread of democracy throughout the 19th century had only partially freed them from the hegemony of hierarchy. The authority of traditional hierarchs had taken a blow. The monarchy, aristocracy, fathers and leaders might be challenged. Little by little, democracy had become an integral part of Western European and North American political reality. But people still heeded the advice of supposed experts and people of high standing and they took their models from above. Of course, people challenged traditional authority figures, but only so as to replace them with new ones. States, mass ideological organisations and companies took advantage of this hierarchy deficit to establish new chains of command that served to discipline employees, consumers and militants.

It might have been expected that the trend towards individualism would have led to a fragmentation of people's patterns of behaviour. Paradoxically, however, the three decades immediately after World War Two saw these motivations driving people en masse towards the same pleasures, the same consumer goods, the same forms of entertainment and the same patterns of behaviour. Though they were just emerging from a cultural and moral system that preached the virtues of duty, suffering, sacrifice and the repression of urges, feelings and emotions, people didn't splinter off in many different directions. Instead, they all lived through the same determining experiences. They became aware of the forms of acute suffering that they were enduring and they began to dream of escaping them: basic insecurity, the drudgery of the long working-day, domestic chores, sexual frustration, lack of affection, boredom... Most of the time, this awareness was vague and tenuous. Most of them had not yet reached the point their successors would ultimately arrive at. They were not yet in tune with the feelings and emotions that could bring them happiness and pleasure. They were still learning and were more than happy to let themselves be guided along the path.

Westerners in the 1930s and 1950s were still not fully autonomous and were easily convinced by apparently rational arguments or by the weight of authority. They allowed themselves to be swept up and towards goals that they would later discover to be partially illusory.

This individualist and hierarchical mass society was governed from on high. But those in power couldn't just manipulate the masses as they pleased. Peering down from their lofty organisation charts, many political or business leaders deluded themselves into thinking that the decisions they took were simply handed down and executed just so by their subordinates. In fact, whilst individuals were governed from on high, it was only insofar as those in power managed to stimulate the appetites and ambitions of the masses. The way this society worked and developed was still largely dependent on informal, living processes, of which the powers-that-be were unaware and which they could not control. And, with time, people continued to learn from their gradual emancipation. This process, and others like it, gradually began to chip away at the mighty edifice of this individualist and hierarchical society based on mass consumption.

Chapter 3

A crucial decade: the threshold between the First and Second Modernities (1965-1975)

The ten years stretching from 1965 to 1975, which began shortly before the student uprisings of May 1968 and ended two years after the oil crisis of 1973, mark the end of the 20th century's First Modernity. They also ushered in a second one.

The century's First Modernity had been driven by the initiatives and innovations of big business, states, and political and technocratic elites. In contrast, it was ordinary people, and especially women and the young, who were the precursors of the new cultural revolution. As they still are today.

The relationship between the First and Second Modernities is one of both continuity and rupture. Continuity, because the quest for emancipation remained the major driving force behind the changes that took place. But also rupture, because the First Modernity had allowed for only a narrow and constrained development of individual freedom, whilst the Second Modernity saw this freedom really come into its own.

Between 1965 and 1975, an earthquake rocked Western society. The first tremors were provoked by student rebellion. But things didn't stop there. The effects of these student uprisings reverberated throughout society, affecting two main groups of people: first, their parents (at least the middle class ones) and, second, young working class people. Both now dared to admit and to express the resentment and disenchantment that had been building up over the last few decades. This, in turn, gave rise to the idea that each of us could and should strive to express ourselves and to fulfil our own potential. Seeking a way of expressing themselves, ordinary people began to undermine the hierarchical society based on mass consumption that had developed during the First Modernity.

At this point, it was once again the United States, France and Scandinavia that were the precursors. It was here that the old order and authority were most effectively challenged.

Young people teach their parents a lesson

Around 1965, the West saw the beginnings of a true cultural revolution. At first, this was most evident in the explosion of new pop music and in the behaviour of young people. Beatles' songs were heard around the world; the first hippy communities appeared in 1966; the student uprisings of May 1968 forced people to think again about the society they lived in. Many contemporary observers were initially inclined to downplay all of this, seeing it as little more than a widespread youth crisis – the folly of a generation who had had things too easy. With hindsight, though, it is obvious that they both marked and initiated the collapse of the First Modernity.

Hippies and the Beat Generation

This challenge to society did not, however, come as a bolt from the blue. From the late 1950s onwards, some young people had begun to turn away from the institutions set up by adults to keep them in line: scouting, youth wings of the major political parties, Christian youth movements, etc.

For the beat generation, marijuana, mescaline and LSD became the tools of self-liberation. They wanted a clean break with the values of a consumer society. And so the hippy movement was born. Many young Americans, especially those from middle or upper-class backgrounds, turned away from their families and formal education and set off for California. The first communities were formed in the forests and on the beaches around San Francisco and New York. This was not a philosophical or intellectual challenge to society. It was the hippies' way of life, their music and their arts and crafts that challenged the prevailing order, both bourgeois and proletarian. They rejected work, money, business, city life and militant action. Refusing to be side-lined, they challenged all forms of authority and fought for the right to make their own rules. This was a culture of spontaneity. Hallucinogens, dance, music and psychedelic lights were all ways for people to expand their minds. They stood for nature, for a return to balance and harmony, for liberation from the social constraints that divide and isolate people, for love, compassion, brotherhood and sisterhood, for a jumble of Eastern philosophies, for pacifism. Hippies created a new type of family based on the collective: free love and shared responsibility for children.

This movement quickly spread throughout the United States, Scandinavia and Germany and gave rise to many new newspapers and magazines. The universities of Berkeley, Berlin and London became hotbeds of dissent. The underground even had its own theorist, Herbert Marcuse, an American philosopher born in Germany, who developed a radical, Freudo-Marxist critique of consumer society.

People abandoned their jobs or their studies, left to join hippy communities, or just left for leaving's sake. During the summer of 1966, more than 200,000 hippies travelled across the United States. Among them were many Northern Europeans. On the 6th of October, 30,000 young people took part in the first 'love in' at San Francisco's Golden Gate Park. There were 400,000 people at the Isle of Wight festival and 800,000 at Woodstock in 1969. California, Asia (especially Kathmandu and Goa) and the Balearic islands (especially Ibiza and Formentera) would continue to attract people for generations to come.

The upheavals of May 1968

Young people revolted. All the major industrialised countries were affected. Further afield, Mexican students turned the 1968 Olympic Games into a 'happening'. In Eastern Europe, these events were echoed in the Prague Spring. It seems to me that the almost perfect synchronicity of these spring uprisings is an indication of the growing cohesion of a Western civilisation in flux. The common denominator was a generation that had lived through similar experiences and experienced similar frustrations across the industrialised world. They had been raised by parents who were more egalitarian, more liberal, more in touch with their feelings and more psychologically aware than the parents of previous generation. They had known the same material comforts and were aware of the traps laid by consumer society. They had listened to the same music and smoked the same joints. They had been frustrated by the same impersonal, authoritarian structures at school, at university and at work. The roots of these different student uprisings were practically identical in all developed countries. On top of this, the international network built up by the beat generation and the global audience for the new mass media doubtless played their part in the timing.

Even so, these uprisings took a different form in each country and had a different effect on the older generation. In the United States and Northern Europe, environmentalism quickly spread. In France and in Italy, meanwhile, the most active groups were strongly influenced by intense ideological debate and by the prevailing climate of Marxism, which still dominated left-wing politics.

Italy and Germany stand out by virtue of the extreme violence that emerged out of the May 1968 movements. In 1970, an Italian sociologist called Renato Curcio founded the Red Brigades. Between 1969 and 1987, there were around 15,000 terrorist attacks, killing more than 400 people. The most famous is undoubtedly the kidnap and murder of Aldo Moro in 1978. Things were not much better in Germany. Andreas Baader and Gudrun Ensslin were condemned to three years in prison for the arson of a department store in Frankfurt in April 1968. Two years later, they were sprung from prison by members of the Red Army Faction, only to be recaptured along with 15 other members of the Baader-Meinhof gang. A Boeing 737 was hijacked to win their release. Many killed themselves in prison. The Red Army Faction continued to target politicians, judges and businessmen, as well as American military bases and NATO personnel, until 1986.

In the United States, this youth rebellion had far-reaching consequences. It broadly overlapped with and fed into the three major fault lines. First, people's vague awareness of racial inequality was jolted awake by Martin Luther King and the Civil Rights Movement. Violence followed. Second, the ongoing war in Vietnam split America down the middle. The majority of the generation labelled 'baby-boomers' were against the war. A peace march in Washington in November 1969 attracted 250,000 demonstrators. Environmentalism was the third new dividing line in American politics. Young people were at the forefront of this movement, but tens of millions of adults were behind them. According to the press, the first Earth Day (on 22nd April 1970) mobilised 50 million Americans. These divisions, which criss-crossed America in the late 1960s, united many adults with the younger generation, while others set about strengthening the dam in the face of this revolutionary tide. The divisions were there to stay.

In May 1968, France witnessed an extraordinary drama played out on the public stage and involving student rebels, the wider public (some strongly supportive, some terrified and shocked), traditional party-political forces and trades unions trying to regain control of the situation, an authoritarian state brought to its knees, and companies paralysed by a general strike that they could not begin to understand.

It began in the universities. In early spring, wildcat strikes sprung up all over the country. Young workers were sometimes supported by student rebels. Maoist, Trotskyite and anarchist groups thought the universities could act as a revolutionary vanguard. The influence of these groups was felt strongly in the university campuses around Paris, and the student body began to stir. The '22nd of March movement', led by Daniel Cohn-Bendit, was born.

Mistakes by the authorities compounded matters. Uprisings provoked repression, which in turn led to further uprisings, culminating in days of student rioting and a massive general strike that largely bypassed the official trades unions. The violence of the language used throughout May 1968 was astonishing and there were repeated riots, involving clashes between demonstrators and the police, but the only deaths were accidental ones. The physical violence contained itself: people clearly knew not to go too far.

This socio-drama was strongly influenced by the Marxist climate that prevailed in leftist circles. It was reinforced by the highly centralised nature of contemporary France, with its codified social relations, hierarchical structures, strong attachment to order and its overweening bureaucratic state. But the Marxists had no real revolutionary blueprint.

Cofremca observed and interviewed student rebels and young strikers throughout May and June 1968. We also explored the reactions of their contemporaries in the months that followed and over the next year, when events were still fresh in people's minds. The press described these young people as highly politicised and revolutionary. We, on the contrary, found them to be angry, but not particularly political and not particularly revolutionary. They had not been indoctrinated, nor had they been especially influenced by political and philosophical books and pamphlets or by ideological thinking. Their protest was something that came from the gut. It emerged from their lived experience, which each tried to explain to us in their own way. They did not like the affluent, consumer society in which they had been raised: to them, it all seemed idiotic and meaningless. They did not want to seize power; rather, many of them told us they 'just wanted to change their lives'. In France, as in the United States and Scandinavia, the urban middle classes often understood and sometimes supported these young radicals.

The events of May 1968 signal the beginning of major cultural change

With several decades' hindsight, it is clear that these student movements were a sign of change to come and the events of May 1968 were the catalyst for this change. This phenomenon was most obvious in France and the United States. The experience of May 1968 radically changed the way people lived their lives. It brought to the surface a series of socio-political stances and new tropisms that had been present in latent form throughout the 1950s and '60s. Parents saw their children fighting for ideals that they knew they agreed with deep down. Many finally felt able to acknowledge these beliefs. Interviews show that people began to recognise that they believed in things they had not even known they believed. Teachers and lecturers followed their students. In the United States, the army was held up to ridicule; in France, the politicians were baffled and business leaders afraid. What was so surprising was that the movement did not appear to be driven by any known ideology. Communism was criticised in the same breath as capitalism.

Self-expression and self-fulfilment

The twin myths of modernity and progress were rapidly losing their appeal. In their place, a new myth sprang up, at least for the time being: that of 'self-expression and self-fulfilment'.

In a few short years, the simple and incredibly widespread idea that anything modern, anything that represented technical progress, was necessarily better both for oneself and for society lost its grip. People began to experience doubt. This doubt affected the middle classes and sometimes even the working classes. Being modern and being seen to be modern lost its attraction. For some, it became old hat to pursue modernity and the modernist ideal. Maybe, they thought, the remarkable technical and economic developments of the previous fifty years were not progress after all. Maybe they were on the road to perdition. The Club of Rome, founded in April 1968 by a group of renowned intellectuals and experts, was pessimistic about the future of the industrialised world. Its 1972 report, 'The Limits to Growth', lent respectability to people's doubts about the possibility of continued progress.

This was not simply a case of changing public opinion. Consumers had grown tired of change for change's sake. They realised that they were not necessarily benefiting from chasing after ever newer and more modern products. The women that we interviewed realised that they were caught in a vicious circle, which wore them out and cost them dear. They did not, however, find themselves in the same position as women a generation before, who had been actively afraid of innovation and had tried to stick to what they knew. They were neither systematically for, nor against, new products. They were alive to the possibility of innovation, but they wanted to see for themselves. For example, many women who had been on the lookout for more modern kitchen appliances began to realise that they cluttered the kitchen, often broke down and, at the end of the day, made life more complicated, rather than simplifying it. Instead, they preferred robust and multi-purpose kitchen appliances. In the same way, rather than focusing on outward signs of one's modernity, people turned their attention to whether such and such product actually improved their quality of life.

One of the main strands of the First Modernity's chain of mass consumption (desire for modernity → purchase of new products and appliances → economic development and increased innovation → desire for modernity) had been seriously weakened.

The 'me' generation

All the groups who were monitoring socio-cultural change in the 1970s considered the social current we called 'self-expression and self-fulfilment' to be the most widespread, the most obvious and the most likely to bring about change. Daniel Yankelovich argued that this current was behind transformations in American society throughout the 1970s.[10] Cofremca made similar observations in France, as did Taylor Nelson in England and SIFO in Sweden. In Germany, the current was weaker, but still visible and one of our Italian colleagues, Professor Giampaolo Fabris, remarked that by the end of the 1970s the current was almost as important in Italy as it was in neighbouring European countries.

These sociologists reported that by 1970, for those who led the way, this movement was experienced as a spontaneous eruption. People's attempts to free up their feelings and emotions led to a new awareness of the richness of their inner worlds: individuals felt themselves to be unique and this came as a wonderful surprise. But it soon also became the norm. General disenchantment with mass consumer society paved the way for a new ideology. And so a new myth and a new norm replaced those of the First Modernity and took on the same role as levers of social change. Westerners seized hold of a few basic beliefs, which came to define the new myth:

- Everybody has their own personality, which makes each of us a unique and precious individual.

- Part of this personality is latent or submerged, it has been repressed and deformed by social conventions and has been manipulated by those in power.

- Everybody has to free their personality from this strait-jacket, to express it in the way they live and to fulfil their true selves.

---

10   Yankelovich D. *New Rules: Searching for Self-Fulfillment in a World Turned Upside Down*. New York: Random House, 1981.

A spontaneous eruption

For the trailblazers or precursors, this self-expression was above all experienced as a spontaneous leap forward. As early as the 1950s, we met a handful of men and women who were discovering their feelings, their emotions and how these fed their desires. Though the initial discovery came about by chance, they soon tuned into it and cultivated it. They learned new things about themselves. They discovered that they were richer, more complex and more special beings than they had thought. They felt that they had a personality and they wanted to explore it and express their uniqueness in the choices they made. Slowly but surely, increasing numbers of men and women began to undergo this sort of personal odyssey. And many ventured further. They set out to explore their uniqueness, to allow it to flourish and to free it from the old constraints and shackles.

These voyages of self-discovery seemed all the more remarkable to us as researchers because we ourselves had set similar processes in motion when we were conducting non-directive interviews in the 1950s. During the interviews, our subjects had discovered an inner richness of which they had previously been unaware. We saw some of them again several years later and they told us that the interviews had been the beginning of a journey of self-discovery that had helped them to choose where they wanted to go with their lives. This process that we had, in some cases, inadvertently set in motion in the 1950s, occurred spontaneously for large numbers of people in the 1960s.

This spontaneous self-expression carried them towards other forms of expression. Being more in touch with their own personalities, they were also in touch with other people's and this opened up a space for intimate dialogue. This phenomenon was particularly evident among the radical students involved in the events of May 1968. Many of them had a deep and finely tuned understanding of themselves and others, as well as of the systems of interaction and influence in which they were implicated. Having watched their parents chase conspicuous consumption and modernity, having seen them pursue often illusory forms of happiness and having understood the motivations and frustrations of their parents' generation, they had a good feel for what they would rapidly come to think of as the problems of a society based on mass consumption and bureaucratic industrialisation. Few had read Marcuse and they only rarely found themselves in agreement with Maoist leaders who dreamed of toppling capitalism and representative democracy. Rather, it was their perspicacity and ability to understand these mechanisms intuitively that drove them to act, allowed them to discover themselves and each other and made them challenge society at large.

This intuition was one of the students' principal weapons in their struggle against the prevailing order. Young people understood their opponents' mentality and anticipated their every move. They mocked the authorities. They intuitively understood how to raise awareness of issues and how to win people over to their cause. The interpersonal and social awareness they displayed in their relationships with others, especially their parents, was a powerful force for change. In 1969, Cofremca undertook field research into this 'new society' for the then Prime Minister, Jacques Chaban-Delmas. This research helped us to understand how this awareness had spread to society at large, especially among young workers in the cities. It was evidence of another important socio-cultural current, which we called 'intraception': the intuitive capacity to interpret and decode oneself and others.

Self-expression becomes a moral and social imperative

The current of self-expression and self-fulfilment was not simply a question of people's desire and ability to express themselves more fully. It also contained an ideology and a moral code. The ideology of self-fulfilment originated in the writings of a few intellectuals. It flourished among the student body and reinforced their critique of the prevailing order, before spreading to wider society and establishing itself as a social norm.

In the early 1950s, Abraham Maslow placed 'self-actualisation' at the summit of his hierarchy of needs.[11] Simultaneously, David Riesman anticipated the extension of independence beyond the three common personality and social types that he had identified. The thinking of Herbert Marcuse also grew in popularity during the 1960s.[12] He criticised industrial civilisation and consumer society, which he saw as creating artificial needs, and argued instead for a form of civilisation that would encourage people to free themselves from repressive institutions. Popular culture and the mass media further popularised these ideas.

The new ideology found fertile ground among Europeans and Americans who were dismayed by the conformism required by consumer society and who had discovered richer feelings and emotional lives. So, on the one hand, we had ideological influences and, on the other, emerging personal tastes and experiences. They reinforced one another, allowing the ideology of self-expression and self-fulfilment to become the dominant social norm of the 1970s.

---

11   Maslow A. *Motivation and Personality*. New York: Harper and Row, 1954.

12   Most particularly, Marcuse H. *One-dimensional Man, Studies in the Ideology of Advanced Industrial Society*. London: Routledge and Kegan Paul, 1964.

This affected people's behaviour in different ways and we can distinguish three ideal types, all of which were present to a greater or lesser extent in people's everyday experience:

1. For some, this norm merely reinforced a pre-existing, spontaneous and largely joyful tendency. They expressed themselves naturally; their emotions, feelings and desires affected their day-to-day lives without their having to push things; self-discovery was a pleasure. Listening to them, it seemed that the congruence they felt between their personal drives and the prevailing norm was a source of comfort.

2. Others felt no real need to express or to fulfil themselves, but they were aware that in the prevailing social climate of the 1970s it was better to be seen to have a liberated and original personality. They copied the lifestyle and behaviour of their more expressive peers and derived some pleasure from this. In so doing, they gradually learned how to express themselves better. These two stances (spontaneous expression and the imitation of expression) were equally present in both Europe and North America.

3. The third stance was more common in the United States. For this group, the quest for self-expression and self-fulfilment was experienced as a personal obligation, almost a moral constraint. The search for one's unique personality and for ways of embodying it in everyday life became a sort of militant act of introspection. It could take people down paths they did not want to pursue, force them to make unpleasant choices and even become a torture of sorts.

More and more, the media offered practical psychological advice to viewers, listeners and readers. It encouraged them to think about self-expression as something that required effort. Everybody was held to have a unique and clearly defined personality, but it only existed in embryonic form. Not only was it thought to be hidden deep inside, but also often deformed by the individual's personal history and by social conditioning. Forms of authority, norms and social constraints all prevented people from fulfilling themselves and prevented them from expressing their inner emotional states.

In the 1970s, the language of pop psychology informed people's search for self-development. They had to satisfy their needs, realise their potential, continue to grow and express their true emotions. They needed to be recognised as 'real' people, with emotional, sexual, material, intellectual, physical and social needs. The more needs one satisfied, the more one fulfilled oneself. Their emotions were somehow sacred and it was a crime not to satisfy an emotional need. Yankelovich observed that many people spent a great a deal of time weighing up the pros and cons of related life choices. How much should they invest in their marriage, their job or their life, and what should they expect to get out of them? Should they remain faithful or should they seek sexual fulfilment wherever they could find it? How should couples split household chores and responsibilities? How should women divide their energies between their roles as mothers, wives and working women? They not only had to choose, but also to be creative in their choices. Rather than focusing on the world and its vagaries, they turned their attention on themselves. Many analysts began to suggest that American society had entered a phase of acute narcissism.

Learning to navigate one's way in life

Unlike in the First Modernity, people's life paths were no longer well defined and clearly mapped out. They had to choose for themselves whether to continue or give up on their studies, whether to live in the countryside or the city, whether to stick at their job or look for a change of career, whether to stay at home with their children or go back to work, and whether to work on a relationship or look for another, more fulfilling one. Tradition and authority were challenged and the signposts and beacons that people had used to navigate their way through life had disappeared. People experimented. Families broke apart and individuals had to look for new ways of living. Young people, middle managers and city workers were at the forefront of this process of change. Some failed and others succeeded; but everybody learned.

Still, it was not only a question of major, life-changing decisions. In the 1970s, the management of day-to-day life became problematic for many people. They stumbled around looking for roles, rhythms and social environments that suited them. They agonised over whether this or that item of clothing, this or that way of receiving guests really expressed their true personality. Couples began to talk intimately and to try to help one another. All this took time and effort. Many felt that they had no time for themselves. This was especially so for women who held down a job and looked after their family.

At first, people would often reject all social norms and conventions as a matter of principle. Later, they would start to find ways of embodying their personality *within* the prevailing social order. Thus, hippies in the United States began by setting up communities that existed entirely outside society and its norms and conventions. Later on, most would rejoin society. All over the modern world, young people ran away from their families in the search for autonomy and self-expression. Later on, they were able to return to their families, which had, by then, become more open and tolerant.

It was often women who chose to follow this path, seeking independence from forms of authority, pre-ordained roles and social constraints. In France, women very quickly went from a position of outright rejection or rebellion to one which was both flexible and which offered them greater independence vis-à-vis their husbands, children and bosses.

The edifice of mass consumerism begins to crumble

At the same time as the myth of modernity and progress began to fade away, two other attributes of the First Modernity also started to collapse: the pyramid of status and prestige (based on conspicuous consumption) fell apart and the world of fashion began to lose its hierarchical character. We also saw the first signs of the selective and cautious consumer emerging.

The pyramid of status and prestige falls apart

The system of conspicuous consumption began to break apart in the second half of the 1960s. This was a complex process. The system was already crumbling in better-off households and among younger people, but the quest for status and prestige as a driving force continued to spread among the working classes for another ten years or so. Overall, however, the system lost more members than it gained.

It was obviously American students and hippies who first rejected the idea of conspicuous consumption. But it is harder to pinpoint precisely where this first spread more widely among the middle classes. It is possible that the commercial failure of Ford's Edsel in 1958-59 was an early example. Yankelovich, though, claims that throughout the 1960s, most Americans, with the exception of the student rebels, continued peacefully to live their lives very much as they had done before.[13] According to him, you had to wait until the 1970s to witness truly radical change.

In France, Cofremca noticed subtle changes as early as 1967. The first signs of this emerged in a survey we conducted for Renault. We were asked to help with the development of a new model, the Renault 5, which finally appeared in 1972. Our fieldwork suggested that previous trends were being turned

---

13   Yankelovich 1981: pp. 13-14.

on their head. Well-off middle managers, for whom a show of conspicuous consumption had long been a major factor in their choice of car, appeared to be less concerned with this aspect of things than before. Instead, they dreamed of a car in which they felt comfortable, which would improve their quality of life and which would be practical, not impressive. They wanted a car 'to feel good in', not a car to show off.

In the same year, similar research carried out for construction companies in and around Paris came to much the same conclusion. Well-off middle managers who had, until recently, chosen their apartments on the grounds of prestige and status, were now motivated by other concerns. They wanted a comfortable apartment where their family would live and interact happily. At the same time, people's notions of the ideal home layout began to change. They no longer wanted apartments with clear divisions between the kitchen and the living area, between private and public space. Instead, they looked for flexibility and rooms that gave space for improvisation and easy communication between different members of the family. By 1975, it was clear that changing lifestyles throughout the Western world had severely dented the importance of conspicuous consumption. They undermined it on two fronts: blurring hierarchies of affluence and consumption and sapping its motivational force.

The blurring of hierarchies of affluence and consumption

In the 1950s and '60s, a small number of products, like kitchen appliances and cars, helped clearly to define status. However, although these objects briefly conferred a certain position in the pecking order upon their owner, they quickly lost their significance as they became more commonplace. Refrigerators are a good example. Their rapid adoption across the social spectrum stripped them of their distinctiveness – first, for the moneyed classes and then for everybody else. On top of this, the very fact of using a refrigerator altered its symbolic value. For early adopters, who had no experience of using one, a fridge seemed like an unnecessary luxury and so conferred prestige and status. But people quickly realised how useful they could be: they were hygienic, practical and made life easier. And so when it came to buying a new one, these practical considerations became more important. Other, new consumer products also failed to fill this role as status symbols. Televisions, for example, took France by storm (in 1962, only 23% of households had one, but by 1973, that figure was 78%), but take-up was higher among the working classes than among some sections of the upper middle classes. Accordingly, questions of prestige and status were less significant in people's choice of a television.

At the same time, multi-car households blurred the complex relationship between cars and status. The clear-cut correlation between one's social standing and the size, horsepower and price of one's car was undermined. As some people climbed the career ladder, they bought ever bigger cars, but others chose to buy a second, smaller one. We saw people trying to work out which of these two choices had greater status value. Car-manufacturers adapted to these changes and confused things further by offering expensive small cars and relatively cheap big ones. Many of the smaller cars were also extremely desirable.

Status and conspicuous consumption lose their power as motivational factors

There were many reasons behind the declining importance of status symbols. In the 1960s, many students (especially the better-off among them) realised that the race to consume and to acquire status was a trap. They had observed their parents and learned their lesson. They had seen their fathers wear themselves out trying to climb the career ladder and come away unsatisfied. They had been disappointed by consumer goods they had long hankered after. Some of them had become immune to the desire for prestige and status derived from conspicuous consumption.

Many adults had also experienced things that weakened their desire for status and prestige. They had derived all the satisfaction they could from status symbols and had had enough. They stopped wanting to compete with their peers. Other types of motivation, like self-expression and self-realisation, became more important. The tropism of conspicuous consumption did not vanish, but it did become a secondary factor and was easily swept aside by other forms of motivation. By the 1970s, middle managers were abandoning successful careers to pursue a more meaningful life.

This was true even for the working classes, who often had not as yet derived much satisfaction from the pursuit and acquisition of status symbols. Consumers, who had worked hard to be able to afford prestigious objects that quickly lost their prestige, were profoundly disappointed. This disappointment undermined their desire for possessions and made them think about their way of life. They had longed for this or that appliance, seeing it as the next step up, but then they realised that everybody had one, even people they tended to look down on. They felt frustrated and cheated. They realised that they had been caught up in an accelerating spiral of consumption and they wanted out. They had grown wise to the trap.

Simplicity now became something to be proud of. Being – and being seen to be – down-to-earth people showed that other things were more important for them. From 1973 onwards, this new approach was reinforced by the economic crisis and its accompanying hardships.

The hierarchy of fashion begins to collapse

The world of fashion is the best example of these wider changes in the social fabric. People stopped following their supposed superiors and instead took their lead from their peers or elsewhere, following the example set by young people and the working classes. This was clear in the widespread adoption of jeans, peasants' corduroy clothing, Afghan coats and clogs.

People's respect for authority and tradition was replaced by a new spontaneity. We conducted a series of surveys charting French women's changing sartorial habits. In 1965, women often said things like, 'I might wear a pair of trousers if I go away for the weekend, but I wear a dress or a skirt to work; otherwise, I'd feel uncomfortable and, anyway, the boss might notice'. In 1970, some of the young women we interviewed bluntly declared, 'I wear trousers to work, because I'm my own person'. By 1975 they said, 'A few years ago, I always wore trousers to work, but then I realised that was just as conformist as always wearing a dress. So now I mix and match. Some days I wear a dress, on others I wear dresses and sometimes I wear a miniskirt. It depends on how I feel.' In ten years, the norm had been replaced by a counter-norm and then by a more flexible approach that took into account people's personality and moods, as well as changing circumstances.

It was the influence of these young women that sounded the death-knell for 'institutional fashion'. From around 1968 onwards, the great fashion houses lost their sway. Alongside their fashions, new ones emerged. Some of these came from the streets and some were dreamed up by stylists or dress makers. Several types of fashion co-existed: women wore skirts of radically different lengths; some opted for dresses and others chose trousers. Everybody had greater choice. By 1975, the same women we had interviewed five and ten years earlier had been reconciled with the fashion world and now said, 'I love fashion. There are loads of pretty things and I can choose what I like, depending on my mood and my personality. That way, I can really be myself.'

It was the same young women who, in 1965, were saying, 'I love fashion, I always try to be fashionable', that five years later came out with statements like, 'I don't care about fashion, I'm not a mannequin and I'm my own person'. In this short period, people had begun to reject fashion, which they increasingly experienced as a sort of authoritarian imperative. In 1971, Cofremca carried out a survey for *Printemps* (the large Parisian department store) that allowed us to explore this phenomenon. The store's customers tended to be fairly cutting edge, much smarter than the average Parisian woman. Their clothes' racks were covered in huge signs, with arrows and slogans saying "The latest style!" We interviewed the women who were browsing among the rails and asked them what they thought. Most responded, "Who cares about their styles? I wear whatever takes my fancy". People were so sick of the tyranny of fashion that they often deliberately wore supposedly unfashionable styles or items, or dressed as simply as possible, cultivating a look that said, "I just threw on the first thing that came to hand".

The rejection of artificial, mass-produced goods

People's rejection of mass-produced goods went hand in hand with a newfound appreciation of the natural world. We saw the first signs of this in France as early as they in the United States. Cofremca came across examples of people rejecting industrial modernity as early as the 1950s. In 1956, interviewees declared that *vin ordinaire* (the cheapest category of wine available, which was industrially produced and treated) was a suspicious, chemical product. Very early on, the chemical industry was accused of poisoning the environment. Both then and now, this rejection was widespread and present in all social groups. Such positions were common to young people, trying to distinguish themselves from their parents' generation, and to more conservative interviewees, nostalgic for the rural life they had known in their childhood. When young people's rejection transformed into collective protest, their elders suddenly felt they could express their nostalgia without having to apologise for it.

This rejection of industrial and artificial goods and techniques overlapped with their appreciation of the natural world and gathered pace throughout the 1960s. Together, they helped to change people's lifestyles and consumption patterns, as well as favouring the emergence of development organisations and consumer and environmental groups.

The growing desire for a return to nature was omnipresent. This was both a physical return to the natural world and a nostalgic return to products people remembered from their childhood. City-dwellers drifted out to live in greener suburbs. Gardening, hiking, horse riding and cycling all took off. There was a new trend for houses with little gardens or balconies, which gave people the impression of being in contact with nature. Cosmetics, food, clothes and other products benefited from these changes if their manufacturers managed to highlight their natural qualities and their intimate relationship with plants, country living, traditional crafts and the land. Consumers, though, grew wary. They felt that such products were not what they had been, that pesticides, insecticides, artificial colourings and preservatives had all, so to speak, denatured nature. People complained that they could not find the tasty, healthy and natural products of their youth.

Here, as elsewhere, it was Americans who first made something of this widespread environmental undercurrent. Leaders emerged and people set up consumer and environmental organisations and ran media campaigns. In 1962, Rachel Carson published her hard-hitting critique of industrialisation.[14] The chemical industry's outraged response only strengthened the movement. Just under ten years later, France created a Ministry for Nature and the Environment.

Selective and cautious consumers

Our research showed that, towards the end of the 1960s and throughout the '70s, consumers were becoming more cautious. They began to ask themselves whether particular products would really satisfy them, whether they were worth the money or the effort. Such questions helped them to think more clearly about the issues surrounding pleasure, desire and happiness. Of course, they still hankered after consumer goods and, though they were less hampered by convention, they were more susceptible than ever to marketing and advertising. But, as their suspicion of advertising claims grew, they were less likely to make spur-of-the-moment purchases.

This move towards more selective consumption depended a great deal on social class. Whilst most members of the middle classes were clearly becoming disenchanted, many working class people remained in thrall to the urge to consume. In early 1974, when this decade of change was drawing to a close and the oil crisis was still in full swing, Cofremca carried out a survey using a representative sample of French people in order to gauge their reactions to various political and economic scenarios. The vast majority of managers, middle managers and members of liberal professions felt that the crisis was an opportunity to tighten their belts and try to build a less competitive and more harmonious society. Most working class people, on the other hand, rejected this scenario and refused to even think about reducing their levels of consumption.

---

14   Carson R. *Silent Spring.* Boston, MA: Houghton Mifflin, 1962.

Nevertheless, many young people from working class backgrounds were aware of the consumption trap. In 1976, Cofremca carried out a series of in-depth interviews with unemployed young workers, which showed that they tended to know their own minds and were able to analyse situations much more clearly than their elders. They had begun to question the race to consume and commercial attempts to manipulate them into buying. They realised that if they wanted to avoid the trap, then they had to drop out of the race altogether. But they could not countenance that. They refused to give up their little pleasures, their desire for the odd luxury item. They thought they could pick and choose, giving in to certain desires, putting off others for another day and rejecting some altogether.

Consumption was also beginning to become less monolithic. More people wanted personalised products tailored to their needs and they shunned ready-made solutions. Women, for example, had tended to use make-up in stereotyped and conventional ways. Now they started to choose their make-up according to their personality, mood or the needs of a given situation. But this new breed of consumer often struggled to find products that really met their needs. Cofremca began systematically to record the 'product and service gaps' that they identified. For example, despite car manufacturers' attempts to diversify, the range of vehicles on offer was still too restricted to meet consumers' tastes.

Casting off the shackles of society

The students involved in the events of May 1968, as well as those of their parents who were experiencing similarly radical change, realised that their newfound desire for self-expression was being hampered by social conventions, traditional family relations, national identity and the moral strictures handed down by the church. Thus was born a powerful movement that rejected social constraints and blew apart the barriers that stood between people and freedom.

The breakdown of sexual taboos

The rejection of sexual taboos began seriously to change people's behaviour in the 1960s as the numbers of those in Europe and America cohabiting, divorcing and having children outside marriage soared.

This new sexual freedom was clearly visible in the interviews we conducted with young people towards the end of the 1960s, as well as in students' diaries and journals. People now demanded the untrammelled right to have sexual relations however and with whomever they pleased. These sorts of sexual relations were neither old-fashioned romantic love stories, nor were they reducible to the brute physical act. Instead, they combined sexuality, tenderness, the exploration of each other's bodies, intimacy and mutuality. It was no longer simply a question of man the predator and woman the seducer, but of two lovers who chose one another, at least for the time being. Nevertheless, for most of our interviewees, the idea of one day finding true love was still present.

Young people's forthright approach to these issues helped their parents rid themselves of the remaining taboos. Until the early 1960s, it was still the norm to marry for life, even among people who had shrugged off Christian morality. But our interviews in the late 1960s and early 1970s showed that divorce was no longer taboo for the French. Of course, most still wanted to find a partner for life and to raise children in a stable marriage, but this was being replaced by an emotional pragmatism. Many began to feel that if the love went out of a relationship, or if it became too stormy, then it might be better to break up and look elsewhere for these things.

Gender roles blur

It was not only men who were demanding the right to self-development and self-fulfilment. For the young people involved in May 1968, it went without saying that women should be freed from their social shackles, should be able to exercise their sexuality as they saw fit and were the equals of men. Even though they were heavily under-represented among the leadership, there were as many women as men on the barricades.

Equally, until 1965, there was only a handful of militant feminists who radically challenged traditional gender roles. Many of our female interviewees were trying to free themselves from the drudgery of housework, but at the same time they still wanted to fulfil their traditional roles as mothers and wives. Men, of course, behaved much as they always had. In other words, the old order was still strong, even if it seemed clear to us that it was fighting a rearguard action. Traditional gender roles were widely understood as part of the natural order of things. Men and women were different. And so, many of our interviewees, whether male or female, working or middle class, found themselves torn between conflicting tendencies which they did not fully understand. Desires born of their emotional and physical reality drove them to behave in ways that seemed to run counter to their pre-determined gender roles. Men found themselves wanting to sunbathe or to use aftershave.

Women, surprised by a sudden desire to drink strong alcohol, wondered whether there was not something wrong with them. Many experienced profound feelings of guilt and shame.

However, as they watched the young student demonstrators, many also realised that the done thing was little more than a convention. They could aspire to something different. Their role as housewives had lost its clearly defined contours. Up until then, they had tried to reduce their workload without really calling the role itself into question. Now they began to wonder whether they should really do all the housework and why their husbands could not lend a hand. Initially, it was young women who posed these questions, but their mothers quickly followed suit, then intellectuals and the modern middle classes, and finally the population at large.

From the middle of the 1960s onwards, more and more French women began to think of themselves as active members of society: not objects, but subjects. Women wanted something different. In 1964, Dim started to market tights. A survey carried out by Cofremca in 1969 showed that more than any other piece of women's underwear, stockings and suspender belts were seen as clear markers of their subjugation. For many interviewees, they symbolised an imposed eroticism, the free rein of male sexual desire and an outdated form of sexuality. It wasn't that these women who voted for tights with their feet were prudes. *They* wanted to choose the right time for sexuality and eroticism, depending on their mood and on the situation.

Women rapidly won greater freedom and improved their position vis-à-vis men, but these changes were played out very differently in different countries. In this regard, the United States and France are at opposite ends of the spectrum. In the United States, many women continued to adopt clearly defined and very demanding roles. They had to be beautiful, slim, well made-up, good mothers and good lovers, but when it came to asserting their rights, they were quick to challenge men in general and their husbands in particular. In contrast, French women in the 1970s placed fewer demands upon themselves and tried to improve their status without directly confronting men. They managed to bring about social and legal change without resorting to militant and extremist feminist politics. These achievements were less the result of a war waged by women against men than the fruit of men and women's collective action, especially among the young. Twenty-five years later, it seems that in the decade that stretched from 1965 to 1975 France witnessed a silent feminist revolution. Many women had carved out enough freedom for themselves to be able to control their sexuality and birth rates plummeted. They gained a new confidence and independence from their husbands. The result was falling numbers of marriages, increasing divorce rates, soaring numbers of cohabiting couples and people marrying later. Their newfound political power led to the legalisation of the contraceptive pill and of abortion, to simplified divorce procedures and to the recognition of the legal equivalence of male and female adultery.

More open and equal parent-child relationships

For many middle class and urban families with teenage children, parent-child relations were changing dramatically. In some cases this was a source of conflict, but everywhere it led to relationships based more on equality, dialogue and participation. Often the parents were just as keen as the children to see a change in inter-generational relations. The events of 1968 allowed people to make these desires a reality. In-depth studies of family relations at the time show how children managed to make use of wider societal changes to re-educate their parents. It was not uncommon, for example, for children to slam the door on their parents, and for the parents to take the first steps towards reconciliation.

Both in families and in society at large, inter-generational mimesis was turned on its head. One of the clearest signs of this shift of power was the change in who led the way when it came to fashion. In the 1960s and 1970s, young men and women stopped copying their parents and innovated. Parents, meanwhile, began to dress like their children.

Families developed more liberal, less regimented and more egalitarian relations. Traditional markers of respect began to vanish. Parents stopped giving orders and notions of what was or was not acceptable behaviour (especially when it came to sexuality) began to change. In some cases, children were even allowed to bring home casual sexual partners.

In France, these changes were particularly noticeable in eating habits. Previously, meals had been minutely orchestrated events, but all of a sudden the sorts of change people had been vaguely imagining for the last ten years began to occur. People still had lunch and dinner at fixed times, but now there was some room for manoeuvre. A course might be dropped from dinner and courses could be served in a different order.

In traditional French middle and upper-middle class families, children had rarely been allowed to speak during meals and had to ask permission if they wished to do so. This now seemed absurd. Instead, parents began to cultivate their children's spontaneity and to help them learn how to have a conversation. Increasing numbers of families stopped trying to instil discipline in their children and instead tried to give them room to develop their own personalities. Even very young children were allowed to have their own tastes and preferences and they began to influence their parents' shopping habits.

Although many people still lived in cramped apartments, research showed that they were making different use of the space. Rooms set aside for the father or the mother began to disappear. Each member of the family tended to have the same rights as any other. Ideally, everybody should have his or her own space (for example, his or her own bedroom), where they could have a little privacy and see friends without disturbing – or being disturbed by – the rest of the family. Living rooms and front rooms became communal spaces, open to everybody, both parents and children.

Rejection of hierarchy and bureaucracy

Young people's rejection of the cold, hierarchical and bureaucratic society they had grown up in had a lasting effect. This was obvious in all major modern countries, but was particularly striking in France, where these hierarchies had a long and venerable history.

The May 1968 movement was fundamentally anti-hierarchical. The students were not opposed to any particular instance of hierarchical organisation, but to the principle of hierarchy itself. They ridiculed the authority of parents, policemen, university apparatchiks, political parties, trades unions and even General de Gaulle. They said it should be forbidden to forbid. They set out to undermine the state, the dogmatism and repression of the Catholic Church and the constraints placed on them by society. They railed against the principle of a selective higher education system that set people's future prospects in stone and so bolstered the existing hierarchy. They wanted more participation and more of a say in how things were done.

They were also trying to challenge the stifling rule of bureaucracy and regulations. 'Spontaneity' was one of the movement's leitmotifs. Nothing should stand in the way of individual spontaneity. Their very way of speaking was a challenge to the formal rules of syntax. Frustrated and constrained by petty bureaucracy and outdated moral strictures, something deep inside these students snapped, and the result was revolt.

Cofremca also carried out interviews with young state and private sector employees who were on strike. Though they had experienced different frustrations and expressed themselves in different ways, they were essentially protesting against the same thing as the students. Their demands were entirely new and they baffled union leaders. Essentially, they were less concerned with questions of pay and working hours, and more interested in questions of hierarchy, dignity and relations in the workplace. They were protesting about foremen and working on production lines. Responsibility was also a key issue and gave rise to interminable debates.

Young people were calling into question the whole edifice of hierarchy and bureaucracy, and very soon middle class and urban adults were raising similar issues. Hierarchy had seemed instinctively correct, as if it were a natural characteristic of humankind, just like it is for so many other animal species. The same was true of formal rules and pre-ordained social roles and expectations. All of a sudden, though, large sections of the population saw them for what they were: mere conventions. And they were seen as limiting people's spontaneity and their capacity for self-expression.

What's more, in the late 1960s and early '70s, people began to see that they were being manipulated and they tried to defend themselves. As early as 1965, Cofremca had identified this trend and continued to investigate it over the coming years. Previously, nobody had much thought about these things and they never emerged in interviews. People's idea of themselves left no room for such thoughts. People saw themselves as rational and responsible individuals who decided what to do and then did it. If they followed fashion, obeyed social conventions or imitated their social superiors, it was because it suited them or because it seemed the rational thing to do. In any case, it was *their* decision.

This world was, however, beginning to come apart at the seams. People's idea of themselves was less predicated on notions of rationality and choice making. They became aware of their unconscious and that they could be influenced and conditioned without knowing it. They realised that they had often been manipulated in the past, both by business and by the state, and they didn't thank them for it.

People became more suspicious of authority. Advertising was hit hard by this turn of events. Advertisements were increasingly seen as deceitful and duplicitous. As soon as people spotted a commercial, their hackles went up. This was not just a question of public opinion. Marketing teams found consumers increasingly hard to influence. They had to become much more subtle and much more sophisticated if they were to succeed.

Workplace relations also became strained. In some of the smaller and more cutting-edge companies, management worked alongside employees to transform conventional relationships. This, though, was the exception rather than the rule. Large companies and the public sector were still organised in the same hierarchical manner. In some cases, employees won minor personal freedoms that were not directly related to their work. Women might be allowed to wear trousers or men to wear their hair long. This was more common in France and Sweden than in the United States. It acted as a sort of safety valve for self-expression. But it was not enough. Workplaces in the 1970s were difficult environments for those who longed to be able to express themselves. There was a growing contradiction between people's new outlook and the way in which work was organised – and people began to challenge this. They dreamt of a world where work was a source of creativity and fulfilment. Some tried to break free, changing the way they worked or looking for new, more fulfilling careers. Such life choices were never very widespread, but they were telling. By the end of the decade, however, hope was being replaced by disappointment. People looked for ways to avoid or limit unpleasant, work-related obligations and they started to put their work into perspective.

Parallel studies carried out in the 1970s by Cofremca in France and Yankelovich, Skelly and White in the United States discovered that growing numbers of mainly young men, both employees and managers, were beginning to reject prevailing workplace norms. They refused to compete, to place their jobs before their personal lives and to prioritise career advancement. They might reject a promotion, and some began to behave in ways that previously had been restricted to women. They arrived late for work because they had to drive the children to school, left work to do the shopping and took time off when their children were born. Although such behaviour was tolerated, it was still exceptional.

Even the army was not immune. Officers and private soldiers questioned prevailing notions of military authority. In the United States, this took the form of massive anti-war demonstrations and the film MASH, which won the *palme d'or* at Cannes in May 1970, portrayed life in the American army as a sexual free-for-all, awash with dissent and improvisation; in so doing, it ridiculed traditional ideas of military authority. This streak of anti-authoritarianism also affected Europe. In early 1975, soldiers publicly demonstrated in several French and German cities. In November of the same year, conscripts assigned to a regiment based in Besançon released a joint statement with a major trades union declaring that they had unionised. All these actions were attempts to challenge existing military structures, which had failed to adapt to modern life. These efforts were sometimes supported by officers, who were, in their own way, voicing similar concerns.

The forces of law and order were less respected than ever: judges were kidnapped and killed, policemen were shot at. In France, it was no longer trades unions that directed protest movements but informal organisations that had sprung up in response to particular situations. They oversaw the struggle, worked to get public support and sometimes acquired real power, but then they simply dissolved when the situation changed, ready to re-emerge if needs be. Most formal organisations (bosses, the state, trade unions) remained convinced that these informal organisations represented a real threat to their very existence.

* * *

The imposing structure of this individualist and hierarchical society of mass consumption had first begun to crumble and then collapsed in on itself. Consumers had been subject to constant pressure to catch up with and outperform the people who sat just above them on the ladders of affluence, modernity and fashion. And time and again they had been disappointed. They had realised that the race to consume had failed to bring them the happiness and emancipation they had hoped for. They also realised that they had been manipulated. So they broke ranks with society as a whole and went looking for happiness and autonomy. This ushered in the Second Modernity.

Chapter 4
People in touch with their vitality

Just as the First Modernity was reaching its peak, a central theme of the Second, *Polysensuality*, was already beginning to emerge and carve out a niche for itself. I first spotted it in Sweden, in 1952, and then in France, in 1954. By the 1960s, the term formed part of Cofremca's standard vocabulary.

So long as people's physical and emotional sensations had been inhibited, repressed and channelled, their relationship with the world had been primarily a visual one. But little by little, and sometimes without realising it, they began to be aware of the variety of their emotions and sensations. They stopped describing and representing and started to feel and experience. They developed a somatic awareness of their emotions and their feelings and began to lean more towards their emotions than their intellect.

First described in the 1950s, this trend quietly developed until the late 1960s without business or marketing specialists making any concerted effort to exploit it. It really only affected the First Modernity marginally, but it did prepare the way for the eruption of another current, that of self-expression and self-realisation. In the last three decades of the twentieth century, it underpinned practically all the different dynamics that helped to shape the Second Modernity. Under the influence of polysensuality, tens and then hundreds of millions of people gradually learned how to tap into their vital energy. We called these people *Vitalists*. By the 1990s, they probably constituted more than half the population of the most developed countries.

A step back in time: the gradual emergence of polysensuality

The repression of emotions and physical sensations

Norbert Elias has described the long historical process by which Westerners gradually became self-disciplined and civilised and learnt to subjugate their emotions and control their drives.[15] The nineteenth century constituted a high-water mark of prudishness, the inhibition of sensations and emotions, the primacy of the intellect, and the arrogance of reason.

---

15   Elias 1939.

In the 1950s, the emotional and sensory life of most people we interviewed was inhibited and channelled. This supports Elias's thesis and helps us better to understand what it was like before the arrival of polysensuality. In interviews, people talked about their thoughts and only rarely mentioned sensory perceptions like touch, hearing, taste and smell. On the rare occasions when people were consciously aware of them, they were felt to be somehow threatening or immodest. They were dismissed as bestial. They could drive people to commit cardinal sins. Out of the five senses, only sight was seen as noble and particularly human – it was linked to the intellect and to intelligence. With the exception of a few artists, people did not think of sight as a sense at all, but as the means by which the mind might grasp reality.

Conventional child-rearing techniques repressed and channelled children's senses. In France, education was articulated around sight. Its principal aim was to teach children to read and to write. The other, lesser senses were not thought worthy of being taught. There were no classes intended to refine children's sense of smell or taste. Schools did not teach people how to touch: they learned for themselves. (Except for the blind, who were taught Braille.) Opportunities to indulge the senses were avoided. It wasn't that long since young girls in boarding schools had had to take their daily bath wearing a shift.

Only hearing received any special attention. Not that any effort was made to develop children's aural capacities in the way that happens in societies where a good sense of hearing can mean the difference between life and death, if, say, there is a snake in the grass. We did teach music, but only reluctantly and with particular emphasis on visual learning. This reticence was obvious in the fact that it was only taught to young girls: boys were not supposed to waste their time on such futile distractions. And music was written down. Westerners read their music.

Children raised in such conditions undoubtedly develop very different neural connections from those raised to make the most of all their senses. The former will tend to prioritise the linear and the Euclidean – that which can be clearly visualised. Rather than experiencing the world, they represent it to themselves. In such cases the intellect dominates. And in fact, most people we interviewed in the 1950s had a tendency to intellectualise their emotions, to describe them in words and to neglect physical perceptions in favour of ideas.

In this pre-polysensual world, displays of emotion might be acceptable for women and children, but they were strongly discouraged among men, except for a few clearly directed and channelled emotions that were linked to dominant ideologies: things like patriotic fervour and revolutionary ardour.

Little by little, polysensuality would overturn these old habits. Modern society reacted violently against the previous state of affairs and embraced the lesser senses: touch, hearing, taste and smell. It also embraced sexuality. Slowly but surely it overcame the inhibitions that had constrained people's perceptions, urges, emotions and intuitions. With hindsight, the emergence of polysensuality seems to be one of the most important occurrences of the twentieth century. It profoundly changed both the Western personality and the whole feel of our culture.

Sweden and France: first contact with polysensuality

My fieldwork in Sweden and France at the very beginning of the 1950s first made me aware of the beginnings of this radical change. When we first arrived in Sweden, we were struck by the intensity of our young interviewees' sensory and emotional sensitivity. They revelled in nature and in the sensations derived from warmth and cold, from feeling their muscles glow as they practised gymnastics, skiing and hiking and from feeling the sun on their skin. The Swedes without doubt took the lead when it came to the pursuit of pleasures like these. They also promoted ideas of comfort and well-being, be it at home, at work or in public transport. In the 1950s, the comfort and furnishings of Swedish households were probably unparalleled anywhere else in the world. The Swedes were the first to design chairs that aimed both to support the body and allow it to relax. Nor was this a purely physical idea of well-being; it was also a psychological one. The Swedish word 'stämning' gives us a good idea of this. It denotes a warm atmosphere and the sensory and psychological happiness that results from feeling comfortable somewhere. Sport, alcohol, exercise, a fire, songs and physical comfort can all contribute to it.

A short time later, I found a similar dynamic emerging in France whilst investigating women's emerging attitudes towards washing, towards their bathrooms and towards toilet soap. The young French girls I interviewed in 1954 had begun to pay attention to physical sensations that had previously passed people by. They enjoyed them and tried to cultivate them.

French women and toilet soap (1954)

At the time, an advertising war was being waged for the lucrative soap market. A few big brands were struggling to break the market dominance of *savon de Marseille*[16], and they were gradually winning consumers over. Four brands were vying for this market: Unilever marketed Lux, L'Oréal had Monsavon and Cadum and Palmolive had still not merged. Though they each had enormous advertising budgets, none had yet managed to outmanoeuvre its competitors.

People in the business assumed that one of women's key concerns was to protect their skin and not to damage it by using harsh products. Accordingly, most advertisements focused on how a particular brand of soap affected your skin, how it cared for it, made it softer, more beautiful and even more seductive. Lux gives you skin like a star; Cadum gives you baby-soft skin; Palmolive brings you the combined softness of palm oil and olive oil. One of the main Monsavon advertisements, designed by Savignac, showed a bar of soap coming straight out of a cow's udder and seemed to say, 'When you use Monsavon, you're washing yourself in natural, wholesome milk'.

Comfremca was invited by Unilever and their advertising agency, J. Walter Thompson, to carry out the first European survey of this market. The interviews we conducted were extremely revealing. Most of our interviewees seemed not to care about skin-protection and it had very little impact on their choice of soap. Questions of prestige, modernity and seduction were luring them away from *savon de Marseille*, but one particular set of motivations (which surprised us) emerged in a number of interviews. Some women seemed less concerned with the effect a particular soap had or with its social connotations, than they were with the sensations or emotions they felt when using it.

The women we interviewed could be divided into three main groups and this typology highlighted the existence of a particular social dynamic that the client might be able to make use of:

1. The first group, about 10% of the sample, consisted mainly of young women who often lived in large cities and who described themselves as modern. They enjoyed the interviews and often let them overrun. They were clearly 'Hedonists' and took real pleasure in their beauty regime. Some had only recently discovered the joys of the bathroom and of soap. They mentioned the pleasant smells and the feeling of

---

16   Although it is once again fashionable, the huge cube of unscented olive oil soap known as *savon de Marseille* was usurped by scented, more highly processed soap bars.

their skin. For example, one said, 'We've only had a bathroom for three years. I really like having one now. I can shut myself away and spend hours in a hot bath. And I really like modern soap bars. They're so soft and all that foam... They're warm and they smell nice. They glide over your skin. I enjoy washing more and more.' They all mentioned how the soaps felt. How gentle they were, what the lather was like, how they felt in their hands. They talked of hot and cold, of the contrast between the warmth of a bath and a cold shower, of smells and sometimes of colours. They tried to make us understand the feelings of intimacy and serenity they derived from these experiences. For these young women, soap bars simultaneously evoked sensations and emotions. They made the link between these underlying physical sensations and the emotions they provoked. They also experienced these emotions in new ways. They were not channelled and directed by social codes but emerged straight out of each woman's sensory experiences.

2. We called the second group 'Renewal'. It covered about a third of our sample. Just like for the first group, their soap and their beauty regime were important and they were happy to discuss them. They mentioned the pleasure they derived from washing, but they presented it in intellectual and moral terms. Washing was a sort of renewal: it washed away discomfort, dirt and tiredness. This was very pleasant. They were also very keen on lather, but their feelings towards it were ambivalent. It was necessary and enjoyable, but it would be outrageous not to rinse oneself properly, not to wash away every last bubble. The occasional slip allowed us to see the sensory pleasure they felt but did not as yet explicitly acknowledge. One clear example of this tendency was a forty-year-old Parisian secretary we interviewed. She was married with two children. 'I like to wash in the evenings, after work. I can wash away the day's dirt and relax. I feel like a new woman when I've had my shower, all scrubbed up and rinsed clean... My husband's an animal, he never rinses properly. And I really like soap. A shower without soap would be like a steak without a nice glass of Bordeaux.' This woman could discuss the pleasure derived from her beauty regime because she made it acceptable by moralising it. But her last sentence, where she mentioned Bordeaux, revealed the underlying presence of a real sensory pleasure, which she was unable to admit openly.

3. The third and largest group covered roughly half of our sample. They tended to be older women and were much more common in provincial towns than in Paris. We called them 'Repressed' because they stoutly refused to discuss their washing habits, except in the most perfunctory manner possible: 'One has to wash and that's that!' The interview made them uncomfortable. They often cut it short, sometimes fairly trenchantly. The stiffness and aggression with which they asserted the purely functional nature of washing and of soap seemed to indicate defensiveness or self-censorship.

The example of soap points to an underlying social dynamic

This range of attitudes led us to suspect the existence of a new social dynamic. We hypothesised that most of the 'Repressed' group were censoring the possibility of pleasure, while those in the 'Renewal' group felt this pleasure but disguised it. These latter seemed to be half way down a path already taken by the 'Hedonists'. This hypothesis was reinforced by three distinct considerations.

- A sociological one: the 'Hedonists' were few in number, but they were over-represented among young women from Paris and other large cities who declared themselves to be modern. They were the trailblazers.

- A socio-cultural one: over the previous twenty years, the Western world had witnessed the development of a strong hedonistic current, most evident in the assertion of the individual's right to pleasure and happiness.

- One involving both economics and people's lifestyle: for young women who had grown up washing in cold water over the kitchen sink, the discovery of the bathroom was an experience that was likely to awaken their senses and give them a feeling of well-being. Meanwhile, bathrooms only became widespread in working class households from 1950 onwards, as buildings were rapidly modernised.[17] Hedonism and the bathroom combined forces. The one was a sort of permission to feel pleasure and the other an opportunity to do so. Together, they helped people to discover polysensual pleasure.

---

17   In 1954, only 17.5% of French households possessed a bathroom; by 1975, this figure was 70%. Borne D. *Histoire de la Société Française Depuis* 1945. Paris: Armand Colin, 1989, p.41.

We concluded that alongside the roles of modernity and prestige/conspicuous consumption as twin motivating factors, another, stronger factor, based on sensory pleasure, was influencing women in their choice of soap. A bar that seemed more polysensual than its rivals would be particularly attractive to women, especially if the advertising was subtle enough for women to be able to imagine the pleasure it would bring without really being aware of it, and so without provoking feelings of prudishness or guilt. Our client could benefit from this by marketing a foamy, rounded soap whose sensual smell and vaguely erotic promotion would chime with this new social current.

This survey also taught us something else. Simply explaining how things were to our clients was not always enough to convince them to act accordingly. Our contacts, who worked in advertising and marketing departments, were afraid that their superiors would be shocked by the tenor of Cofremca's conclusions: 'You can't just completely change strategy like that. Maybe you've been reading too much Freud! We can't be having all this stroking the body and what not. Our bosses will never understand.'

In the end, it was another company, Procter and Gamble, who a few years later were the first to market soap (Camay) in a radically hedonist and sensual manner. It worked like a charm and helped to speed up the emergence of polysensuality. Later, Cofremca carried out other surveys looking at women's beauty regimes. These highlighted the existence of a growing numbers of 'Hedonists' and 'Renewals'. By 1967, the 'Repressed' category was an endangered species among urban women under sixty-five.

Groundswell

Even during the First Modernity, polysensuality was both present and considered acceptable in a few limited, but important, areas of society. Two types of emotion quickly became acceptable and gradually became associated with a high degree of sensory interaction: romantic love and the parent-child bond. It became acceptable for couples and for parents and children to show their affection by openly touching one another.

But it was not until the 1970s that the freeing up of physical sensations and emotions became widespread. In 1979, a seminar was held in Villequier, Normandy, to discuss the major axes of socio-cultural change in Europe and the challenges faced by multinational companies. It brought together 22 of Shell's senior managers and seven sociologists from Germany, France, Italy and Great Britain. We also had comparative data from Sweden, Norway and Switzerland. One of the sessions dealt with the identification of major social currents common to all seven countries. It was clear to everybody that the most noticeable current was that of self-expression, but polysensuality also figured prominently. Contributors remarked that it tended to affect women and young people most strongly. Feeling fit and at ease with oneself had become more pressing goals than looking good, not sticking one's neck out and in some cases even more important than trying to express oneself. We remarked that sensations, emotions and feelings had become more important than ideas.

This change was first picked up in life history narratives, but periodic quantitative analysis told a similar story. Particularly well documented from 1974 onward in France, the trend towards polysensuality was rapidly spreading and it was beginning to affect society as a whole. Initially, it had been confined to young people and white-collar workers in large cities. Between 1974 and 2000, the rest of the population began to catch up. Our fieldwork allowed us to identify three particularly clear indicators of polysensuality and it is interesting to look at these indicators across representative samples of French adults (over the age of fifteen).

The percentage of people who agreed with the statement 'I like to relax in a hot bath, go sunbathing or have a massage' went from 44% in 1974 to 51% in 1990 and 61% in 2000. This increase was visible across all age groups, but was particularly marked among 15-24 year-olds, and also among the over-45s who were beginning to catch up. In the 1990s, the increase was four times larger for women than for men.

As regards the parent-child relationship, in 1977, 30% of French people thought that it was 'more important to have an intimate physical relationship with a child, to stroke and cuddle them, than to teach them verbally how to behave'. This figure increased to 39% in 1990 and 48% in 2000. Women were more inclined to favour physical contact than men, but the latter were gradually catching up. Older people (the over-55s) were less likely to go down this path, but they too were gradually closing the gap.

The third indicator was only used from 1983 onwards, when 33% of people declared that they would like to 'experience new emotions every day'. This rose to 41% in 1990 and 49% in 2000. These figures were largely independent of gender. There were, however, marked age differences. 15-55 year-olds showed strong increases over the period in question, but among 55-64 year olds, there was no real change. In 2000, as in 1983, only 20% of them wanted to experience new emotions every day. It was as if old age withered the desire to seek out new emotions.

It was not only France that witnessed such rapid change. Comparable surveys in Canada also showed significant increases in the numbers of people who wanted to experience new emotions every day. The figures went from 68% in 1984 to 78% in 1998. In Italy, Professor Giampaolo Fabris' indicator of overall polysensuality also showed regular increases. According to his data, in 1985, 42% of Italians could be considered properly polysensual. By 1988, this had risen to 52%, and in 1996, the figure was 54%.

Our sociological microscope highlighted three processes that together had encouraged the development of polysensuality from the mid-1960s onwards. One of these was the way in which children were brought up. The second was children's day-to-day lives, which provided adults with a learning opportunity. And the third was the complex relationship between physical sensations, emotion and technological progress.

Polysensual Education

The 1950s saw major change in the fields of education and child rearing. Received wisdom was turned on its head by developments in psychoanalysis, child psychology and the study of learning. The ideas of Sigmund Freud (1856-1939), Jean Piaget (1896-1980) and Maria Montessori (1870-1952) combined to undermine parents' and teachers' faith in traditional techniques. Maria Montessori revolutionised traditional education. Previously, it had focused on imparting knowledge, but she showed how to liberate young children from obstacles to their development by prioritising the senses.

Even before the 1950s, private Montessori kindergartens and then primary schools had been set up. They focused on discovering life, movement and the realm of the senses. They used non-visual and non-analytical teaching methods. During the 1950s, in France at least, these techniques began to spread to state education. As a result, large numbers of children born in the late 1950s received a completely different style of education from that experienced by previous generations. In 1955, many parents spoke to us of how surprised they had been by the way their children were taught at school. They were no longer immediately teaching children to read and write or imposing strict methods on them. Instead they tried to stimulate children, make them play and encourage them to explore their bodies and their movements: touching, feeling, singing, dancing and experimenting with colour without prioritising representation. These new educational techniques necessarily affected the way in which these children's personalities developed. It was these same children who came of age around 1968.

These wider social changes reflected the inner changes experienced by hedonist parents trying to raise their children in a warm, loving environment. Child rearing became less rule-bound and authoritarian. Mother and child shared more emotions and had more physical contact with one another. The strengthening of the mother-child bond was reinforced by the declining numbers of domestic servants employed by the upper-middle classes. Fathers also developed more sensory and emotional relationships with their children. They were allowed to. They fed them and changed their nappies. In the early 1970s, it became acceptable for fathers to attend and participate in the birth of their children. They were allowed to touch and hold their partners during labour and their children as soon as they were born. These became important memories for all concerned.

Women's improved status in family life helped to encourage the spread of so-called feminine values, which were much more accepting of polysensuality than traditional, patriarchal ones.

Learning to be intimate with oneself

In the 1960s and 70s, many had a chance to sit back and reflect on their experiences. In so doing, they set in motion a process of learning and self-discovery that would prove unstoppable.

Many people were just beginning to break away from social conventions, taboos, prudishness, guilt and shame, and they still only had a very vague idea of which sensory experiences and emotions would bring them pleasure. But as they set off on this voyage of self-discovery, they gained experience and began to learn. People initially threw themselves into certain forms of pleasure, but quickly tired of them. For many Swedish and French people, their initial 'gluttony' soon turned into a more refined and selective search for pleasure. This transformation was encouraged by the combination of vanishing taboos and new products, techniques and experiences. Bathrooms and soap bars allowed people to discover new sensations. The same was true of the development of contraceptives. For many women, now freed from the fear of getting pregnant, love-making became a whole new experience into which they could plunge, using it as an opportunity to discover and explore new forms of sensuality alongside their partners.

From the 1950s onwards, and thanks to the media, growing numbers of Westerners became aware of their unconscious. Knowing that you and everybody else had an unconscious mind and a complex inner world led people to explore them and strengthened the process of learning about themselves.

Learning about self-awareness becomes more widespread

Throughout the 1980s and 1990s, people developed a deeper and more profound connection with their inner selves. Most of the life histories we analysed were full of tales of new realisations, learning and understanding. Our interviewees were learning from their experiences. Thanks to the way they had been brought up, young people seemed to be developing faster than their elders, but everybody was moving in the same direction. We saw people experimenting, trying things out and then reflecting on why particular experiences had been a success or a failure. Each new experience enriched their understanding and increased their emotional intimacy with themselves.

Life was hard for many people in the 1980s and 1990s, but periods of stress or unemployment were often opportunities to work on oneself. People realised that they could be just as happy when times were hard as when life was good. For those people who experienced retirement as a freedom from constraints and responsibilities, it was a catalyst for further exploration. New technologies like PCs, fax machines and Prozac encouraged people to communicate and deepened their awareness of themselves and others. The vast majority of the population benefited from this learning process, which with the passage of time began to appear as one of the primary vectors of modernisation.

The myth of personality loses its appeal

We have already seen how the myth of discovering one's personality and fulfilling one's potential reinforced people's growing self-awareness throughout the 1970s. But as our interviewees ventured deeper and deeper into their inner worlds, their vision of their personality became less clear-cut. Although people were still searching for self-fulfillment and self-actualisation, the myth of a fixed personality gradually began to break down.

The first signs of this change of direction emerged during our 1976 annual conference in Switzerland. We were all presenting the results of our research over the previous year. Cofremca described a discovery it had made. In the course of our sociological fieldwork among young French people, we had come across some whose behaviour showed a marked contrast with what we had observed in previous years. They were basically saying, 'Self-actualisation is all well and good, but it's a hassle. I've had enough of that. I want to have fun, I want to feel alive.' Cofremca declared that it was intending to study a new socio-cultural current, which it called 'vie riche et animée'. Arthur Shapiro, who represented Yankelovich, Kelly and White, said that they had encountered the same phenomenon in the United States and called it 'full, rich life'. The coincidence was all the more striking because our respective teams had had no contact over the course of the previous twelve months.

In the mid-1970s, then, living a full, rich life had become a major motivating factor for many groups of young people. This quest spread throughout the rest of the population over the next twenty years. People were no longer striving to actualise a personality buried deep inside by struggling against authority, norms, constraints and social conventions. Instead, they wanted to live a full life and embrace the gamut of emotions and desires, letting them find their direction in life just by living it. This was a new form of fulfilment.

Deepening their connection with inner selves made many people realise how diverse and inchoate their personalities really were. They realised that they changed from one situation to another. Their mood and personality changed, depending on the circumstances and on the company they were in. Their drives and their reactions did not always correspond to the idea they had of themselves. They realised that this personality was vaguely artificial and could become a prison. Instead of thinking they had a clearly defined personality, they felt themselves to be in constant flux. They were a mosaic of sensations, emotions, drives and states of mind. Those who clung on to the idea of a fixed personality, started to speak of a 'multi-faceted personality' and set out to explore these different facets. The 'truth game' and 'truth or dare' symbolised the 'me' generation's approach to life. They were very popular in the 1970s and were intended to reveal players' true identities. Games played in the 1980s and 1990s, on the other hand, encouraged people to adopt multiple, different personalities. Role play was one clear example of this trend, as was the growing use of assumed identities on the Internet. American pop psychology exploited this tendency throughout the 1990s, encouraging many Americans to believe that they had multiple personalities, each of which acted independently of the others, sometimes engaging in illegal or immoral activities. Lawyers made use of such theories to exonerate their clients.

Clearly felt sensory and emotional experiences

In the 1950s and '60s, most of our interviewees found it easier to talk about their emotions than to actually live them with intensity. They waxed lyrical, using words and phrases that intellectualised or poeticised their feelings. In the 1980s and '90s, many of them discovered that their emotions first made themselves felt as physical sensations: mouth dry, hair standing on end, face frozen or drained of colour, a knot in the stomach or tears coming to their eyes. Only then did they seek to verbalise these sensations. People said things like 'a shudder runs down my spine and I feel drawn towards him. I love him', or 'I get a lump in my throat when I see things like that on the TV'.

In so doing, they discovered and experienced new emotions and physical sensations, and these enriched them. But many of our interviewees lacked the words to describe these nuances: the subtle realm of textures, tastes, sounds and physical sensations that they experienced. People also struggled to find words that would do justice to the emotions provoked by interpersonal contact: friendship, love, warmth, union, sexual excitement, coldness, repulsion, hatred and many more. Where once only poets, artists and epicures had had such a refined sensory and emotional palette, now ordinary people were developing one.

Sexual drives and amorous feelings were at the forefront of such exploration. Despite AIDS, young people, both gay and straight, were much more sexually liberated than in previous generations. And their experience of sexual interaction was very different from that of young people in the 1960s and '70s. It was no longer a matter of sexual freedom (which went without saying), but more a question of deepening the physical sensations, emotions and feelings that arose during sex or in the intimacy of a relationship. Our interviewees spoke increasingly freely about such things. When it went well, making love without feeling guilty and without seeing it as a conquest, but rather as an opportunity for pleasure and happiness, was a marvellous way of discovering powerful emotions and sensations. People responded to this in different ways. These emotions and sensations often either led to feelings for the other person, or reinforced existing ones, thereby strengthening the relationship. But it was not uncommon for them to drive people to look for new and different experiences. And so, the duration of a relationship began to depend less on social conventions and more on the emotions, sensations and sentiments that either brought couples together or drove them apart.

Emotions, physical sensations and electronics

Developments in the fields of electronics and communication technology helped people to free up their senses and emotions and to deepen their self-awareness. The Canadian sociologist Marshall McLuhan argued that the dominance of the visual was tied up with the invention of the printing press and the spread of 'cold', written media.[18] The pre-eminence of writing was finally undermined by advances in communication technology and the development of 'hot' media, like radio and television, which targeted people's emotions rather than their intellect. According to McLuhan, this led to the transformation of sequential and rational modes of thought into simultaneous and emotional ones. McLuhan goes so far as to suggest that the birth of electronic media actually caused wider changes in people's mindsets.

Our own observations do not support this causal link. Our French and Swedish interviewees were showing the first signs of nascent polysensuality a good twenty years before they had access to televisions. Electronic media did not set the ball rolling, but they did contribute to the process, both feeding into and being fed by it. Along with LPs and the cinema, they reinstated sound, music, the spoken word, images, pictures and movement at the heart of society. Perhaps one day they will do the same for touch and smell... Polysensual and affective people were more open to television and radio than individuals who remained trapped in the intellectual and rational. Listening to the radio and watching television increased their sensibility and sharpened their emotional reality. They identified with characters from television and films, rather than from books, and this enriched the range of emotions and physical sensations they were gradually discovering. Throughout the 1970s, we repeatedly explored the relationship between polysensuality and hi-fi systems. It worked both ways. People with a sensitive and refined ear were more likely to buy cutting-edge musical equipment and the fact of having such equipment, and so listening to better quality music, improved people's aural sensitivity, thus giving them access to more nuanced emotional worlds.

In the 1990s, the Internet, mobile phones, ever smaller and more interactive laptops, and video games spread like wildfire. Their users gradually reduced their use of formal, written forms of communication, turning instead to less intellectual and less rational ones, like speech, music, images and pictures. As communication became more immediate, so it became imbued with more intense emotionality, in that it communicated people's emotions almost as soon as they felt them. All this increased the fluidity and vitality of people's networks and communities and reinforced the 'soft', 'virtual' and 'free' in dialogue, where 'hard', 'practical', 'real-life' and 'paid-for' had previously held sway.

Remote controls were an immediate success because they met the need to be mobile, flexible and immediate and because they increased the fluidity

---

18   McLuhan M. *The Gutenberg Galaxy*. Toronto: University of Toronto Press, 1962.

of people's everyday lives. The intense frustration people felt when their remote control broke or when somebody else grabbed it testifies to the importance of these gadgets. Wireless technology and credit and debit cards had a similar effect.

Towards the end of the 1960s, we noticed that many young Americans and Europeans had begun to accord a central place in their lives to music. Their numbers increased over the next few decades and they were not drawn from any particular social group. Vast numbers of young (and then older) people spent several hours a day listening to music. This music tended to be very invasive and often targeted the body as much as it did the ear. In the 1920s, people had begun to discover jazz, a form of music that was not written down, but instead emerged during jam sessions and drew directly on musicians' emotional states. It was also a style of music whose rhythms colonised the body. From the 1960s onwards, many young people used electronic music to enter a sort of trance. This music not only targeted the ear, but also the solar plexus and even the skin.

This combination of polysensuality and music seems to mark the beginnings of a shift from a culture dominated by the intellect and writing to an emotional and musical culture that was open to the possibility of ecstatic experiences.

A society of Vitalists

Polysensuality continued to spread throughout the 1970s, '80s and '90s, and there is nothing to suggest that the trend is flagging. The more people explored their emotions and physical sensations, the more it changed them, putting them in touch with their inner and somatic worlds and with those parts of themselves they had once dismissed as bestial: their instincts, drives, physicality, emotions and intuition. People experienced this renewed vitality and we observed it. The change was so evident that, in 1984, Cofremca decided to call those people most affected by the trend (about half the population at this time) *Vitalist*.

Flexible, alert and generally calm

By the late 1990s, these Vitalists had developed a good understanding of their inner energy and of the impressions and intuitions that emerged from their interactions with people and things. It was this understanding, rather than old ideologies, their superego or the internalisation of conventional models of behaviour that drove them to act. They were emotionally supple, reactive and adaptable. They worked in flexible ways, had few hang-ups and were able to make the most of both their potential and of the circumstances they found themselves in.

So long as their energy was not blocked or frustrated, it did not become over-excited, febrile or aggressive. At the end of the 1990s, it seemed as if they were happy just to get on with their lives. Ideally, they aimed to be attentive to others and to their environment and they wanted to have enough freedom to make the most of their opportunities. Our interviewees told us that in such circumstances, they really felt they were living life to the full and they experienced a sort of biological and psychological fulfilment. They talked about the pleasure of feeling the blood course through their arteries, their muscles flex and their minds at work. Vitalists tended to focus on the moment (the 'now'), on what they were doing and on how it made them feel. They realised that this approach to life made them happy and so they stuck with it, making new discoveries as they went. Most of the time, they were calm, but a few rare cases made us realise that if this contentment and happiness seemed to be threatened, then they might take to the streets and become violent.

Vitalists were able to make the most of a wide range of situations. Research carried out between the mid-1980s and late '90s suggested that they flourished equally in periods of intense economic activity, characterised by a multiplicity of opportunities, and when faced with the challenges posed by economic downturn or unemployment. Their energy manifested itself in a constant state of alertness, in the exploration of possibilities and in a readiness to change their approach and re-enter the fray as soon as possible. They were confident. They derived pleasure from action, from surmounting difficulties and from confronting challenges.

Vitalists depend on moments of happiness[19]

Happiness remained a key objective for these people, but they experienced it in new ways. It was no longer a question of material possessions or of actualising some mythical personality, nor even of finding true love or dreaming of utopia. Above all, it was about cultivating a state in which one always felt comfortable in one's skin and good about oneself.

They also realised that a happy life is made up of a succession of moments of happiness. They stopped looking for one definitive form of happiness. They intuitively understood that if they pursued every possibility of pleasure,

---

19   'Microbonheurs'

then they would end up feeling empty. They had gone from being gluttons to having sensitive and refined palettes. Rather than contenting themselves with crude distinctions (pleasure/suffering, happiness/unhappiness, interest/boredom), they had learned to identify and distinguish between a wide array of subtly different forms of pleasure, happiness, sorrow and stress.

Many interviewees mentioned the pleasure they got from physical and mental exercise. The huge numbers of health and beauty products on the market improved their physical well-being. As well as jogging and aerobics, they also indulged in hiking, mountain-biking, skiing trips with family and friends, yoga and a whole range of other more or less esoteric activities. 'Sliding' sports, like surfing, skiing and skating, were particularly popular and more intense pleasures were to be found in extreme or dangerous sports and activities.

In order to be happy, Vitalists turned to their environment for energy and stimulation. They preferred their social and business circles to be supple and flexible, with no unnecessary friction. They also liked to take part and help things to grow and change. Sometimes, they found this satisfaction in new companies, charities or mutual support networks. They preferred organisations that behaved like non-bureaucratic and flexible living organisms, able to realise their potential, and which, by the same token, allowed them to express their vitality and engage with reality.

They found moments of pleasure at home, with their family, with friends and in their sexuality. Evenings or weekends spent with loved ones, time spent at home reading, listening to music, watching television or chatting were all moments of peace, harmony and warmth that they increasingly savoured. Such things played a key role in their dreams and in their lives. The household, family, friends and sexuality were the best sources of emotional warmth and harmony and also among the best remedies for stress. At the same time, friends, evenings out and sexuality could also offer the intense emotions and feelings of transgression that some craved.

Vitalists tried to create social environments that gave them a sense of well-being. They preferred social shapes and spaces that were not restricted to the visual realm, but were explicitly polysensual. These interviewees disliked the harsh lines and architectural gigantism of tower blocks. They wanted spaces that were impervious to the intellect, that were built to be touched and felt: spaces to live in and constantly rediscover. Ideally, they should be neither geometric nor repetitive.

In 1974, Cofremca alerted Renault to the possibility of taking advantage of cars' polysensual potential, and things developed from there. Cars became vehicles to be experienced and enjoyed, rather than displayed. They became spaces of physical and mental well-being. European car manufacturers started to market Vitalist cars. These were fast, powerful, responsive and comfortable, they let you know when you accelerated, and they contained sophisticated electronic equipment that gave the driver a feeling of control. Such vehicles were ideal for Vitalists. SUVs and other 4x4s offered something different. They gave drivers a feeling of power: they had an overview of the situation, were connected to the passengers and they felt safe in them. Drivers could choose their own route without having to worry about the condition of the road. They felt good in them.

Hedonists or warriors?

During the 1990s, we had the opportunity to observe Vitalists in many different countries and situations. The vast majority of them were Hedonists, preferring peaceful solutions to confrontation. They were good at diffusing tension. If placed in highly competitive environments, they were able to enter the fray and fight their corner, but they tended to prefer win-win outcomes. Even in the United States, where the economic climate of the 1990s combined with the prevailing culture to encourage people to compete, Vitalists showed their preference for cooperation. Like their European equivalents, they looked for situations that would allow them to explore their emotions and feelings of affection, communion and fulfilment, seeking to avoid ones that might provoke anger or aggression.

They tended to look for ways to escape oppressive or stressful situations without entering into conflict. From 1976 to 1982, Cofremca and its partners were involved in joint seminars with Shell's planning and strategy teams. We showed that the more modern sections of French, English and Italian society were abandoning the stifling institutions of officialdom and quietly withdrawing into familial, friendly and neighbourly forms of relational behaviour. These seminars led to the idea that a new social fabric was being woven – one based on informal, warm and hedonist micro-societies.

In the 1990s, the implications of the dislike felt by Vitalists for oppressive business and social environments became clearer. They would refuse to vote, criticised their bosses and considered the world of politics to be a farce. They might also withdraw physically: choosing to be self-employed, to move to the countryside or to look for work in a start-up. On leaving university, they shunned big business and public service in favour of smaller, more flexible work environments.

Alongside their non-confrontational approach, they tended to feel that their problems were in the order of things, rather than deliberately created by other people or institutions. They would take responsibility for their part in things and make the most of whatever opportunities they had.

However, in the 1990s, most observers of socio-cultural change highlighted the existence of two behavioural patterns that contradicted the dominant, hedonist model.

Subversive behaviour. Be it at work, in their neighbourhood or in clubs and social groups, some Vitalists began to adopt subversive attitudes and behaviours. They had the advantage of acute interpersonal intuition and highly developed social radar. If they came to the conclusion that their lives were being hindered by a particular institution, and that that institution was vulnerable, then they derived great pleasure from thinking about how to undermine it. We found that many young people were tempted to engage in forms of subversion that were reminiscent of those used by the May 1968 demonstrators.

Aggressive behaviour. Vitalists could also be caught up in strong emotions, which might drive them to do things they would never normally consider doing. And some of them took pleasure in these things. To reach this point, they had to feel rejected or frustrated. Instead of feeling that their problems or difficulties were part the order of things, they might begin to feel that society had it in for them. There were two distinct examples of this. In one, they felt that their way of life, the little pleasures they derived from their family and friends, were threatened. In the other, they felt that they had been unfairly treated by society – their situation was getting worse, while all around them things were looking up. Their resentment and aggression then began to build. The slightest spark might lead to individual or collective violence. In 2000 and 2001, whilst the economy was performing fairly well, both we and our German, Canadian and American colleagues noticed that increasing numbers of Vitalists were leaning towards aggressive behaviour.

Like Janus, Vitalists have two faces. Most of the time, they wear their smiling and hedonist face, but the other violent and confrontational face is never far from the surface. This is undoubtedly at the heart of one of the central uncertainties faced by contemporary society. Large sections of the population, perhaps the majority, are above all characterised by what we have called their vitality. They are naturally hedonistic and look for warmth, cooperation and intense, but peaceful, emotions. The more comfortable and the less stressed they are, and the more they have access to warm and fluid interpersonal interactions, the more they tend to fit this description. They have an intuitive ability to improve their sense of well-being and to repair deteriorating relations. But if times are too hard, or if they feel rejected or targeted, then they can become aggressive and violent, and the more so because of their intense emotionality.

In sum, the balance and harmony of a society of Vitalists are highly dependent on people's levels of stress, living standards, overall well-being and the extent to which they feel that they are an integral part of the social fabric.

Chapter 5
Smart people looking for meaning

In the early 1980s, there occurred yet another shift in people's lived realities – one that both complemented and disrupted the trends we have previously noted towards self-expression and vitalism. This shift first took place among people who had freed themselves from the grip of conventional authority, sexual taboos and social conventions. Their sensory and emotional experience of life was becoming less inhibited and they had learnt to express themselves. They had, in other words, integrated the modern ethos.

A Westerner who had fallen asleep in the 19th century would, upon waking in 1980, have thought that mankind was regressing rather than progressing, moving towards a primitive or bestial state. However, rational analysis had not been eclipsed by the rise and rise of physical, sensory, emotional and intuitive awareness. The 1980s and '90s saw large numbers of people groping their way towards a more integrated balance of reason and the emotions. This integration improved their ability to live a 'smart life'. It led them to search for greater meaning in their lives and opened up the possibility of a dialogue between their spiritual experiences and their rational selves.

This chapter deals with this process of integration and the major changes that it brought about. First, however, it is important to have a clear idea of how far the modern ethos had affected Western society by 1980.

The modern ethos circa 1980

Making quantitative international comparisons of the development of different socio-cultural currents is a delicate business, confused by differences in survey methodology and problems of translation. That said, it is possible to draw some general conclusions. So we can estimate that by 1980, about a quarter of the population of the most modern countries had been profoundly affected by the modern ethos. Adding in those who had been affected to a lesser extent brings the total to about 80%.

Members of the International Research Institute on Social Change (RISC)[20] performed typological analysis on surveys carried out between 1978 and 1980, allowing them to estimate the relative impact of the modern ethos on

---

20   Basis Research in Germany, SRI International in the USA, Cofremca in France, Demoskopea in Italy, Taylor Nelson in the United Kingdom and SIFO in Sweden.

different populations. The typology best suited to international comparison drew on the work of Arnold Mitchell at the Stanford Research Institute. It distinguished between three types: the least modern type tended to focus on making ends meet; the second group was typical of 1950s and '60s modernity and were motivated by questions of prestige and esteem – how other people saw them. It is the third type that interests us here, because their primary motivations were self-expression and personal development. This type encompassed between a third and a quarter of the population in Sweden, Britain and France, about a fifth in the United States and significantly less in Italy and Germany.

At the Villequier conference organised by Royal Dutch Shell in 1979, our German and Italian colleagues reflected on the relatively slow spread of this type in their respective countries. Giampaolo Fabris analysed the socio-cultural situation in Italy, focusing on the collapse of Christian values, which had previously regulated family life and (especially sexual) relationships between men and women. Here, with the exception of a few narrow social groups, it was less a matter of personal development than individual emancipation. However, he remarked that although ten years earlier Italy had lagged far behind the United States and France, it was now catching up rapidly. Carmen Lakaschus suggested that her fellow Germans were taking a breather after the long reconstruction effort. With few exceptions, Germans in the late 1970s were not trying to construct a personality for themselves. Instead, they were pursuing the sorts of pleasures and sensations that had been so appealing to the French in the 1950s.

As for France and the United States, it was possible to tighten the comparison by drawing on the results of quantitative socio-cultural surveys carried out by Cofremca and by Yankelovich, Skelly and White. In the late 1970s and early '80s, the modern ethos had profoundly affected 17% of Americans and 25% of French people. It would continue to spread throughout the 1980s and '90s, taking on new forms as it did so.

Combining reason and the emotions

It was that quarter of the population who had been most affected by the modern ethos, and especially its younger members, who would be at the forefront of the move towards integrating reason and the emotions.

Emerging from the shadow of 1968

In 1979, Cofremca undertook a comparison of two generations of young people born ten years apart. The older group was made up of 25 to 30 year-olds. Born between 1949 and 1954, they were of an age to have taken part in the events of May 1968 and they were the last representatives of the generation that had set out to challenge consumer society. Attentive to questions of personal development, their profile was unsurprising. They could be broadly divided into two categories. On the one hand, were people who valued their drives and emotions, but mainly for reasons of principle or ideology. They intellectualised them, rather than feeling them. They built a tower of rationality around their physical and emotional awareness and their personality. In the main, they were inclined to intellectualise, philosophise, theorise and protest. On the other hand were a group of people who had a much more intimate relationship with their physical sensations and emotions. They embraced and cultivated them. They valued them highly and let their emotions guide them, rather than rationalising them. They were often involved in New Age practices.

The younger group was aged between 15 and 20. The eldest of them were only nine years old in 1968 and had not participated in the events of that year, though those events had, in some cases, affected their upbringing and education. They had lived in a society of abundance, but from early on they had been aware of challenges to this society and had experienced its growing complexity and uncertainty. Some were secondary school or university students. Others were in employment. None, though, was really established in life. The surprising thing was the way in which some of them managed to combine an acute somatic understanding of their emotional worlds and a capacity for rational analysis. They were realistic and pragmatic. They tended not to theorise about things, other people or themselves. Instead, they were attentive to what occurred around them, had a clear understanding of their own mental processes and of the situations they encountered, and had an intuitive awareness of the interconnectedness of things in the wider world. They were intraceptive and understood how personal and social networks could change and what opportunities might emerge from those changes. They analysed these things in an apparently calm and lucid manner. They embodied an approach that was new to us: they privileged neither reason, nor emotion, but harmoniously combined the two.

Their ability to analyse their emotions and intuitions rationally was undoubtedly linked to their education and upbringing. This generation had been through secondary and often higher education. Never before had such a high proportion of people received a higher education. Between 1950 and

1960, the numbers of people in higher education doubled in the United States, more than doubled in Germany and tripled in France. A few decades earlier, the vast majority of Westerners had only been educated to primary level; by 1990, such people were a tiny minority. In the process, most people had learned how to make connections between different ideas and, more useful still, how to compare their observations with their ideas.

Their upbringing and education had been very different from that of the older group, the generation of '68. As we have seen in previous chapters, their parents had been more loving, more attentive to their emotional and sensory lives, less authoritarian and more open to dialogue. They had been less rule-bound and, having grown up in an environment where women and mothers were making their presence felt, they had known more physical affection. In Europe more than in the United States, they had grown up in a world where God and religious traditions were largely absent from their daily lives. They had made love younger and more freely. They had attended schools and universities where the old order was being challenged. Television had played a central part in their upbringing. They had experienced drugs and hypnotic music. They had observed the generation of '68 struggling with ideas of self-development. And unlike them, they had not had to struggle against authority and outdated moral codes. Growing up in a climate of freedom where they faced new difficulties, many of them had had to choose their own path in a society that had lost its sense of self-satisfaction and in which unemployment and hard times were once again part of many people's daily existence.

The process continues throughout the 1980s and '90s

The life histories we collected showed that once people began to overcome the emotion/reason and intuition/deliberation divides, the process was unstoppable. The younger of the two generations we interviewed in 1979 continued to develop this capacity through the next two decades. Many analysts highlighted the differences between this generation and that of '68: they were less ideological, less messianic and more realistic; they were in tune with their drives, emotions and authentic desires; they knew how to identify and sometimes manipulate them. They had a clear understanding of objective reality and of the competition they faced and they were well equipped to think through their problems. Digging deeper, we found that they were developing a system for navigating their way in life in profoundly different and constantly improving ways.

This capacity to combine emotion and reason was not restricted to the generation that discovered it. Life histories analysed during the 1980s and '90s show that many people from the older group (the generation of '68) were also learning to do similar things. Not only did they savour their physical and emotional experiences, but they were also able to step back from them and analyse and understand them. In so doing, they discovered that other people had emotions and feelings and they became more aware of the feelings provoked by interaction with others. They developed their empathy and interpersonal intuition and they sharpened this empathetic intuition, which acted as a sort of social radar and played a central role in transforming the fabric of society.

At the same time, many people were developing a subtler understanding of their different cognitive modes and the diversity of their mental states. They learned to distinguish between them and to call on them at will. Some examples: intuition and reasoning, analytic observation and shape-recognition, forming mental images of others and having an intuitive awareness of their intentions, attention and distraction, concentration and letting the mind wander.

When interviewees talked of difficult choices and decisions, they often spoke of how their intuitions and emotions had overcome their reason, or vice-versa. Analysis of these interviews showed that they did not seem to parcel up their physical sensations, emotions, drives, mental states, intuitions, reflections and reasoning into different categories. On the contrary, they were all thought of as emerging from one holistic, living organism. And none of these dimensions seemed necessarily to dominate any of the others. Hundreds of millions of Americans and Europeans reflected on their experiences and made progress towards a better integration of emotion and reason.

In this same period (1980s and '90s), not only did the most 'modern' no longer reject reasoning and reasonable behaviour, but they even valued them, whilst simultaneously keeping them in their place. They turned their attention to their ways of reasoning, just as they had with their physical sensations, emotions and intuitions. For them, reason had become one tool among many, and one that did not always work.

The conditions that allowed this integrative capacity to emerge

It is possible that, once again, this was a case of adults copying the young. But it is reasonable to suggest that people's increasing self-awareness naturally led to the development of this capacity to integrate different forms and levels of awareness. Indeed, careful quantitative analysis of Cofremca's 3SC Monitor data from 1984 reveals a series of correlations that confirm this hypothesis.

The integration of emotion and reason occurred among those people who were most advanced, in terms of four different socio-cultural currents: deepening polysensuality, intraception, hedonism and self-expression.

- These people had highly developed polysensuality and emotionality. They were so in tune with their sensory and emotional life that they no longer felt the need to reject anything whatsoever out of principle, be it the intellect, rationality or ancestral rituals.

- They had refined their intraception, relating to others and to their environment using multiple channels of perception and understanding (empathy, emotional awareness, rational understanding, etc.). They had sophisticated social radar. They intuitively understood other people, society and their relationship to the world around them. It was not the same sort of intraception as fifteen years earlier, which had been based on moments of intuition about oneself, one's relations to others and one's position in society. Instead, it was a permanent and systemic understanding of one's place in one's ecosystem.

- These people were Hedonists, but their hedonism was not that of the 1950s, based on the rejection of constraints and taboos, nor that of the 1960s and 1970s, which had been greedy and limiting. Their hedonism was more refined and controlled. They knew how to sideline or delay certain pleasures that they felt might not be good for them.

- They were also 'expressives', but spontaneous ones, freed from the shackles of the relentless quest for self-expression.

Everything suggests that, in the middle of the 1980s, large numbers of Westerners had travelled sufficiently far along these four social axes to have crossed a sort of threshold, beyond which lay the integration and equal incorporation of emotion, intuition and reason.

From dichotomy to unity

The transformation described above cannot be reduced to a simple change in people's inner mechanics. It also describes a fundamental shift in the cultural representation of human reality.

As I've said, it was in 1979 that Cofremca first described the emergence of a new capacity to integrate two aspects of human reality (emotion and reason) that our civilization had previously tended to counterpose. It was also in

1979 that two of our colleagues (then at SRI), Peter Schwartz and James Ogilvy, were preparing a report discussing precisely the same phenomenon.[21] They adopted a completely different methodology to that used by Cofremca, analysing changes in the world of science and ideas, rather than focusing on ordinary people's lives. Nevertheless, they too highlighted the disappearance of this dichotomy so characteristic of Western visions of mankind and the universe. Body and soul, reason and emotion, spirit and matter were no longer seen as radically separate entities, but as elements of a larger whole.

Hitherto, the vast majority of Westerners had understood themselves as split in two; possessing a body and a soul, human and animal aspects, emotions and reason, all of which were not only seen as distinct, but as antagonistic. They now began to conceive of themselves as holistic ensembles composed of different elements working in harmony and on an equal footing.

In the process, the idea of the brain as a rational machine, seen for a while as analogous to a computer, began to lose ground. New representations emerged. More and more people saw themselves as possessing an infinitely complex brain, comprising a more sensitive right hemisphere and a more rational left one, a powerful neocortex and an equally powerful reptilian hypothalamus, all working together. The popularisation of neuroscience by the mass media contributed to people's self-awareness. Books and articles discussing the brain and the immune system sold well and communicated new discoveries to a wider public.

Strategic opportunism

Further ethnological research, carried out among young French people in 1984, offered us additional insights into a complementary aspect of this process. We knew that the dissolution of the myth of personality was well under way. This research helped us to understand what was replacing it. It showed us that the idea of the personality as an arrow pointing in a definite direction from birth or like seed programmed to grow into a particular plant was giving way to a radically different representation. Now people were starting to see themselves as hazy entities whose life gave them direction, and as organisms in evolving ecosystems, changing and being changed by them.

---

21   Schwartz P. & Ogilvy J. *The Emergent Paradigm: Changing Patterns of Thought and Belief*, VALS Report No. 7. Menlo Park, CA: SRI International, 1979.

Draw a picture of yourself in life

Observing young people helped us to get a better idea of the phenomenon at hand. Our goal was to explore these profound changes in the way people lived their lives. Cofremca came up with a novel survey technique which we tried out on a few dozen 15 to 25 year-olds. We had to avoid approaching the subject too directly and so we tried to come at it from an angle. The researcher gave each person a large sheet of paper and some coloured pens and said: 'This is a game. Take your time. Draw something that symbolises the idea of you in life'[22]. After leaving them to draw for 15 or 20 minutes, the interviewer sat down with each one and discussed what they had drawn. What does this or that shape or colour signify? What were you thinking about when you drew this red line? The technique revealed how each person thought about his or her life and about the future.

Five or ten years earlier, similar groups of young people tended to tell us what they wanted to achieve and how they intended to go about it. They often said that they wanted to free their inner selves. What we heard in 1984 was, in many cases, completely different: 'I don't know where I'm headed, but I'm headed somewhere. I'll change along the way. Sure, it's vague, but that doesn't bother me. It's exciting. I know I'll adapt'. This allowed us to understand that we were faced with a new socio-cultural current. Cofremca called it *strategic opportunism*. A short while later, our English and American colleagues confirmed that they had discovered the existence of an identical current, which they dubbed *adaptive navigation*.

Making it up as you go along

Our young interviewees did not think that they had a clearly defined personality that needed actualising. Instead, they tried to come up with a way of life that suited them by turning away from ready-made or conventional models, and without having any preconceived ideas of what it should look like. They spoke of making the most of the situations that arose and of trying things out to see what improved their sense of well-being and what detracted from it. Our Anglo-Saxon colleagues called this a *do it yourself way of life*.

This constituted a radical change of stance: from planning to improvisation and a reactive form of navigation, with a flexible sense of direction. With a navigator who reacted in real time according to the sensations and intuitions he or she felt and the feedback received. The direction and destination were subject to change, depending on the difficulties and the opportunities encountered.

---

22   *'Vous dans la vie.'*

The underlying conception is an 'ecosystemic' one: one's position in life is understood as being similar to that of an organism in its ecosystem. These strategic opportunists were aware that they were at one with their environment and with the people they interacted with. They felt that they were the outcome of these interactions. They felt as if they were immersed in a complex and evolving system that they might just be able to alter but which might also alter them. And yet they felt confident and self-assured. The future depended on them, on others and on the turn of events and they thought they would be able to make the most of their opportunities. The growing practice of playing role games, complex video games, war games and simulations was ideal training for the development of an understanding of reality as a system that called for skilful navigation.

For these strategic opportunist, the idea of having a clear forward plan for one's life was replaced by one of anticipation, of multiple visions and possibilities, and of trial and error. Our interviewees said that the important thing was not to cling onto goals that might be momentarily or permanently unrealistic, and not to set one's motivations in stone. But one should also keep sight of them and be able to intuit the long-term future and sense the opportunities on offer.

Strategic opportunism/adaptive navigation often manifested itself as a rejection of strict forms of morality, especially in the United States and, in 1985, Robert Bellah and his US colleagues[23] stressed the moral aspect of this stance. Those who adopted it rejected both rigid goals and rigid moral standards, which they saw as limiting their flexibility in life. In order to make the most of things, you had to be flexible, adjusting to the particularities of different situations. More precisely, they said: 'If the self is to be free, it must also be fluid, moving easily from one social situation and role to another without trying to fit life into any one set of values and norms, even one's own'.[24]

These young people were realists. They analysed the constraints imposed upon them and looked for ways to overcome or get around them. If they were unavoidable, they were prepared to put up with them, at least for a

---

23   Bellah R. Madsen R. Sullivan W.M. Swidler A. & Tipton S.M. *Habits of the Heart, Individualism and Commitment in American Life.* Berkeley, CA: University of California Press, 1985. The fieldwork from which this book emerged took place between 1979 and 1984. It involved more than 200 subjects, who were interviewed (often repeatedly) and in some cases observed as they went about their daily business. In the early 1980s, I asked David Riesman who in the United States was continuing in his footsteps. Without hesitating, he replied: 'Bellah'.

24   Bellah et al. 1985: p.77.

while. This was neither fatalism, nor a feeling of impotence. Instead, it was a calculated choice, designed to save their energy for more important things. As we listened to and observed these young people, we could not help but feel that they were truly well equipped to face the difficulties they would encounter in a society that was growing ever more complex and ever more unpredictable. They were also well equipped to transform this society. They seemed to be mutants, better adapted than their forebears. And strategic opportunism rapidly spread to different age groups and marked the course of the 1990s.

Out of this permanent dialogue between, on the one hand, emotion and reason and, on the other, oneself and one's life, emerged three new step changes: smarter and more astute self-conduct in life; a tendency to be highly attentive to the meaning of one's life; and an openness to spiritual experiences that did not disregard the rational.

Smarter self-conduct

Over the last two decades, people's integration and use of the strategic navigation skills described above has constantly improved, in all age and social groups, although at different speeds in each. These tools seem to have helped people to pursue their goals in smarter ways, to do so more efficiently and to gain a new independence.

People's life histories shed light on this process. Vitalists have learnt to challenge their own rational analysis of a situation if it makes them uncomfortable or is at odds with their intuitive response. But they choose also not to be slaves to their own drives and desires. They take the time to decide whether to gratify them now, later or at all. Intuition and analysis work in concert to find the best solution. Even altered mental states and bouts of spiritual ecstasy can be compatible with rational analysis.

These complex internal dialogues lead to behaviour less calqued on social rules and forms than on personal points of view. People were smarter in that they tended to avoid crude traps and followed paths that suited them and served their own best interests. They became better and better at constructing for themselves a life that really suited them.

Therapeutic navigation

I have described the emergence of strategic opportunism and shown it to be an ecosystemic approach. It was also a therapeutic one. People began to attribute their anxiety, stress or depression either to themselves or to the social nexuses in which they were implicated. Beyond a certain point, they identified the existence of a pathology in either themselves or in the system. And they set out to cure it.

Strategic opportunists often became relatively well-informed self-therapists, able to manage their peace of mind and to deal with stress and anxiety. For example, they permitted themselves moments or bouts of pleasure in order to maintain their well-being and their sense of inner balance in periods of tension. From the early 1990s onwards, our American observers also noticed that people increasingly used occasional outbursts of Dionysiac excess to manage their stress. Calm, organised, reasonable consumers suddenly gave themselves over to pleasure in excess (to help them deal with stress and maintain their emotional balance), before returning to their routine. The same phenomenon quickly became evident in Europe.

It became clear that if life was going badly, then the problem lay either in oneself or alternatively in society. When our interviewees felt unhappy in themselves, with their lives or with their relationships and social networks, then they tried to work out which aspect of their behaviour led them to place themselves in uncomfortable situations. Some set to work on themselves, others turned to therapists or neuroleptic drugs, and still others turned to neo-spiritual practices. Where psychotherapy had previously been confined to very specific social groups, in the 1980s and '90s many different sorts of psychotherapy became increasingly widespread among the American and Western European middle classes. At the same time, a sort of indefinable socio-therapy also began to develop.

The light shed by neuroscience

These new skills of integration and strategic opportunism led many people to access previously untapped human resources. A few recent discoveries in the neurosciences can help us to understand the extent to which people's integration of emotion, social intuition and clear reasoning constitute a major step forward for humanity.

Antonio R. Damasio was head of the department of neurology at the University of Iowa when his book, published in 1994, brought his work and that of his colleagues to a wider public.[25] Their observation of brain-damaged patients showed that lesions to the pre-frontal cortex severely impaired their ability

---

25   Damasio A.R. *Descartes' Error: Emotions, Reason and the Human Brain.* New York: A.Grosset/Putnam Books, 1994.

to live a well-adjusted life without affecting their capacity for abstract reasoning. It seems that there is a specific part of the brain that deals with the complex neurobiological processes that regulate people's ability to behave appropriately in social and interpersonal environments. Apparently, such damage to the pre-frontal cortex even prevents monkeys from behaving appropriately in their social environment and from developing social relations, leading them to be rejected by their group.

Damasio uses a series of examples to clarify the opposition he establishes between 'practical reason' (life-management) and 'theoretical reason'.[26] Practical reason involves problems like, 'choosing a career; deciding whom to marry or befriend; deciding whether or not to fly when there are impending thunderstorms; deciding whom to vote for or how to invest one's savings; deciding whether to forgive a person who has done you wrong or, if you happen to be a state governor, commute the sentence of the convict now on death row'. These are regulated by the pre-frontal cortex. Theoretical reason, on the other hand, involves problems like 'building a new engine, or designing a building, or solving a mathematical problem, composing a musical piece or writing a book, or judging whether a proposed new law accords with or violates the spirit or letter of a constitutional amendment'. These are dealt with by other parts of the brain. Damasio remarks that everyday observation supports this opposition between two different types of reasoning.

More in-depth analysis led Damasio to conclude that four different families of neurobiological processes overlap in the prefrontal cortex and the ventromedial region of the frontal lobe: the ability to feel and express one's emotions; a feel for social relationships; the ability to think through concrete problems concerning social behaviour in one's personal and social environment; and working memory – i.e. the ability to keep track of multiple different variables and to think them through for long enough to be able to make a decision. Conducting a normal life requires people simultaneously to mobilise emotion, reasoning, social skills and working memory.

Damasio, then, helps us to understand a biological substratum of which philosophers like Descartes were simply unaware and which clearly shows that making good decisions requires the use of both emotional and cognitive processes. He also explains precisely how his work clarifies the different roles played by emotion and reasoning in decision-making processes.[27] Problems of managing one's daily life (or a company) are much too complex and uncertain to be resolved by reason alone. This is all the more so

---

26   Damasio 1994: pp.217 and 220.

27   Damasio 1994: pp.224-240.

because many decisions have to be taken very fast. According to Damasio, emotions here act as 'somatic markers'. The body immediately accepts or rejects different hypotheses. Some hypotheses are thus sidelined (and so left unexamined by reason) whilst others remain viable. Our emotions quickly let us know what is good or bad for us. We imagine a particular scenario, see where it might lead and we get a lump in our throat or our stomach knots and we sideline that hypothesis. The emotions provoked by different scenarios alter the decision-making process, rejecting negatively charged scenarios and favouring positively charged ones. Damasio points out that the process does not have to be conscious to be effective.

These neurobiological analyses shed new light on the significance and the extent of the processes of socio-human evolution already described. They allow us to understand why uninhibited feeling and emotion and many people's newfound ability to combine emotion and reason, coupled with improved sociosystemic intraception, constitute a spectacular leap forward in the smarter conduct of life.

Christian and Cartesian culture repressed physical sensations, feelings and emotions; instead favouring a clear conscience and an awareness of the difference between good and evil. It dichotomised mind and body, spirit and matter. It imposed forms of education, upbringing and social control that cut us off from our senses, feelings and emotions. It allowed us to perfect our reasoning, but prevented us from making the most of sensory, emotional and intuitive capacities. However, the socio-cultural change that occurred over the second half of the 20th century (especially the spread of polysensuality and the renewed vigour of the right brain, followed by the integration of intuitions, feelings and emotions on the one hand and reason on the other) allowed ordinary people to make the most of their potential and made them better able to lead their lives and manage the organisations that some of them were in charge of.

Meaning and meaninglessness in everyday life

Over the last twenty years, our research has put us in contact with men and women who ask themselves questions about, rejoice in and worry about the meaningfulness or meaninglessness of what they do, what happens to them and, more generally, about their direction in life. We have also come across people who act in ways that make their lives more meaningful, even if they do not explicitly discuss the problem of meaningfulness. This movement gathered speed in the period after 1990.

In 1983, we became convinced that this was a major socio-cultural dynamic. This realisation emerged from a meeting held in Paris with our colleagues then at the Stanford Research Institute. The comparison of different data showed that the same phenomenon was to be found in both Europe and the United States and that, in some cases, it was having a significant impact on ordinary people's lives. The search for meaning in one's life was becoming what became known as a shaping trend.

The problem of the meaning of life

In the 1950s and '60s, people were rarely troubled by the meaning or otherwise of their actions. The thousands of interviews we conducted at the time showed that people always had ready-made explanations to justify their actions. And the explanations that came to mind and that made their actions meaningful often appeared straightforward, obvious and logical. They were rationalisations and justifications borrowed from the dominant intellectual and religious systems of the time. People were satisfied with them because they were uninquisitive and disinclined to make the effort to dig a little deeper. 'Why did I vote Communist? Because I'm working class.' However, if we encouraged them to think about their underlying motivations, then they sometimes realised the meaning of their actions. And perhaps they also realised that they could dig deeper still.

There is doubtless a natural, hardwired human tendency to interpret events and one's own actions, to attribute meaning to them and to make sense of them. Young children drive their parents to distraction by constantly asking 'Why? Why? Why?' Future developments in neuroscience will certainly shed light on the mental processes that regulate and underpin these phenomena.

In the late 1980s, I read Michael Gazzaniga's book on the networks of the mind and I felt it helped me to understand the mental processes I had observed among my interviewees.[28] Gazzaniga and Roger Sperry carried out experiments on the split-brain, which led to the discovery of hemispheric specialisation. He surmised that our cognitive system was organised into modules. A large number of relatively independent modules evaluate data received both from the outside world and from the inside. They may or may not communicate this data to the conscious verbal system, but they can also express their reactions by ordering the body to act in a particular way. The role of specialised modules in the left hemisphere is to interpret these actions and attribute meaning to them. Gazzaniga stresses that this left-brain interpreter

---

28   Gazzaniga M. *The Social Brain: Discovering the Networks of the Mind.* New York: Basic Books, 1985.

has to find reasons for what we do and for what happens. His hypothetical representation of mental processes seemed potentially very useful to me. Indeed, it helped to explain not only people's apparent obligation constantly to come up with rationalisations, justifications and theorisations of their own behaviour (which we came across in most of interviews), but also the possibility common to both interviewer and interviewee of having some idea of the real intentions that underpinned their actions.

The people that we observed throughout the 1990s were no longer in the same situation as those we had interviewed thirty or forty years earlier. They no longer looked for meaning outside themselves; instead they looked at their own history and experiences. Culture and society no longer provided them with signposts and guides. The whittling away of traditional forms of knowledge and belief (religions, ideologies and worldviews) had deprived them of ready-made responses. Without them, they were forced to face up to new and often surprisingly different experiences that they had somehow to explain to themselves. They often felt uncomfortable in this new society and tried to understand their discomfort.

Their new knowledge and skills would serve them well. They had a 'left-brain interpreter' that was far more adept at communicating with other brain modules than anything their predecessors had had. The result was a greater ability to understand the meaningfulness or otherwise of what they did and what happened to them.

Experiences that generate meaning

In the interviews that we conducted, the sense of meaning or meaninglessness was sometimes immediately clear. It might result from an intuition or an act of meditation or reflection. Or it could emerge from analytic reasoning. Sometimes it could be all these things in concert.

This sense of meaning or meaninglessness emerged when people took a step back. They often had the impression of having created space for thought and for examining the situation at hand, as well as the available alternatives. A sense of meaninglessness often arose from a stinging setback that was later reassessed. Many people realised that they were chasing shadows. They devoted themselves to work, to spending and consuming, to earning ever more money and to winning every competition they were dragged into. This gave them brief moments of satisfaction, but also anxiety, stress and long-term tension. Their families and social networks were damaged in the process. Many of them both looked for and found ways out of these traps. By the end of the twentieth century, many modern Europeans and Americans had realised that when all was said and done their life and their social environment did not really suit them. To different degrees, they looked for realistic ways to change their way of life and to build themselves a new life that they could accept: a life, for example, that allowed them to make the most of their energy and creativity, to escape the tyranny of time, to develop a sense of harmony with their dominant feelings or natural rhythms, to live in an environment where they felt comfortable and which left room for a social conscience, etc.

Meaningfulness sometimes appeared as a sort of revelation born of a feeling of living life to the full, of helping somebody out or of contributing to the building of a community or system. It also materialised in practices that offered people peace of mind, exaltation, ecstasy or a feeling of fusion and communion. People were very much focused on the long term. They analysed the past and imagined the future, learning from past experience. They observed what they had felt and tried to understand what it meant and where it was taking them. Ephemeral pleasures and satisfactions were only meaningful if they contributed to long-term self-development.

This led people on to new discoveries about the meaning of their lives and about the meaning of life more generally. Gradually, they laid the foundations for a new moral order that would privilege self-development and the holistic experience of life.

The neo-spriritualist resurgence

As they got in touch with their senses, feelings, emotions and intuitions, they also gained access to remoter parts of their inner worlds. This focus on their mental processes led many of them to experience altered states of consciousness, to savour them and to try to reproduce and expand on them. The rationalism and materialism of the 19th and 20th centuries had dulled the Western world's capacity for wonder and its openness to hidden forces and religion. The Second Modernity reawakened our latent spirituality and channelled it in new directions.

The words 'spiritual' and 'spirituality' are perhaps not entirely appropriate descriptions of this resurgence. For some, they accurately define their explorations, but many others, travelling down similar paths, refuse to describe their experiences as spiritual. As a way of highlighting this divergence, I propose that we call this phenomenon 'neo-spirituality'.

This resurgence was already in evidence in the New Age movement of the late 1960s and early 1970s. This emerged in the United States in about 1970[29] and it was in the United States that it was most powerful, most naïve and most clearly defined. Over the next three decades it would spread to the rest of the Western world. It was characterised by the rejection of a society based on consumption and wedded to rationality, by a fascination with esoteric traditions (be they Western, Eastern, shamanic or Amerindian) and by people's expectant wait for a massive upheaval – less the coming of a messiah than the dawn of a new age. This new age was written in the stars in the form of a transition from the constellation of Pisces to that of Aquarius. It might be accompanied by a spectacular increase in the human brain's hidden potential, by a new understanding of nature and life and perhaps by the arrival of aliens bearing a message. It was pantheistic and incorporated Eastern wisdom and new environmental concerns.

Thirty years later, the neo-spiritual resurgence is no longer marginal, nor is it dominant. It is probably more present, and is certainly more visible, in the United States than in Europe. But even in Europe, it affects between a fifth and a third of the population. It includes many different types of people from all walks of life.

Experiencing altered states

Many of our interviewees have told us about the altered states they have experienced and how these experiences seemed to offer them a new emotional palette and to open new doors for them. These include a range of mental states, stretching from heightened consciousness to deep trance, which people often have trouble describing. They speak of hazy states, floating in oceans, meditation, fusion, dreams and waking dreams, premonitions, hallucinations, revelations, ecstasy and the warmth of collective gatherings.

Such altered states can occur in both the strangest and the most everyday situations: visiting a church, going on a monastic retreat, being carried away by Gregorian chants, attending an electronic music concert, being swept up in a passionate and all-consuming love affair or even attending an exhibition.

Many young people describe how their mental landscape was opened up by their experience of collective emotion. They have the feeling that their mind or soul enters into contact with the crowd and is energised by it. They

---

29   Ferguson M. *The Aquarian Conspiracy: Personal and Social Transformation in the 1980s*, Los Angeles, CA: J. P. Tarcher, 1980.

mention raves, music festivals, collective religious experiences or the fervour of the days following Princess Diana's death. They sometimes mention having used hallucinogenic drugs.

A variety of physical and mental exercises can be used to encourage altered states. Some of our interviewees sought them out; others stumbled on them by chance. A number talked about praying alone or in groups. Others mentioned yoga, Zen Buddhism, meditation or martial arts. Such practices seem to be one of the major paths to neo-spirituality. In 1991, more than 30% of French people said that they regularly engaged in one or another of them.

Many people mention reading books that opened their eyes and some describe how their boredom, rage or despair led them to seek solace in a sect. Though they might have left it a few months or years later, they remained open to parallel spiritual planes. Others mention watching charismatic preachers on the television every Sunday.

Altered states of mind have a reputation for being calming or ecstatic, sometimes unpleasant or even terrifying. But our interviewees only mentioned having had positive experiences and many continued to seek them out. They reduced levels of stress and tension and brought them a feeling of harmony, calm and peace. They allowed their mind or soul to commune either with others or with the universe at large or with God. They witnessed wonders and this helped to re-enchant often sad or cold lives. Some said that these experiences improved their mental or physical health or taught them to heal themselves. People make use of them to improve their intuitive feel for the future and derive a feeling of being at one with their destiny. Some use astrology, clairvoyance or other forms of divination to shed light on their future. The I-Ching is fairly popular in the West.

Altered states give many people a sense of meaning and, for them, this sense is clearly something that they suddenly experience and that sweeps them up – it exists independently of the words they use to describe it. But they can also interpret their altered mental states after the fact and then construct theories about them. These states speak to them of nature and humanity, God and the cosmos. In the context of a general decline across the Western world in cold and institutional churches, and of a profound de-Christianisation in Canada and Europe, these theories offer syncretic alternatives that are strongly imbued with a sense of personal choice and tend to focus on immanence rather than on transcendence.

Adventures in syncretism and personal choice

Just as with the New Age movement, all of these interpretations draw on the collective wisdom of traditional religions, esotericism, pantheism as well as on visions of modernity. Their integrative characteristics bring to mind the various syncretic cults that once emerged from the ruined cosmologies and belief-systems of primitive cultures colonised by Western powers.

Modern science and technology are often present, in the form of references to the brain, the cosmos and interplanetary travel. We are told that aliens visit Earth, that the human brain is developing new powers and that the Internet will allow humanity to reach a superhuman state (the Omega point). There are often millenarian undercurrents and references to coming upheavals, catastrophes and emergencies. They almost always merge different exercises and rituals drawn from ancient religions and modern psychology. And they always amalgamate scraps from different religious and cultural traditions, rather than relying on a single, pre-existing tradition or philosophical approach.

Christianity and Buddhism both contribute to these theories. Buddhist wisdom, practice and ritual play an important part in contemporary neo-spiritualist syncretism. Of all traditional faiths, Buddhism is probably the most in tune with modern Western sensibilities.

Hitherto, Europeans and Americans tended to follow the religion or philosophical approach of their parents or their peers. The modernising process administered, here as elsewhere, a strong dose of personal self-determination. Today, ordinary people are inclined to choose a religion or philosophy that suits them under the circumstances and then to change when circumstances change.

But there are two distinct paths that may be followed. On the one hand, there is the 'pick 'n' mix' approach to religion popular in Europe and Canada, where everyone invents their own religious system. And on the other, there is the possibility of choosing (although perhaps not permanently) one's religion off the peg from the wide range available. This is much more common in the United States.

Pick 'n' mix. Wherever they may be, most spiritually inclined people today are not involved in sects, cults or official churches. Though they may not be alone in their search, they are not looking for institutional environments. They are engaged in a personal spiritual quest. They flee from dogmatism and attempts to enlist them in institutions. They borrow here and there and build up a wealth of personal experiences that together constitute a sort of inchoate philosophy. Though they may draw on non-monotheistic oriental wisdoms, they normally refrain from permanently adhering to any particular doctrine. And so, sometimes alone, sometimes with others, and sometimes with the help of one or more guides or gurus, they knock together a sort of vague, individual syncretism. This in no way shuts them off from other people, each of whom has their own unique blend of practices and experiences and with whom they may be happy at times to engage. This path tends to lead to tolerance and ecumenicalism. Networks are formed, with more or less clearly defined boundaries, but most of the time they are not hermetically sealed. This is less a search for something in particular than the pursuit of a sort of self-development where people can share a sense of complicity that gives them the impression of belonging to a vast, open-ended community of seekers.

Off the peg. In Europe, a small number of our interviewees are clearly involved in sects or cults. In the United States, charismatic cults and sects, which may be hard to distinguish from churches, are widely accepted. They multiply and prosper. Both charismatic Catholics and especially Protestant evangelicals incorporate ecstatic chants and dancing into their services and make widespread use of mainstream marketing techniques. There is a wide range of different faiths on offer. This is so pronounced that our American colleagues describe large numbers of their citizens as going shopping in religious supermarkets. People who opt for this or that cult or sect take on a ready-made set of beliefs, practices and rituals which they import from outside and in which they seek solace. But they still retain a certain independence because they can always change their minds: there is no social stigma attached to changing faiths.

The move towards immanence

Our interviewees hold an extremely wide range of different beliefs. Some refer to an extremely anthropomorphised God (over the last thirty years, such references to God have grown increasingly rare and only remain relatively common in the USA). Others speak of a higher power, which may be divine. Others still mention the great wheel of nature. Still others see their altered states as the result of normal brain activity.

This search for spiritual experience now extends beyond the confines of traditional churches, God and transcendence. We have perhaps reached a major junction in Western history. Surveys carried out by Cofremca in 1989 showed just how modern this divorce between spirituality and God really was. More than half of French people said they were interested in spiritual development, but they had very different conceptions of what that meant. For 60% of them, spirituality was a natural dimension of human existence, a para-rational exploration of their humanity. For the other 40%, cultivating their spirituality was a way of drawing closer to God. The radically opposed psycho-socio-cultural profiles of these two groups were significant. The first group (the humanists) were heavily influenced by the major socio-cultural dynamics of the time. They were attentive to their feelings, senses, emotional experiences and altered mental states. They had highly developed empathy. They were independent and stood apart from hierarchies, authority and social conventions. They were Vitalists, strategic opportunists, connective, and open to others, the outside world and change. They were confident and rarely at a loss. The Deists, on the other hand (those who placed God at the heart of spiritual experience), were largely unaffected by these currents.

Equivalent surveys were carried out in Canada in 1998, as part of the Canadian 3SC Monitor, and these showed similar findings. The vast majority of the Canadian population still claimed to believe in God, but people's ideas of God were changing. Many did not envisage God as described by the church, but 'in their own way' or 'as a powerful force of which both they and nature were but a part'. The most modern among them were also far and away the most likely to say that life was nothing but biology and that God was a human creation. In France and Canada, but probably in other European countries as well, modernisation favours Godless forms of neo-spirituality.

Among those people whose daily life revolves around the search for meaning, a rationalist, humanist, neo-spiritual and radically modern philosophy is slowly being born. Those who follow this path are looking for spiritual meaning, but without supposing the existence of God. They are wary of interpretations that appeal to the supernatural and deliberately choose to focus on immanence. They encourage dialogue between these altered states and their reason. The latter tells them that the former are the result of normal brain activity. They surmise that the brain has hidden reserves of perception, anticipation and communication that go beyond mere sensory and logical capabilities. These phenomena strike them as neither supernatural nor pathological. They seem to be a genetic endowment of mankind. They think that Western civilisation has tended to marginalise them, but that throughout history people have experienced such altered states, whatever culture they belonged to.

They are still rationalists, but modern ones. Nowadays, we hardly ever come across old-school rationalists in our surveys, except among the very oldest generations. And even their ardour is waning; the passions of yesteryear are being forgotten. Unlike their predecessors, modern rationalists focus on the whole person: a being that is the product of evolution and that still has untapped potential that needs to be understood and developed. They believe that the experience of ecstatic states of consciousness is written into our very nature.

For the neo-spiritualist rationalists we have interviewed, the different forms and expressions of human wisdom are evidence of the parallel development of human spirituality. What unites them is their refusal to sideline or dismiss any of these different paths to wisdom, but instead to step back and try to assess them.

The questions that these neo-spiritualist rationalists are asking themselves are informed by developments in the life sciences. They are on the lookout for new discoveries that might help them to better understand both mind and consciousness, as well as to understand how they communicate with others and the place of humanity in wider evolutionary processes. They hope that future discoveries in the field of neuroscience will give them new insights into the hidden depths of the human mind, into the relationship between the mind and conscious states, into dreams, altered states, and the nature of spirituality. They expect that genetic and ethological research will allow us to understand better who we are and what distinguishes us from other mammals and our close cousins, bonobos and chimpanzees. Perhaps this will provide them with new *raisons d'être*.

Happiness in everyday life

Interviews looking at people's search for happiness can be extremely interesting. By the year 2000, our interviewees were no longer chasing the idea of happiness, which had been people's primary goal from the 1930s to the 1960s: perfect happiness, one true love and the revolution to end all revolutions. Instead they focused on amassing a multiplicity of often ephemeral moments of happiness: warm and affectionate relationships; physical, mental and spiritual well-being; sensory pleasure; harmony between oneself and the world; the feeling of being in control of one's life; confidence in one's ability to deal with the future.

When circumstances conspire to prevent or destroy these moments of happiness, people respond in different ways, but all of them try to refocus on happiness and meaningfulness. Sometimes, they just make do and lower their expectations. Often, they try to escape, looking for a new social environment or a new life that will satisfy them. It is not uncommon for them to try to destroy the obstacle to their happiness, by undermining or attacking it. Some of them set out to reform society so that it gives people more opportunities to find happiness and meaning, and in so doing they also experience moments of happiness and meaningfulness.

Most contemporary Westerners are smart enough and live in societies that are tolerant enough to allow them to create their own moments of happiness, and which make the constraints, stress and pain of their lives bearable.

A warm and loving home which day-to-day sustains loving couples and family relationships is often the best antidote to the suffering and stress inflicted by the outside world.

Chapter 6
An organic social fabric emerges

The changes discussed in earlier chapters together form a series of concatenating chains of learning and discovery. But they also intertwine with changes in the architecture and structures of society and with particular developments in communications technology. From these multiple interconnections and inter-reactions has emerged an extremely complex, organic social fabric.

The social fabric that I try to describe here is changing and evolving: my description is simply a snapshot of a moment in a process that already has a direction but whose precise outcome we cannot yet discern.

Anomie or organic social fabric?

It was around 1975 that we first began to understand the nature of these changes to the social fabric. In the mid-1970s, the annual conferences that brought together Cofremca and its international partners highlighted both similarities and major differences of opinion. Our English, German and American colleagues spoke of an explosion of narcissism and anomie. As they saw it, those ordinary people who were blazing the trail of modernity were more interested in themselves and in discovering their true selves than with other people and society. They seemed to be discreetly stepping away from formal and conventional society and withdrawing into themselves. Some observers predicted the emergence of a broken and fragmented society – almost a non-society.

At the same time, however, people were being drawn towards small communities – ones that were based on, and valued, warmth, intimacy and feelings. The challenge was how to interpret this phenomenon. For some observers, it was nothing more than a symptom of people's nostalgia for a vanishing society. Others, though, saw it as the beginning of a new dynamic that would lead to more affectionate and emotionally informed relationships between people, and perhaps to the emergence of a new type of social fabric.

In France, we opted for the latter interpretation. Surveys carried out by Cofremca between 1954 and 1970 had provided us with a wealth of data that contradicted the theory of fragmentation. More and more French people were trying to create and maintain warm and affectionate relationships with others and to develop their capacity for empathy. They felt drawn towards older forms of society where strong emotional ties bound people together in small groupings. It was these observations that had, even before 1970, led Cofremca to explore three socio-cultural currents that could be understood as precursors of a new type of social cohesion: *Openness to Others, Intraception* and *Ethnicity* (also called *Rootedness*). Between 1975 and 1979, parallel studies carried out by our European and American partners confirmed that these three currents indeed constituted one of the major tropisms of the Second Modernity.

Later on, quantitative surveys supported this hypothesis. The 1970s, for instance, witnessed large increases in the number of Americans who wanted to be part of small, intimate communities. Regular surveys carried out by Yankelovich, Skelly and White showed that the current known as *Search for Community* grew from 32% of the population in 1973 to 47% in the early 1980s. In France, similar, if less dramatic, progress was evident for the *Rootedness* current (which was very close to Yankelovich, Skelly and White's category): in 1974, it affected 27% of the population; in 1980, 31%; and in 1986, 36%.

Spurred on by Royal Dutch Shell's Group Planning department, our German, English, French and Italian colleagues set out to explore major trends affecting the social fabric. In 1979, we met with Shell's management to discuss types of change to be found in all four countries. We concluded that there were five trends that all pointed in the direction of new social forms:

- social emancipation: people breaking away from social constraints, norms and authority

- a growing tendency to flee from established, larger, institutionalised society and social structures, and a search for smaller, more informal and more intimate groups

- a rise in pluralism, tolerance and versatility: these emerging communities were neither hostile to, nor hermetically closed off from, one another

- increases in intraception and empathy, which allowed emotional communication to flourish and intensify and made interpersonal and social relationships more transparent

- a rejection of institutional authority, which was most pronounced in France, weakest in Germany, but everywhere on the increase.

We had known from the early 1970s that people increasingly felt uncomfortable in fixed, authoritarian, cold and bureaucratic structures and that they felt less and less attached to them. As they moved away from these structures, so they began to strip them of their vitality, thereby undermining nations, social classes, religions, political parties and trade unions. By 1979, observers of socio-cultural change in Europe and America realised that people's growing search for autonomy and rejection of institutional and authoritarian society did not necessarily cut them off from one another and was not fragmenting society. On the contrary, it led them to reinforce their emotional ties and interactions with others and to recreate open and communicative micro-communities. A new social fabric was emerging. During the 1980s and '90s, these trends continued.

People and the social fabric

The actions and interactions of autonomous people shape a new social architecture

By the 1990s, most men and women were in touch with their emotions and intuition, socially autonomous, smarter and in search of happiness, fulfilment and meaningfulness. They now chose which groups they wanted to affiliate themselves to and which to avoid on the basis of their feelings, moods and interests. They were less and less likely to put up with social conventions and rules, with the dictates of any particular elite or with the real or imagined restrictions previously imposed by being born in a particular place or into a particular class. They wanted to, and did, choose freely whom to mix with.

In order for people to make a connection with one another or join a group, something had to click. This might involve a spontaneous attraction or a careful choice, similar tastes, intuitive awareness of synergy, or shared feelings, interests or goals. In this way, 'modern people'[30] would link up with each other and then grow apart, join groups or networks and then leave them, strengthen, loosen or discard connections, and they would do so of their own volition, without reference to others and often on little more than a whim.

Modern people were thus happier to engage with fluid networks and groups in open-ended and negotiable ways than to join fixed entities once and for all. They would establish connections and overlapping interests with loose,

---

30   In any Modernity and for any of the trends discussed here, the term 'modern people' (in French, *moderne*) describes those who are actively participating in, or who identify themselves with, that trend or current.

malleable and sometimes ephemeral collectives. The important thing was not to become a prisoner of them. They would enrol warily and try to remain free to break off contact if things did not turn out as promised.

Be they emotionally based or more functional, these sorts of relationship could be fragile or solid, brief or long-term. But, above all, people would look for emotional intensity: love, strong emotional connection and authentic and profound human interaction. Modern people appreciated stability because it offered security, intimacy, confidence and warmth. But the relationship would need to be subject to review at any time if either affection or shared interests disappeared. Modern people would strive to remain free to break off relations, whilst simultaneously investing a great deal in those they held dear.

If forced to associate with people they found unpleasant or untrustworthy, then they would feel stressed and unsettled. Their immediate reaction would be one of avoidance: they would turn away from any conflict that might trouble their peace of mind. If they could not avoid contact, then they might feel repulsion, anger or aggression. In the 1990s, however, the majority of connections we observed were characterised either by warmth and closeness or by complete absence of contact. When people recognised difference, even fundamental difference, they would try to avoid the outbreak of hostilities and especially vendettas. Rather than declare war or erect frontiers, people would establish a no man's land. We will return to this aspect of 1990s modernity in the next chapter, which looks at peace and violence.

So we could see each following their own path, adapting it to their circumstances, emotions and interests. However, these paths shared much common ground: they overlapped, mutually reinforced one another and clustered together, thereby creating a new social fabric that was neither woven from norms and traditions nor dictated from on high, but which was an emergent property of the actions of many individuals. This was a social fabric both tightly and loosely woven, and intensely interactive; a social fabric dominated by interpersonal networks and characterised by fluid boundaries, multiple overlaps and frequent shifts. Its extreme complexity, coupled with its self-organised nature, made it a living, organic thing.

Happiness is other people

For modern people, it is essential to create a life that suits them. They both feel and, increasingly, understand that the success or failure of this quest depends on the people they feel close to and on the relationships they develop with them. They need to feel loved. They also need other people's support and advice. In order to feel integrated, they have to find points of similarity and of difference. Otherwise, they have the impression that they are lacking in consistency, direction and even identity.

This has provoked a fundamental transformation in Western society that is doubtless still far from over. Westerners have centred their lives around their emotional reality and their relationships. These relationships are one of the most important things in their lives – more important than God, country, success or consumption. As they grow increasingly attuned to their emotions, so modern people also become aware of the impact that other people have on their way of life. The actions and reactions of other people are a source of both positive and negative emotions, bringing them happiness and sadness, pleasure and stress, meaning and meaninglessness.

Of that half of the European and American population that we call 'modern', the vast majority claim to be generally happy. They almost all give similar answers when asked to describe their moments of happiness. Sometimes these include moments of solitude. Much more often, though, they mention time spent in company, with friends, family or their current partner. Without emotional dialogue and affectionate relations, their lives would be cold and meaningless. For most of them, it is impossible to find moments of happiness if they are alone, deprived of emotional networks or in tense and stressful situations.

Learning how to see and how to be in society

It is increasingly important for our interviewees to feel in touch with others' intimate selves. And of course, these 'others', so important to modern people, are not quite the same as they were a generation or more ago. They feel alive and feel that other people are too. They are living human beings in their own right, not just members of a community, a crowd, a class, a political party, a trades union or a socio-demographic category. The 'significant others' on whom our interviewees increasingly depend are not only their loved ones and close friends and family, but also people they see or hear in the media or whom they meet by chance and for whom they feel a sudden surge of affection or aversion.

Contemporary Westerners better understand their own psychology and so pay more attention to other people's, thereby developing their intuitive capacities to read the faint signs they give off. They have an instinctive feel for the ways in which others are different from or similar to them and they seek to understand this better. They rely less on cold, external assessment and instead try to empathise, stepping into the other's shoes.

What is more, voyages of self-discovery are not undertaken alone. They rely on interaction with real and imagined others. Being aware of the intimate depths of other people's inner worlds helps them to understand their own. It is no longer society and their place in it that determines their identity. They construct their own identity as they go, exchanging emotions and feelings with others. In couples, people mutually construct one another through talking and interacting. Parents and children do the same. As do friends. Novels, films, television series and reality TV all provide new frames of reference. More and more often people participate in self-discovery and personal development groups, which provide them with excellent learning opportunities.

As they build new relationships, modern people have to reveal enough of their private and intimate selves in an unthreatening way, so that the other can get a feel for potential points of convergence and then, in turn, offer admission to their own intimate thoughts, feelings and selves.

Experience of life and social interactions allows people who are part of complex societies to behave in efficient and harmonious ways. In a social environment that has been stripped of its rules and codes, it is imperative to have a social radar that allows you to negotiate your way through life: to save a damaged relationship, to raise your children, to escape from a spiral of conflict, to take charge when authority has broken down, and to build a social network or a friendship group.

Through my analysis of life histories, I have come to the conclusion that most adults continue to make progress and that 20 year-olds in the year 2000 disposed of a much subtler and more sophisticated social savoir-faire than did their counterparts in 1980. A large majority of people both old and young now possess social skills that allow them more or less to construct a close, interpersonal environment which they find satisfying and which they say makes them happy.

Sensitivity to the intimate inner worlds of oneself and others prepares people for the intimate world of society. People have the feeling that they are involved in a process of social osmosis and that society has become more transparent. They engage with society less on intellectual and ideological grounds and more in terms of emotion and intuition.

From the decline in the hierarchical tropism to the emergence of a heterarchical social fabric

The decline in the tropism of hierarchy, coupled with progress that has been made towards autonomy, has had a major impact. modern people do not appreciate receiving orders from above nor being treated like pawns. And most of them are not even happy to elect a member of parliament or political representative to take decisions on their behalf. They want to participate directly in things that concern them, giving their opinion and feeling that they are being listened to. They like to take the initiative and to feel that their actions have an effect on the situation. They only feel comfortable when they are on an equal footing with others. They like to be involved in authentic dialogue – i.e. interactions in which each party tries to understand the other, takes their position on board and accepts the possibility of mutually influencing each other.

Though they do not like being forced to follow orders, they no longer feel the need to challenge authority systematically. They are recalcitrant when people or institutions issue commands without explaining or justifying them, but they may follow an inspiring and trustworthy leader. The social fabric with which they feel comfortable and which they are spontaneously helping to create is best described as heterarchical. It admits of no permanently fixed hierarchies and no stable chain of command. Influence and leadership rotate. In France, for example, the percentage of people who, given the choice, would opt for a social environment based on influencing people rather than giving orders went from 54% in 1983 to 65% in 1994. More than 70% of the French population said they felt more comfortable in groups where the leadership can change depending on the circumstances than in ones with only one leader. This tendency is particularly marked among young people.

This rich micro-social fabric plays some important social functions

Throughout the 1990s, most people demonstrated their ability to create close social 'cells' and networks that provided some of the emotional exchange that they needed in order to be happy, to feel integrated into society and to flourish. This micro-social fabric was essentially made up of new types of couples, families and networks. They offered those who built them a certain degree of emotional balance and helped them find their place in society.

The architecture of this micro-social fabric

The old micro-social fabric had essentially been made up of clearly defined and stable families and kin groups, of links between these families and groups, and neighbourhood and work groupings. Participating in small, local communities, in clubs, charitable organisations, charity shops and local church or party political groups played an important role, especially in the United States.[31] People used to join these communities for the long-term. Modern people, though, stripped this social fabric of its vitality and established new and much more open-ended personal relations, weaving a fabric of interpersonal, flexible and biodegradable groups and networks.

A new form of family takes hold. Research carried out in the 1980s and '90s in Western Europe and North America suggested that the family was not collapsing, but reinventing itself in new ways. Family situations that would have seemed bizarre, if not scandalous, in the 1960s, now seemed normal to many people. Accordingly, I use the term 'household' rather than 'family' to describe groups of people living most of the time and fairly permanently in one house. 'Family' is too tied up with images of clear and formal boundaries.

Throughout the 19th and early 20th centuries different types of family co-existed and the idea of family constantly changed. But behind these transformations lay a particular model. The family was an institution sanctioned by ritual and law; it was based on the concept of a lifelong marriage, which was approved of and sometimes arranged by the couple's parents. It consisted of a man and a woman who bore and raised numerous children (with high infant mortality rates). Their union consecrated a social tie between two extended families. The man was the head of the family and the role of this family was to transmit wider social norms to its children.

The First Modernity witnessed the ephemeral emergence of one particular variation on this theme that both drew on the past and presaged what was to come: the erotico-affective household, based on consumption and still hierarchical in nature. Love marriage replaced parental and social choice with personal choice. In such unions, a man and woman, who were ideally in love, formed a couple for life and raised children. The man was in control. He brought home a salary and earned enough money to ensure that the family could consume. The woman did the housework and looked after the children, even though she might also hold down a job.

---

31   The decline of these communities is discussed in Putnam R.D. *Bowling Alone: the collapse and revival of American community*. New York: Simon & Schuster, 2001.

Very soon, there were signs of the breakdown of this model. It was in the family, rather than in business or residential arrangements, that the social fabric first began to change. Nevertheless, it was not until 15 or 20 years after the end of the Second World War that modern people really imposed the idea of a biodegradable couple (cohabitation and divorce), which allowed them to give up and try their luck again if things went wrong. It was only then that statistics began to tell the same story and that legislators began to adjust the legal framework to suit the new situation. In a few short decades, beginning in the 1960s, the family model that had dominated the Western world throughout the 19ᵗʰ and early 20ᵗʰ centuries came apart.

The biodegradable couple. People no longer had to get married in order to have a relationship and bear children. Nowadays, 50% of children are born out of wedlock in Scandinavia, and more than 40% in France. The figure is slightly lower in Britain and the United States, and far lower in Germany and, especially, in Spain and Italy. Whatever the different figures reached by the end of the 20ᵗʰ century, the increase in births outside wedlock that occurred from the 1960s onwards was remarkable throughout the Western world. Between 1970 and 1980 they more than doubled, and then doubled again between 1980 and 1990, before falling slightly in the period from 1990 to 2000. France has one of the lowest marriage rates in the West: 4 marriages per year for every 1000 inhabitants. In the United States, in contrast, there are more than 9 per 1000. More than half of French women are unmarried when they give birth to their first child. Out of every ten married couples, nine have previously cohabited. Indeed, cohabitation has become a permanent lifestyle choice. The *Institut National d'Études Démographiques* has shown that 30% of couples who started cohabiting in 1990 were still together and still unmarried ten years later. Marriage is no longer indispensable to life as a couple. But for heterosexuals the couple (whether married or not) is still the predominant form of relationship. The family, then, is changing, but not disappearing. In both Sweden and France this social and moral shift is widely accepted, even among very traditional or religious families. The same cannot be said of the United States, where the religious and political right still vigorously protests against such change.

So the couple survives, but it has lost its permanence. People's growing need for emotional and sexual harmony, combined with their rejection of constraints placed upon their desires, has made couples more fragile. From the 1960s onwards, divorce rates rose almost everywhere. In the 1990s, they appeared to stabilise and now in Scandinavia, France, Britain and the United States half of all marriages end in divorce. The increasing fragility of the couple can be attributed to one of two distinct and competing patterns, whose relative importance differs depending on the country. In the United States, people often divorce quite quickly and then remarry. In Sweden, on the other hand, the marriage-divorce-remarriage sequence is often discarded in favour of a series of cohabitations, none of which receives religious or legal sanction. That said, the vast majority of the young people we interview remain attached to the ideal of a long-term couple, raising a family together, helping to ensure the day-to-day happiness and personal development of all the family's members. Couples are bound together by mutual affection and the pleasure they derive from spending time together. This is why so many of them go to such lengths to preserve intimacy and love in their relationship and to maintain sexual intensity. But they also think that if the harmony dies, then it is better to look for another long-term relationship.

Control of fertility. Bearing children has changed radically over the centuries and, nowadays, it is no longer unavoidable, but has become a choice. People can choose at what age to have children, at what time of year, how many they want and soon, perhaps, the child's sex, eye colour and personality. Medical and genetic breakthroughs have overcome biological obstacles to conception and childbirth that a few years ago were insurmountable. But they have not made up for the combination of social trends that have reduced the number of children that people have. Since the 1960s, the most modern countries have witnessed dramatic falls in fertility rates, though at different speeds in different countries.

The rise in fertility rates seen in the United States over the last few years can be attributed to the size of immigrant populations (principally Latinos) whose fertility rates remain high. Elsewhere, we are well below population replacement rates.

Changing fertility rates[32]

		1965	1980	1998	2007
Sweden		2.42	1.68	1.51	1.66
France		2.84	1.96	1.70	1.98
United Kingdom		2.83	1.93	1.72	1.66
Italy		2.55	1.66	1.19	1.29
Spain		2.97	2.16	1.15	1.29
United States	(1970)	2.48	1.84	2.03	2.09

32   The number of children that an imaginary, average woman would give birth to over the course of her life time, if she were to embody the overall average for the particular year shown.

Some commentators have tried to establish a direct correlation between falling fertility rates and the contraceptive pill. In fact, things are much more complicated than this suggests. Fertility rates have fallen sharply both in countries where very few women use the pill (like Spain and Italy) and in countries with very high uptake (such as Sweden, the Netherlands or France). There are huge differences in the types of contraception used from one country to another. This is true of exclusively modern contraceptive techniques (the coil is very popular in Norway and Finland and sterilisation is widely used in the United Kingdom and the United States), but also of modern and traditional techniques in combination. It seems that the type of contraception used has hardly any impact on fertility rates. Instead, falling numbers of births are the result of couples' newfound autonomy and women's improved life-navigation skills. Couples, and especially women, tend to have the number of children they want and to have them when they want them. Women's liberation, improved contraceptive techniques and the work of family planning centres have all contributed to the increase in small families with planned and wanted children.

Flexible household geometry. Now more than ever, there are many different types of couple. They may be married or not, ideally forever, but often not, and they may or may not involve stepchildren; all of them, though are looking for affection, happiness and room for personal growth. These are flexible households with porous boundaries. Sometimes friends or relatives join them, either for a while or for good. Sometimes children from different parents live together under one roof, sometimes the children of one relationship are scattered between several households. Some children move back and forth between households. Exchanges take place. Households break apart and fuse together. Partly because of children and alimony payments, but also partly for reasons of ongoing affection, divorce does not necessarily signal a complete rupture between two people.

People are living longer and older people are healthier than ever. This means that grandparents play an increasingly important role in the ecology of the family and are sometimes more or less integrated into the household. Many grandparents (who are often retired, relatively well-off, free from constraints, looking for affection, and with time on their hands) invest significant amounts of effort in their families. They are the parents of the generation of '68, or even later generations, and their children helped to educate them. When they reached the age of retirement, many of them became social innovators who entered into easy, egalitarian and affectionate relations with their grandchildren. It is no longer rare to find four generations in one family, sometimes living under one roof. Sixty year-olds may find themselves in a pivotal position, ready to help out their own parents, their children and their grandchildren. Younger people often mention how attached they are or were to their grandparents. These ties, reinforced by visits, letters, e-mail and phone calls, are often simultaneously described in terms of the pleasure they bring, the sense of continuity and roots that they offer and the obligations that they constitute.

When families break down, grandparents can be a godsend. Not only in terms of the support and help they offer to one or other of the parents, but also as a source of stability and security that makes the change easier for children to cope with.

Heterarchical households. These new, more or less permanent, households are neither hierarchical nor pyramidical. Instead, they look like cybernetic systems where an outsider cannot tell the top from the bottom, seeing only interactions, feedback loops and influence passing from one household member to another. The climate may be friendly or hostile, but everybody says his or her piece and leadership roles change according to circumstances. The father no longer controls new communication technology. Children have direct access to it and often teach their parents how it works.

In a traditionally hierarchical country like France, this constitutes a spectacular change. Fewer and fewer people agree with the statement, 'the father should be head of the family'. In 1975, 59% of people concurred; in 1985, this figure was 39%; and in 1999, only 29% did. This bears out the hypothesis of a significant double socio-anthropological change discussed in previous chapters: the decline in hierarchy and the feminisation of society. The same transformation is evident throughout the Western world. However, in some countries fathers have retained their privileges more than in others. A survey carried out by Sociovision in 2001 illustrates these differences. Only 10% of Swedes and 19% of Germans thought the father should be head of the family. At the other end of the spectrum, 40% of Spaniards, 45% of Americans, 52% of Japanese people and 74% of Brazilians agreed with the statement. The French (26%), Italians (27%) and the English (34%) were somewhere in between. Sociovision also created a more complex indicator of relative heterarchy, which it applied to representative samples of the German, American, French, Japanese and Swedish populations. It gave more or less the same results as the simpler survey. If we take 100 as the average heterarchy score of the five countries, then France scored 105. Germany (142) and Sweden (134) were much more heterarchical. The United States (81) was less so, and Japan (38) was much less heterarchical.

These changing belief and value systems are reflected in social structures. In 1995, most French families were heterarchical. Mothers and children were less inclined to obey the *pater familias,* had won greater decision-making freedom and were more influential. Asked in 1995 about their family life, less than 10% of them said the man was in charge. The same proportion of respondents said that it was the woman. And the vast majority agreed with the statement 'everybody has their say'. These proportions were scarcely affected by variables like the respondents' socio-cultural or socio-demographic background. It is clear that heterarchy has profoundly altered all walks of French family life. It is interesting to note that heterarchical families also tend to be happier and more harmonious ones. Households where the man is in charge are often characterised by a climate of tension, more or less constant fighting and a cold atmosphere.

Informal personal networks

Social networks are not a recent invention. In the 19th century, the bourgeoisie was already based on networking. One's social ties were determined by family histories, by one's education, by one's political, religious and philosophical persuasion and, only recently, by one's profession. They were often closed networks, which it was all but impossible to break into: networks which fought hard to maintain their identity, culture and influence. And, of course, there have long been other networks: the Freemasons, church groups, the Ku Klux Klan, gentlemen's clubs, old boys' networks and many others.

These were very different from the freely chosen, open and flexible networks we see emerging today. During the 1980s and '90s, spontaneous networks sprang up: people developed ties to other people who, in turn, had ties with yet others. This form of networking developed among all social classes, not only among the elites. Most networks were very different in form from their predecessors. They were freely chosen: people selected one another, instead of having their social ties decided by birth, social conventions or their situation in life. They were informal, not institutional. They were self-organised, rather than being instituted or imposed from the outside. Sometimes they were semi-permanent, but just as often they were short-lived and did not necessarily aim to be definitive or even very stable.

We see networks emerge and then disappear. Their boundaries are often vague, porous and potentially overlapping. Each connection contains the possibility of further connections, and so the fabric of networking is gradually woven.

The tendency towards networking is developing throughout the Western world, but some cultures are more open to it than others. In 1999, Sociovision tried to evaluate the relative development of a networking culture in different countries. Its analysis took into account people's predisposition to network, to choose their own contacts and construct their own micro-social environments, the extent to which they emotionally distanced themselves from institutions and their preference for participative grass-roots action, rather than top-down initiatives. According to their analysis, networking culture was stronger in France, the United States and Sweden than in Germany. Japan was very resistant to it, whereas it seems to form a natural part of Chinese life.

Networks and households are intertwined. Contemporary households are much less introverted than traditional ones were. They are living networks of people. Their members are relatively independent of one another and mutually influence one another. They relate to people from outside the household in freely chosen and biodegradable ways. They are both the origin and the culmination of multiple networks, open spaces adapted to sociability.

This pretty much universal trend is particularly striking in France, where life had typically centred around the house-as-fortress. By the end of the 20th century, however, three quarters of French people described their houses as open to the outside. Barely a quarter of them still claimed to enjoy holing up at home: these were either very conservative people or people who lived in neighbourhoods which they described as hostile, violent and noisy. New communication technology only encourages this openness to the outside world.

The micro-social fabric helps people find inner harmony and integration within society

It is clear that humanity has the potential not only for an enormous range of emotional experience, but also for emotional connections and relationships. Other people's gestures, facial expressions and emotions strike a chord in us. They reach straight into our emotional selves without passing through our cortical consciousness. This potential is visible even in babies, who communicate intimately with their mothers via facial expressions and gaze: facial expressions that convey attention, sorrow, fear, love, anger or any other emotion. These are facial expressions that the baby can decode and that mean the same things for everybody in all cultures.

In the 17th, 18th and 19th centuries, this potential had been repressed in the Western world. Dominant norms, education and child-rearing had all privileged rationality, ideas, facts and words, at the expense of emotions, gestures and facial expressions. They belittled children, in whom it was felt that everything was to be instilled by adults.

Looking back, it is tempting to conjecture that this development of a culture of emotion-based relationships stretches far back into the First Modernity. It was without doubt in the erotico-affective households of the First Modernity that people began to rediscover and relearn these emotional capacities, which quickly became socially acceptable. The two parallel social and personal transformations discussed in Chapter 2 (the spread of affectionate relations between parents and children, and love marriages) probably played a determining role.

Unlike people a century earlier, modern people choose their partners and friends because they love and like them, and they try to keep these feelings alive. They choose whether or not to have children and when to have them. Because they have been chosen, and longed for, children are more likely to be loved, thus ensuring more profound communication and allowing both parents and children to be truly themselves. And, for people suffering from severe stress, being part of a loving couple, or having close relationships with their children or friends, is often enough to help reduce the tension and anxiety, at least temporarily.

The exchange of affection and psychological and physical 'strokes' between parents and children has become acceptable and is widely encouraged by the medical profession and child-rearing specialists. It has become a normal part of people's behaviour and has most likely helped children to develop rich neural connections. These have allowed them to savour emotions in refined ways. And it was probably these same neural networks that helped them to acquire the sort of social savoir-faire that led to the development of a new social fabric. By contrast, children (and young apes) deprived of all affection seem unable to access those skills that would allow them to be accepted by others, to adapt to them and to play a full part in the social networks around them.

This general trend has quickened pace in the course of the Second Modernity. For parents and children who exchange affection, this has not only become the social norm, but also a source of pleasure. Most of the time, this affection and the easy relations it leads to do not stop at the onset of adolescence. Indeed, parents and children have both been affected by the drive for autonomy and meaningfulness. Most young people no longer have to fight for their freedom and for the right to have their say. Accordingly, parents and children get on well with one another and many young adults decide not to leave the family home.

The spread of the love marriage was just as important. Marriages arranged according to social conventions were replaced by unions formed by two people who chose one another largely for reasons of sexual attraction and feelings of emotional harmony. The old system did not exclude love, but it did not favour it either. The new one offers a good way to begin a liaison that can grow in strength and allow its members to explore and enrich their emotional life together.

Over the last half-century, European sexual practices have changed considerably. First, this took the form of emancipation from traditional sexual taboos. But, later on, people turned to the active exploration of the sensations, feelings and emotions tied up with love-making, which often encouraged a couple's sensory and affective development.

We saw the early signs of polysensuality and sexual freedom in Sweden and France in the early 1970s. Our observations focused on the extent to which prevailing sexual taboos had been dismantled: tolerance of adolescent sexual relations, of extra-marital affairs and of public references to sexuality. This liberalising trend came to an end in Sweden in the late '70s and in France in 1982 (among 15-18 year-olds) and in 1986 (among the rest of the population). However, we saw the liberalising trend continue in other areas: the acceptance of homosexuality and increased tolerance of practices once considered perverse or transgressive.

During the 1980s and 1990s, however, we witnessed a change of direction. The tide of sexual liberalism, as it related to sexual values and behaviour, gave way to the search for a sensually and emotionally richer sex life. One of the earliest and most striking signs of this transformation was the shift in France from a sexual liberalism in the 1970s centred on emancipation and challenging convention to a sexual liberalism in the 1980s and '90s based on hedonism and polysensuality, on the quest for the sensations, emotions and pleasures that accompany love-making.

According to our interviewees, this enrichment of people's sex lives had four major characteristics. Many men adopted views that had traditionally been considered feminine: sex and sexuality should be accompanied by feelings, intimacy and a sense of connection with one another. Many women had become more 'masculine' in their attitude towards sex: taking the initiative and actively seeking (multiple) male sexual partners. Together, men and women had set out to explore and cultivate the emotions and sensations connected with love and sex. Finally, these emotions and sensations lasted longer as couples prolonged their sex lives into old age, sometimes making use of new medical treatments.

Italian, French and English life histories collected in the early 1980s show how much couples' lives had changed. The disappearance of the idea of sin and the growing effectiveness of contraceptives combined to allow people to explore the sensual and emotional aspects of lovemaking in a relaxed way. We saw close couples who were able to deal with infidelity, and sometimes even use it as an opportunity to grow, who worked on their emotional relationship to break out of spirals of conflict and ensure their stability. In many cases we saw the blossoming of a happy sexual and emotional life which combined psychological and physical intimacy with eroticism and tenderness.

In the early 1980s, Norbert Bellah and his colleagues observed that in the United States love and lovemaking were also becoming a mutual exploration of each other's infinitely rich, complex and exciting personalities.[33] Their interviewees insisted on the fact that their relationships were much better than their parents' had been, stressing their improved ability to heighten their intimacy, share their feelings and deal with the root causes of the problems they faced. Although couples had become more fragile, they also brought each other much greater satisfaction.

The warmth of friendship networks. Close friends, with whom we can communicate almost without words and in whom we can confide, as well as groups of mates, constitute precious emotional capital.[34] Such friends can be as important as partners or family when it comes to easing tension or stress or to being happy. Sometimes groups of mates can be as important, if not more so, than members of one's own household. Sometimes these two poles balance each other out. Sometimes it can be hard to tell where one ends and the other begins – are the almost-sisters, virtually-my-own-daughters, like-a-second-mothers and adoptive-uncles, whom people discuss in their interviews, family or friends? For some, support groups, like spiritualist circles, Alcoholics Anonymous, Weight Watchers or book or philosophy clubs, also form part of their affective capital. Though they may not include close friends, they can play just as important a role in conserving their members' inner balance as networks of real friends or extended family.

---

33   Bellah et al. 1985: pp.108 and 110.

34   In different cultures, people prioritise close friends in different ways. For example, surveys conducted by Sociovision Cofremca have shown that the Japanese and especially the French and the Germans are three times more likely than Americans to consider perjuring themselves for a close friend. Swedes fall somewhere in between.

Situated somewhere between the household and a friendship network, these extended families often acted as shock-absorbers, especially during the economically and socially difficult 1990s. They sometimes offered serious financial and material support. This intra-familial solidarity is without doubt one of the mechanisms that allowed those societies that suffered real economic and social hardship during the 1990s not to be torn apart.

Essential, but still incomplete. This analysis shows that by the end of the 1990s the micro-social fabric fulfilled not only a utilitarian role, but also a socio-affective one that was essential to the well-being of people and society. For many people, it was their principal source of happiness and personal fulfilment and the locus of affection and of social and socialising interaction. It was no longer coercive, but provided a place of refuge for people who had fallen foul of, or been frustrated by, society at large. Its cohesion still depended in part on its members' self-interest, but much more so on the emotional ties that bound them together and on the support, understanding and help they offered one other. It was a place where people could recharge their emotional batteries and deal with their stresses and frustrations. It could only fill this emotional role because it was heterarchical, comprehensive and tolerant. When it worked well, its members could feel free to be themselves and to be accepted for what they were.

However, this micro-social fabric was not all encompassing. A small minority of lonely people, who sometimes suffered a great deal, were left out by it. For some, the only sources of affection and warmth were visits to the doctor or brief chats with friendly shopkeepers. For some, a smile or a few words could be shafts of light in otherwise dark days.

New macro-social configurations begin to emerge

Even if they are well integrated into their household and social networks, people still feel the need to develop links with society at large and to find their place in it. They are trying to fill the void left by their abandonment of traditional forms of belonging. They are on the lookout for collectives or emergent collectives with whom they feel some sort of harmony. These may be short-lived, their boundaries unclear and their composition in flux; they may be latent or dormant, but ready to burst into life when needed.

Modern people are looking for subtle and very precise points and forms of agreement with others. This tends to encourage small social groups and results in fragmentation. But these groups are also open to the possibility of alliance, amalgamation or absorption, like a system of Russian dolls. And so modern people, who are emotional and reactive, subject to a constant hail of information, and connected to the rest of the world via Internet and television, can synergise at any time with huge collectives that may encompass hundreds of millions of people spread over the entire planet: for example, other young people, other 'Greens', other Christians, other humanists, etc.

Scholarly works and everyday conversations often refer to these collectives as 'communities' or 'tribes'. In my opinion, neither of these words really does justice to the phenomenon. The word tribe conjures up images of primitive societies. When it is used more precisely, it refers to topographic divisions, shared descent or ethnic similarities. All of these uses distance it from these modern groups, which are freely chosen, collectively authored and easily abandoned. I use it only to describe very small collectives with strong, shared characteristics that try to separate themselves off from the rest of society by particular rituals and signs.

During a study trip to the USA in October 1999, I was struck by the omnipresence of the words 'community' and 'belonging' in my conversations with sociologists, consultants and business leaders. They used them to refer to the new collectives that were springing up throughout American society. However, although these words do justice to certain aspects of the traditional American social fabric (with its associations and stable and formally defined political, religious and neighbourhood clubs), for me, they are both too strong to describe most of the modern groups and relationships under discussion here. Perhaps we should speak of quasi-communities or of weak, fluctuating or multiple belonging.

These quasi-communities come in a number of different shapes. Sociovision singled out and described those that appeared most often in the late 20th century. We distinguished between four different types of quasi-community: **halos of emotion**, groups of people brought together and carried along by a shared wave of emotion; **kindred spirits**, groups of people one likes; **mouvances**, people all heading in the same direction; and **isolates**, groups in which people shut themselves away[35].

Halos of emotion

In a sea of otherwise half-hearted identification with others, the vast majority of people today like sometimes to be swept up by waves of emotion or surges of compassion which draw them into a short-lived community of sentiment, be it at the level of their city, their country, their continent or the entire planet.

---

35   *Halos d'émotion, philées, mouvances and isolats* in the original.

Most of these groupings only last as long as the emotions that inspire them. A particular event acts as a catalyst that unites an entire population. Huge numbers of people suddenly feel an intense emotion and realise that it is widely shared. They are in tune with others and so feel close to them. Together, they form halos, vague and transitory social configurations that can sometimes tightly bind together thousands, millions, tens or even hundreds of millions of people. The waves with which they begin can encompass almost the entire planet, as when the Berlin Wall came down in late 1989, when Princess Diana died in 1997 or during the anti-war demonstrations of 2003. They can be national or local, provoked by oil slicks, by a government's failure to prosecute a paedophile network or by people's outrage at the unexpected success of the far right at elections. These ensembles are often marked by solidarity or political protest, but they can also involve joy, hope or fear.

From Tiananmen Square to Kosovo, emotion and compassion cross international borders. We see images of starving, flooded or decimated populations on the television, we cry together and feel the same compassion. Sport also brings people together. Sometimes, spectators feel that they belong to a united community, as when their national team wins the World Cup. But these waves can also be limited to stadiums, where people embrace one another in the heat of the moment. People also enjoy parties and festivals – music festivals or events like Halloween can briefly unite towns, neighbourhoods or villages; raves and festivals can give young people an impression of oneness with their contemporaries the world over.

Many other societies have known such waves, but these emotional waves are a central element for the extremely emotional society that is emerging in the West. Large or small, they gather, swell and then subside. And when they subside people and things sometimes go back to the way they were before, but sometimes they are changed for good. They can ignite informal and biodegradable organisations that are sparked into life, manage the moment and then die down when the wave subsides. Often, the powers-that-be try to make use of or manipulate these waves.

Kindred spirits

Kindred spirits – those we like – are relatively long-term groups of people brought together by similarities or by shared lifestyles, philosophical or spiritual positions, ethnic origins, cultural background, the sense of sharing material or cultural interests, or pastimes. This sense comforts them and allows them to feel they have a place in society and to identify with others.

Most of the time, these groups of kindred spirits do not feel bound together in long-term or stable ways, but instead they feel a fluctuating bond of which they may be only barely conscious or which may give them an impression of temporary fusion with others. Often, this is built on vague similarities: 'we humanists', 'we conservatives'. Sometimes it is built on profound feelings of connection, but ones which lack shared rituals or identifiers: it may be people who share an interest in Buddhism, cycling or opera, or just young people as a whole. If these feelings of belonging seem long-term and people develop identifiers and shared rituals, then we can speak of tribes, like punks, hippies, Harley Davidson petrol-heads, or people who enjoy rap or techno music.

Today, it is possible to distinguish a handful of life-stances that subtend these different groups of kindred spirits. Humanists are very widespread and include people who are interested in human rights and human development. These groups are often political or charitable in tone. They divide up and focus on different aspects of the struggle for human emancipation. Ecologists are equally diverse. They include large numbers of Westerners who are open to the idea of reasonable environmentalism. Music generates emotional and cultural resonances that allow people to commune and bond.

Many groups of kindred spirits are also based on shared interests or leisure activities. They give people the feeling of belonging to a sort of vague fraternity: for instance, people who regularly cycle or walk. People are less inclined to talk to their neighbours, but cyclists and ramblers almost always greet each other. People involved in such networks of kindred spirits enjoy sharing opinions, beliefs, jargon, tastes and rituals.

Ordinary people from different cultures and from all over the world also feel drawn towards older cultural entities, which are more specific and more rooted in particular places. This globalisation of stereotypes or cultural exemplars, often spurred on by the media, is not a novelty. Figures such as 'the Parisian woman' or 'the American cowboy' are classic examples, but new ones emerge regularly. The martyrdom of Tibet, the radiant personality of the Dalai Lama and the spectacular beauty of the Himalayas have created a sense of solidarity with Tibetan Buddhism – one that could always tip into a halo of emotion if triggered by further violence on the part of the Chinese authorities. The Welsh, Irish and Bretons are reviving their ancient Celtic culture and creating a new type of Celtic music, blending tradition and modernity. This offers them another layer of personal and social identity and also fame and fortune, as young people without the slightest link to Celtic culture buy into their music. New forms of fusion-cuisine are also becoming part of people's eating habits.

The Internet is an ideal tool for the development and spread of new groups of kindred spirits. People use it to seek out and communicate with others who share the same passions, sensibilities and interests. The success of many Internet start-up companies has depended on their ability to convince people with latent concerns or interests that they all belonged to a wider culture of users. The dramatic success of social networking sites and Web 2.0 both confirms the continuing pull of the 'Kindred Spirit' quasi-community and also offers the technological means to facilitate and enable ever-easier interaction of this kind.

Mouvances

Mouvances unite people with shared goals or aims. In many ways, they are similar to groups of kindred spirits. They are bottom-up rather than top-down. Most of them are one-dimensional and do not insist on exclusivity – i.e. they do not ask people to renounce their other interests and they do not seek to bind them in forcibly. They are flexible, open, overlapping, biodegradable, and can take on many different forms and operate at different levels of intensity. They feed off waves of emotion that may briefly intensify their members' sense of belonging or draw new members in. Modern people's pacifist tendencies are also visible in these mouvances, but they have grand designs, objectives, leaders and at least embryonic forms of organisation and, if the circumstances call for it, they can become violent.

Mouvances differ from 'Kindred Spirits' in that those who take part in Mouvances tend to feel that they are trying together to play a determining role in influencing civil society. Modern people want to be involved in and influence things that affect their lives. This explains why mouvances spring up as soon as people realise that they are not alone in wanting to bring about or prevent particular outcomes and they realise that together they can change things. They unite, around major or minor issues, to influence the way society works. If leaders emerge and can catalyse events, then mouvances can become more solid and sometimes unite with others in collective action. They fluctuate, weaken or grow stronger depending on people's emotional commitment and the galvanising capacities of their leaders. They can give rise to small associations or even large NGOs.

Modern people do not want to be involved in everything, all the time, but instead to be able to say their piece and be listened to, or to be able to do something about things which concern them when they feel moved to do so. Many mouvances are short-term and very specific: building a bypass, changing some aspect of the local education system, driving drug dealers out of the neighbourhood, changing the way one's company works, closing down a polluting factory, etc. Modern people are often deeply concerned and happy to volunteer to help improve their collective or community, encourage its vitality, make it run more smoothly or deal with its problems. They are ready to defend it against aggression or threats, be they from the state, the local council, a devastating hurricane, Europe or the federal government. Most of the time, though, these are short-term engagements.

Other mouvances have wider goals: liberalising abortion, building Europe, fighting globalisation, defending wider human rights or the specific rights of women, homosexuals, AIDS victims or foetuses, protecting the environment, etc. There are a few, clear meaningful issues that drive modern people: life, human and cultural rights, ecology, environmental harmony and the human spirit. These are very different from the themes proper to old political movements. Similarly, changing values, technologies and conceptions of life can divide those people who favour self-development or protecting the environment from traditionalists. These divisions cut across old-school, political ones.

These new mouvances are better at combining forces to achieve particular goals than old-fashioned organisations or churches. This is made easier by their porous and flexible boundaries. Modern Westerners, especially the young, are becoming more realistic and smarter. They are ready to put their sensibilities on the backburner in order to achieve their goals. This realism allows highly focused or culturally specific mouvances to ally briefly with others, which may have opposing views in other dimensions, in order to achieve a particular goal. The 'anti-globalisation' mouvance is a good example of this. Rejecting materialist culture and economic and financial globalisation, it was formed during the WTO meeting in Seattle in 1999 and created a sort of globalisation of civil society that opposed the purely economic and financial globalisation that had emerged from the Washington consensus. It united highly diverse groupings in one broad church. Most participants were highly determined, but pacifist, although a small number were bent on stirring things up.

Isolates

When people are extremely unhappy, if they feel rejected by wider society, overwhelmed by a sense of meaninglessness or if their personality has been seriously damaged in some way, then they can cut themselves off from society and seek refuge in **isolates**, where they can hide away. In the 1990s, such closed collectives represented an extreme, relatively rare and almost atypical form of the mouvances and groups of kindred spirits discussed above. When people's sense of belonging becomes too strong, when it transforms into an exclusive tie that encourages people to cut themselves off from others and even become aggressive towards them, then ghettos, sects, combative factions or violent action networks can emerge. At the same time, for rather different reasons, the rich, for example, can withdraw into gated communities or 'rich ghettoes'.

A self-organised living society

The proliferation of 'single-storey' sociosystems

During the First Modernity, large swathes of economic and social life were organised from above or determined by social conventions. I have described how this gave way to the process of self-organisation that emerged from the adaptive strategies of different individuals and groups. People attracted and repelled one another. They created couples, households and networks, and got involved with kindred spirits, mouvances and associations. Collectives interacted with each other in similar ways. Where they grew apart, pre-existing social forms withered away. When certain sets of connections broke down, then whole sections of society lost their vitality. And when new connections sprang up and in some cases interwove and became lasting, then they gave rise to yet further new connections.

Strategic opportunism governed the actions of people, collectives and organisations. Their points of connection and points of rupture became less and less clear. Neither individuals nor collectives had fixed programmes or objectives. They adapted their behaviour according to the information they received and the emotions, intuitions and reflections that emerged from their interactions. Connections between people and collectives emerged, were reinforced, grew weaker, broke off and sometimes created synergies and allergies between one another. Thus the architecture of a new society took shape.

Sociosystems have always existed, but since the 1960s and '70s they have increased in number, infiltrating everywhere, regulating growing numbers of micro- and macro-social interactions and shaping changes in ways of life and behaviour. They have also changed in form, moving from hierarchy at work, patriarchy at home and elites in fashion and consumption towards systems characterised by heterarchy, consensus and autonomy. These non-hierarchical sociosystems, which effectively operate with all their members working on an equal footing, I have called 'single-storey' sociosystems[36].

Self-organising micro-sociosystems began in a small way. As one met another, they gradually grew in importance until they formed a larger system operating at a higher level. Modern society tends to work in this way – fractally – with systems emerging at the micro level and self-organising at higher levels until the architecture of a whole new society eventually appears.

Many sociosystems went unnoticed because they were informal and their participants were scarcely conscious of their existence. But, if we pay close attention, we can find them everywhere. In the next few chapters, we will examine the workings of numerous micro- and macro-sociosystems. For now, though, a few examples should suffice.

Unhappiness about their neighbourhood either led people to try to build relationships with their neighbours or alternatively to flee them and look elsewhere for a pleasant life. An aggressive, indifferent or invasive neighbourhood could sometimes drive people to move out, and this reaction encouraged the development of ghettos. But an aggressive neighbourhood could also push people to meet up with their neighbours and try to reduce violence and antisocial behaviour. Most of the people we interviewed claimed to have at least a few good neighbours with whom they had built up ties that might, for example, lead to mutual help networks for babysitting, driving children to school, carrying out home improvements or for lending each other basic items like milk or bread. The growth of local information exchange networks and local exchange trading systems (LETS) are other examples of micro-sociosystems in action.

We have seen how large companies were transformed by sociosystems that grew up in the interstices of their organisational structure and bureaucracy. Some of these increased the company's vitality and creativity by, say, sidestepping formal structures. Others led people to drag their feet or prevent certain decisions from being carried out. Thanks to the sociosystems that developed between customers and staff, many companies and organisations became better adapted to their environment and customers, almost in spite of themselves, and sometimes without even being aware of it.

The social and economic vitality of a region might increase or diminish; some places prospered whilst others faded, depending on whether or not local sociosystems worked positively and effectively. People began to realise

---

36   'Sociosystèmes de plain-pied'.

that, just like groups or organisations, cities would have more vitality and be better adapted for survival if they included large numbers of more or less synergetic sociosystems.

The formation and development of sociosystems were sometimes unexpectedly provoked by the use of authoritarian measures or apparently rational decisions that ignored the human factor. In this way, they could have either negative[37] or positive consequences. In the United States, for example, it seems that the exceptional financial support accorded to single mothers encouraged lifestyles that provoked an increase in juvenile delinquency. Elsewhere, steps taken to legalise and destigmatise abortion reduced the number of unwanted children and promoted more affectionate parenting techniques and so reduced youth violence.

Seemingly strong governments with large majorities were hampered less by the official opposition than by sociosystems that either opposed them or had different priorities. For example, a *de facto* collusion between judges and journalists in countries as diverse as Italy, France and the United States, has, in some cases undermined the authority of politicians and other social leaders. In Seattle, the anti-globalisation sociosystem emerged from the interaction of a number of different NGOs and paralysed the World Trade Organisation.

Mutual support networks like the mafia, terrorist networks and criminal organisations of all sorts spread rapidly. They took advantage of people's lack of respect for the law and bureaucratic states' diminishing authority. They were helped by the worldwide spread of instant communication, which legal authorities struggled to regulate.

The old powers are outmanoeuvred

Self-organisation and self-regulation are characteristics of living systems and have always occupied a central place in socio-human ones. Primitive societies were self-organised and our civilisations are too. The market is the classic example of a self-organised and self-regulating system. It was neither invented by the powers-that-be nor imposed from on high, but was an emergent property of people's behaviour. In the Middle Ages, it developed like a natural system, pushing aside barter and princely predation.

That said, the authorities still endeavoured to limit the sphere of self-organisation and self-regulation. They tried to encompass and set guidelines for self-organising and self-regulating informal systems, or alternatively to

---

37   Boudon R. *Effets pervers et ordre social*, Paris: PUF, 1977.

replace them with organisations that were conceived, driven and rationally administered from on high. Princes, cities and then states set out to regulate and profit from markets by imposing taxes and formal rules, or by appropriating the power to mint coins. Constitutions and company guidelines were written up and implemented. The institution of marriage developed.

In the 20th century, states, companies and large, centralised organisations managed to massively restrict the sphere of self-organisation and self-regulation. They shackled the lives of people and society in legal, constitutional, bureaucratic and organisational straitjackets. Communist states even contrived to do away with the market (if not the black market) and representative democracy, thinking this would allow them to build a more efficient and just society.

The flourishing of self-organisation and self-regulation ushered in by the Second Modernity posed problems for these mass, authoritarian and outdated systems. The ordinary people who helped create and maintain sociosystems were equipped with sensitive social radars and an intuitive understanding of complexity that made fine strategists of them. They contributed to the functioning of these sociosystems, which duly developed their capacity to hamper or enact social change. Many formal leaders felt helpless in the face of this. Political parties, trade union organisations and institutional churches were all affected. The principal victims, though, were the behemoths of the First Modernity: nation-states and large businesses.

Self-organised sociosystems often created parallel and informal organisational systems that co-existed alongside official ones. They sidestepped chains of command and gained real power. They discredited leaders and, in some countries, the entire political class. They often prevented authoritarian decisions from being enacted.

In many cases, attempts by organisations and traditional powerhouses to clamp down were profoundly counterproductive and only accelerated people's drive towards independence: systematic disregard for the (far too numerous) rules, the introduction of slack into the system, antisocial behaviour, people increasingly taking things into their own hands, corruption and even violence. In sum, a degree of disorder that cleared the way for a wave of new self-organising groups.

In this way, an organic socio-technological fabric progressively transformed the process of natural selection as applied to institutions, organisations and companies. Sovereign and welfare states, as well as large multinational companies were particularly affected. They had all been shaped and acquired their power and legitimacy during the First Modernity, in a world where authoritarian chains of command and rational, bureaucratic and Taylorian organisation were the paths to success. Now, in contrast, it was those companies which could go with the flow of self-organisation and make the most of self-regulation that were most likely to be selected for survival. Those which remained monolithic, authoritarian and bureaucratic suffered.

A new form of governance gradually takes shape

A new set of questions now emerged: how to manage a family, business or country in a complex, organic society characterised by self-organisation and self-regulations? How to have a decisive impact on their future? How best to influence and steer people and events?

In family networks and friendships groups, we observed members who, more or less deliberately, set out to provoke collective action or realise internal change. They did this in strategic ways, combining emotion, moments of intuition, observation and rational analysis, and working out how best to go about creating a shift of motivations and/or relationships that would change a situation. In this way, they explored new forms of self-organisational expertise.

In the 1980s, Norbert Bellah and his colleagues dedicated a chapter of their book to the emergence of a new type of relationship, which they called 'therapeutic', similar to the one described above.[38] Bellah thought that the therapeutic approach, which involved understanding, intimacy, objectivity and the attempt to influence people and things, was in the late 1980s becoming a model for all American relationships.

Exactly the same phenomenon was in evidence in Europe at the time. Cofremca's observations highlighted what we called strategic opportunism and adaptive navigation. And it seems to me that this approach is just as much strategic as therapeutic. We could also call it ecosystemic, because the subject's strategic analysis or search for the right therapy also involves a consideration of the wider context of the organism in its ecosystem. In short, it is an attempt to guide the course of events that is both smarter and better informed (either by intuition or careful observation).

Leaders who manage to govern or run huge modern organisations, states or groups go about things in fairly similar ways. They have biodegradable strategic visions (ones which can change if the circumstances require it) and, like ordinary people, they use adaptive navigation. They try to get an

---

38   Bellah et al. 1985: pp. 113-141.

intimate understanding of situations. What is the structure and physiology of the collective to be governed? How is it situated in its ecosystem? What self-regulation is at work and what are the conditions in which it operates? Are other self-organisations emerging and what interventions might speed up, alter or block their emergence? What loose but formal structures might engage with these sociosystems and make best use of them? If they feel they have really understood a situation, then they act decisively. They try to catalyse, facilitate or encourage forms of self-organisation and self-regulation that they deem to be positive, and at the same time they block those that seem counter-productive. One might say that they try to develop a sort of complicity with human and social concatenations. Or to understand which innovations synergise with them. Or to make them work on their behalf. Or even to liberate and actualise the latent qualities and potential of a system.

Over the final chapters we will see how our very future may depend on the speed with which states, companies and society itself can learn these forms of governance.

Synergies between micro-communication technology and the society of ordinary people

By the end of the 20th century, socio-cultural change and the development of communication technology were operating in intimate synergy. Personal and social change was already well under way when, in 1985, it inspired a radical transformation in communication technology. It was this change that shifted the focus away from monolithic, centralised and pyramidical forms of communication in favour of peer-to-peer communication. But as these new micro-communication technologies became part of people's daily lives they rapidly reinforced the pre-existing tendency for socio-cultural change to move towards greater autonomy, freer interaction and more heterarchy. They accelerated the development of open households, personal networks, halos of emotion, groups of kindred spirits, mouvances and sociosystems, as well as the intensification of free communication among them – i.e. they increased their vitality. New interactive, open-ended and overlapping collectives could never have self-organised so effectively, nor on such a large-scale, without the help of information and telephone technology.

Modern people choose which technologies become part of their daily lives

People's dissatisfaction, and especially employees' dissatisfaction, with the difficulties they faced in living, communicating and organising relationships in the way they wanted, created a momentum that pushed technological innovation in the direction of applications that were more personal and less monolithic, more heterarchical and less centralised.

If the civil service, large companies and their IT departments had been allowed to determine the direction of change, then we would doubtless have seen the emergence of a very different range of communications technology: more monolithic, more hierarchical and more compartmentalised. Instead, it was employees, middle managers, ordinary people and their penchants for autonomy and heterarchy that set the tone.

If I stress the importance of this socio-human momentum, it is because we are still haunted by traditional Western paradigms that suggest that causality only works in the other direction: so that technology is usually seen as changing the socio-human sphere.

Some examples of socio-human momentum in technological change:

VCRs. During the 1980s and '90s, television for the masses was a form of torture for more independent-minded people. There were few channels, programmes were broadcast at set times and there was no possibility of interactive dialogue. Video recorders helped to make television less monolithic and more supple, by meeting people's need to record programmes, to choose when to watch them and perhaps to exchange video tapes among friends.

Fax-machines. It was often despite, not because of, management that faxes became so popular. As they spread through companies, they met many people's need to communicate directly with other parts of the company and with the outside world without having to go through a centralised system. You did not have to prepare the documents in a special way, their arrival caused no disruption, and you didn't even need to be there to receive them. As such, they fitted in easily, increased the range of interpersonal exchange that was possible and breathed new life into sociosystems that were crying out for it.

Mainframe computers had favoured consolidated organisational structures, hierarchies and the power of specialists. In contrast, **networked PCs** responded to people's need for independence and autonomy and promoted communication that bypassed the centre. Their rapid spread was driven by employees and middle managers who took on senior management and IT departments, which would have preferred to hang on to their privileges.

Increasing numbers of telephones. The telephone is an interpersonal communication and networking tool *par excellence*. Households jumped at the chance to have multiple telephones (both mobiles and landlines). This increase was a major innovation as far as the social fabric was concerned, allowing for intimate and discreet communication with the outside. Cordless phones were another step down this path: people went to their rooms to talk in peace. In the 1990s, the lighting fast spread of cordless and mobile phones completed this transformation.

In some cases, people and society can hijack particular innovations, using them in ways which their creators never intended or imagined. Users take the initiative and contribute to the emergence of new communication services. The **answerphone** was immediately transformed into a filtering device: depending on my mood and on discovering who is calling, I can choose whether or not to take the call. I remain in control.

In France, a similar thing happened with **Minitel** (a precursor of the Internet). The system and the accompanying machine had been designed and released in the 1980s. It was geared around traditional pyramidical society and put millions of households in touch with information centres. However, its founding fathers lost control of their creation when, in a spontaneous act of self-organisation, a few independent and decentralised operators set up buddy networks and the 'Minitel Rose' (rather like internet dating sites). They had seen the possibility of facilitating a communications explosion.

To a large extent, the **Internet** created itself as a response to the needs of several groups of people. Early prototypes had been created by the military for internal communication. They were quickly adopted and developed in scientific circles and then, later, by ordinary people who jumped on the Internet. Despite its initial drawbacks and its awkwardness, people quickly used it to communicate among themselves and, in particular, to find like-minded users.

Chemically-facilitated communication. People can feel shy, withdrawn and depressed, whereas they would like to be able to communicate easily. All kinds of solutions have been developed to help with this problem: Prozac freed many individuals from their isolation; Ecstasy allowed people to feel at one with each other. (Hopefully, one day they will be replaced by less harmful chemicals.) New forms of therapy, especially group and family therapy, are spreading and have a rosy future, but there remain many situations that lack catalysts for communication. We need new social rituals, new architecture and new sorts of meeting that encourage communication.

The use of new micro-communication technologies reinforces changes in people and in the social fabric

The opposite influence (that of technology on the socio-human sphere) is also crucial. As they become part of everyday life, VCRs, PCs, fax-machines, answerphones, mobile phones, the Internet and Prozac feed into people's personal evolution and promote the development and intensification of their networks and sociosystems. As they use these new tools, men and women discover unsuspected possibilities that reinforce or trigger changes of perspective, often revolutionise their lifestyles and promote transformation in the social fabric. This is true whether or not they have already been profoundly affected by modernising processes. As they use them, they become more autonomous, better connected and their vitality increases.

Research carried out by Sociovision in several European countries in 1998 and 1999 highlighted some of the principal impacts of these new tools.[39] They lessened – even removed – geographic, psychological and social distance within networks and society. Interpersonal communications, family, friendship or business networks, and mafia and terrorist organisations were all able to adapt and self-regulate in real-time and on a global-scale. They allowed people to discover and choose one another on the grounds of psychological affinities, shared tastes or interests and cultural similarities. Insofar as they removed the need for real-world, face-to-face communication, computers and telephones freed people from their inhibitions. They counterbalanced modern phenomena like mobility, migration and unsynchronised life rhythms that might otherwise have broken families and networks apart. They helped people to remain a part of, rather than becoming alienated from, society. Electronic media seem to favour authentic, even brutal, communication. They solicit less formal and more direct forms of speech. Mobile phones also transformed communication. They allowed for instant communication; people were able to say what they felt the moment they felt it, without intellectualising or brooding on it. Recent surveys show that 'on line' communication (by telephone or Internet) tends to intensify relationships within a micro-system. In many families, it has already become

---

39   The central findings of these surveys are summarised in 'Les nouvelles technologies dessinent les contours de la société de demain' in *L'Observatoire de la Cofremca Sociovision* No. 48, March 1999.

unthinkable for any member not to have a mobile. Even young children of 7 or 8 have one so their parents or older siblings can check up on, advise and reassure them.

Despite its disappointing flaws and stock-market bubbles, the Internet casts its net further and more intensely with each passing day. It nourishes millions of people's lives and networks. For most companies, life without the Internet is already unimaginable. It sidesteps many established commercial and intermediary systems. It helps create global civil society and has already facilitated several revolutions. This is only the beginning. The Internet will become much faster and much more user-friendly. Its graphic and sound interfaces will become sharper. Its ability to find the right co-user or the right piece of information will improve. Technological progress will allow the World Wide Web to expand exponentially and this will undoubtedly have a major knock-on effect on the organic social fabric and modern socio-economy.

The unlikeliest of people will meet up, discover their affinities and build multiple, overlapping ties. Virtual communities will proliferate: cooperative forms of communication, living networks that allow individuals to work in groups, to exchange services, share their passions, to chat over vast distances, to change their social practices, and to create new forms of power and regulation. The Web will provide the means for latent movements and sociosystems to self-organise and these may have a dramatic effect on the course of things. Perhaps it will allow humanity finally to exist as one totality.

The widespread use of the Internet will facilitate the creation of a new relational order: a spontaneous order that will look more like disorder to some. The users of new technologies tend to take advantage of their flexibility to undertake initiatives at the right moment and to act when they choose. They can be constantly contactable, in case an interesting connection can be made. Discontinuity, chance and intuition have become paths to efficacy and creativity. The fact that the Internet is not hierarchical, but rather anarchic or heterarchical sits well with this. Its structure is very similar to that of grass-roots, self-organising groups. It replaces classic and hierarchical classificatory systems with a sort of spider's web of hyperlinked texts and messages that allow people to follow an infinity of paths from one point to another. In this way, use of the Internet goes hand in glove with people's evolution away from the linear and hierarchical Western tradition.

The Internet's dispersed structure makes it all but impossible for a single entity to dominate or control it. Internet communication will probably continue to elude governmental and state control. It will undermine their power and reinforce the grass-roots. It will alter or reduce the market share of many large companies and bring them new opportunities. There are many projects underway which aim to install wireless community networks and open-source networks using open-source software. These are run by ordinary people and depend on volunteers. The synergies between the Internet and modernising processes are so strong that the World Wide Web will doubtless be one of the vectors of the Third Modernity. The other vector will probably emerge from the budding synergies between socio-cultural change and the practical applications of life sciences such as biology and sociology.

A powerful and directed dynamic

An extremely powerful dynamic will probably continue to affect social change over the next few decades. It emerged from the dovetailing of personal change, alterations in the social fabric and progress in the field of communications technology. In the last twenty-five years of the 20th century these developments created a directed dynamic in Western society. A sort of self-perpetuating spiral in which these three elements (people's emancipation and coming of age, a new self-organising social fabric and the application of a few micro-communicational advances) fed into and mutually reinforced one another. It is unlikely that it will lose its momentum any time soon, and even less likely that it will turn on its head and go in the direction of hierarchy, centralism and bureaucracy. Even if some states and many large companies try to use micro-communications to regain minute and authoritarian control of their citizens and employees, it will probably continue to be one of the dynamics that will, over the next few decades, help to determine the history of the planet.

Chapter 7
Dreams of peace and the threat of violence

In this chapter, we shall see that in their interactions the vast majority of modern people ensure that their behaviour, whilst not entirely conformist, is acceptable in their social environment. But it would only need a few serious shocks, a few acts of aggression, for their stance and the prevailing climate to become violent. Thus we could envisage a Third Modernity dominated by violence and antagonism.

This is why I have come to think that the maintenance of informal regulatory frameworks is one of the major challenges of our time.

Our research has highlighted three types of interpersonal and social process:

- the first, which developed enormously throughout the 1990s, tends to create peaceful relations and looser regulations

- the second leads to violence and antagonism; so far, its scope and the damage caused has been limited, but our analysis suggests that it could weigh heavily upon the future of our society

- finally, the third type tends to either prevent or interrupt cycles of aggression, but it is only partially successful in this endeavour.

And so we find ourselves faced with a lack of certainty that demands intervention.

Processes tending to support the emergence of peaceful relationships and looser regulations

Towards a humanist morality of personal growth and development

As we saw in Chapter 5, the manner in which people reflexively distance themselves from their experiences leads them to reassess their representations of reality and, explicitly or not, to ask themselves questions about the meaning of their lives. The internal dialogues that people conduct between their actions, their feelings and their assessment of reality, leads them to focus on personal growth and development and to look for peace, not conflict. These desires are probably the precursors of a new moral system.

Older collective systems that provided people with a meaningful framework for their lives have gradually lost their significance. Modernity has steadily and unstoppably chipped away at them. Despite the apparent void that this has created, millions of people still experience moments of meaning and of meaninglessness in their day-to-day lives. Reflecting on these, they feel and judge that some of their actions and some aspects of their existence are meaningful, whilst others are not. They recognise which things are consistently meaningful for them and learn from this. If this learning becomes entrenched, then we witness the gradual emergence of new value systems which are more or less widely shared.

These precursors of a new philosophical or moral system are still far from being clearly organised or fixed. Individuals' search for meaning is most obviously present in the emotions that they feel and which they judge to be justified or appropriate. It is much less likely to be seen in the shape of specific values that they advocate. Their search for meaning emerges as a feeling that intuitively or impulsively drives people to sideline some attitudes or types of behaviour and to seek the company of other people who allow them to feel more comfortable with themselves and with their lives. It is less about belief or moral systems than a sort of tropism or general movement.

That said, this flourishing of individual emotional trajectories suggests that a broader process of reconstruction is under way – one that will recalibrate our belief and value systems. Certain characteristics of these future systems are gradually becoming clear, and they may grow clearer still over the next few decades. They encourage a sort of individual and everyday wisdom, which is perhaps selfish, but which is softened by a social philosophy that focuses on the preservation and expansion of living systems, including human relationships and human development.

A slightly selfish everyday wisdom. Building yourself a life that really suits you, means building a life that allows you, every day and over time, to be in profound harmony with yourself, and that allows you to feel authentic, vibrant and alive. This is a major source of meaning for those who set about it. What really matters for those people who follow this path is not to work harder or better, nor to be more appreciated at work; nor is it to be able more easily to buy this or that object they long for, nor to earn more, nor to notch up sexual experiences, nor even to see their children climb the social ladder. It may perhaps include one or more of these goals, but only insofar as it contributes to building a life that truly suits them.

From one interview to another, the goals towards which people are directing their efforts and energy vary, but they can be grouped together in a few broad categories:

- Self-realisation – for oneself, one's marriage or personal partnership, one's children and one's social network. This is a key goal.

- Taking care of one's body and one's peace of mind. The frustration, tension and stress that characterise contemporary life are all factors that encourage people who are highly aware of their feelings and emotions to focus on their peace of mind. They do physical and mental exercises and try to suppress desires that they find troublesome. They may use recreational drugs or medicines of Eastern or Native American origin or the most modern Western paharmaceuticals.

- Living a peaceful, measured life is a long-term project. It is only in the long-term that self-realisation, as well as the achievement of an emotional connection with loved ones, is meaningful. Preparing oneself to grow old in peace has become a goal not only for the elderly, but also for people in their prime who watch their parents ageing. Old-age is no longer simply decrepitude. It can also be fulfilling if one only knows how to go about it. Growing old and dying in the way that one would have wished afford the opportunity to make sense of one's life.

- Establishing a harmonious relationship with time. For modern people, time-constraints are felt to be a major obstacle to building a meaningful life. The impression of meaninglessness emerges when people no longer feel in control of their time, or worse when they have to submit to a rhythm or to a timetable which seems unfair or unreasonable. Ideally, one should be able to speed up or slow down as the situation requires, to live life at a leisurely as well as a hurried pace, and to make the most of both one's free time and of busier periods.

- Knowing how to keep work in its rightful place. For many people, the most important thing about their work is that it should not be too invasive or overwhelming, and that it should leave enough free time to find fulfilment elsewhere.

- Protecting oneself from the spiral of consumption. Ideally, one should be able to enjoy being a consumer, to make the most of it in the long-term, but without becoming its slave.

In the main, our observations don't show us people driven, who plough on with gritted teeth, nor do they reveal 'self-realisation militants' in pursuit of specific objectives whatever the cost. These are not people obsessed with meaning. They let meaning come to them rather than struggling to capture it. They explore as they go.

In the form it took throughout the 1990s, this everyday wisdom was extremely self-centred. Wisely, but perhaps selfishly, people set great store by harmony and personal development, both for themselves and for their friends and loved ones. This self-centredness was only partially off-set by the emergence of a social philosophy focused on life and human relationships.

The outline of a social philosophy focused on a rich and full life and human relationships. Attentive both to themselves and to others, modern people naturally project the emotions, intuitions and ideas they encounter in their private lives onto other people and society at large. What is more, they assess their social experiences according to how meaningful they are. These experiences, either consciously or not, then give rise to judgements regarding social life and social actors. Different situations, people and societies are felt to be 'good' or 'not good'. These judgements have not yet been translated into precise or clearly defined values. But they follow several trajectories which together sketch out the shape of a humanist morality.

The importance of a very physical humanism. modern people feel themselves to be very much alive, both in mind and in body. They feel pain, pleasure and the gamut of emotions and they have lives to be lived. Except perhaps for their real enemies, they consider other people to be like them. This experience is at once the culmination and a transformation of the ideology of human rights, with the addition of a visceral form of compassion that makes the ideology less theoretical and probably more powerful. The humanity of others, even distant others, is no longer a theoretical principle or a moral absolute dictated from above. The pain of others is also our pain.

The idea of one's fellow human beings tends to encompass everybody and throughout the entire course of their lives – everybody, including those most remote from us geographically or socially – throughout the entire course of their lives, in that people are inclined to pay particular attention to those things that might lead others astray and so ruin their future.

The importance of a peaceful, tolerant and supportive society. Modern people combine acute empathy with an extreme attachment to self-determination, without which their lives would be all but meaningless. To them, it seems fair enough that others are equally protective of their own right to self-determination. This makes them tolerant of different points of view. However, they only tolerate or welcome these points of view insofar as they find in others a reciprocal tolerance. Tolerance thus becomes a key value for them.

Intolerance is dismissed and rejected. For Vitalists from the mid-1980s onwards, things around them need to function smoothly. People who prevent this (extremists, blinkered militants and the intolerant) are at the other end of the spectrum of value and may drive Vitalists to aggression. They tend to consider aggressive or violent behaviour anomalous or pathological and as something which must be eliminated.

The importance of happiness. Hedonist values abound in this society. The pursuit of happiness and different types of pleasure is a strong motivating factor. This seems legitimate. People's concern with meaning moderates this hedonism, but does not do away with it. Even extreme forms of pleasure condemned by society at large, such as sexual depravity, binge-drinking or the use of illegal drugs, may form part of a meaningful life. Meaningfulness is not opposed to pleasure in the way that good was once opposed to evil, and sacrifice and suffering to hedonistic enjoyment. Modern people tend to think that all forms of pleasure can be legitimate so long as they are sensibly managed. Happiness and pleasure are good things, and a good society is a society that makes its members happy.

The importance of a full, rich life. For those who focus on self-development (both for themselves and for others), people have to be allowed to live their lives, seeds must be given room to germinate, their growth encouraged, and obstacles to their development overcome or eliminated. Impediments to these ambitions are seen as illegitimate, whereas combating such impediments and favouring growth are meaningful activities.

For the majority of Europeans and Americans, it is senseless not to take care of the environment and not to at least attempt to leave a healthy planet for future generations. Many feel that it is unjustifiable to harm any group in society, and important to work towards harmonious, sustainable development the world over.

This long-term concern for others favours neither the advocates of an extreme economic liberalism that would see the poor go the wall, nor those who argue for systematic and paternalistic social protectionism. Liberalism seems to sacrifice the potential for development. It stands aside when people and communities follow dangerous paths, whereas with a little help at the right time, they might have developed harmoniously. The paternalistic approach seems no better. Where it is systematic, it leads to welfare dependency – something which is not only diametrically opposed to one of contemporary society's central tenets, individual autonomy, but which is also considered to be socially and economically counter-productive.

Even though they may be used in commercial advertising or in the publications of NGOs, these themes of tolerance, happiness, life and shared humanity are no mere passing fashions. Instead, they seem to be deep-rooted personal and collective dispositions which draw their vitality from the search for meaning that is so present in contemporary society. They will probably last, even if they do so in new guises.

The reassessment of social, economic and political entities. The different trajectories taken by this new everyday wisdom and by this outline of a social philosophy focused on life and human relations are profoundly opposed to many aspects of social, economic and political life in the West. So people are wary of states, governments and political parties, as well as of the financial and economic establishment and multinational companies. They are equally wary of official social institutions and especially of the old elites.

Children who are beaten, raped and killed; poorly educated youth; competent middle-aged professionals who would like to keep on working but are forced into retirement; cold, formal and bureaucratic institutions; the contrast between the protection afforded to some and the extremely precarious social situation of others; between the massive wealth of a few and the poverty of many; politicians who waste their time in pointless jousting instead of dealing with real problems; one law for the powerful and another for everybody else; the bureaucratic organisation of a social security system that encourages irresponsible behaviour; the incapacity of political and economic leaders to consider the long-term and to fight environmental destruction; economic globalisation destroying minority cultures... These themes, and many others like them, repeatedly surface during interviews and they have a negative impact on public opinion and on people's sense of belonging.

Young people who are raised in an affectionate environment grow up to be socially adept adults who seek out happiness

In the past, when individual life paths were more clearly mapped out and were largely controlled by top-down social norms, the question of how to raise children and nurture positive aspects of their personality was less critical than it is today. Unstable individuals damaged the social order less than they do today. Contemporary society is less controlled by top-down social norms, regulations and commandments, and its functioning is fundamentally dependent on individuals' self-determination. In this context, raising well-adapted children is a major challenge. Ill-adapted individuals will be incapable of creating a life that suits them and so pose a threat to the fabric of this new society.

Families and friendship groups are important learning environments. Life in Western societies continues to produce a personality type characteristic of the Second Modernity and discussed in previous chapters.

Families who are, in the main, loving and tolerant and who are more and more attentive to the education of their children managed, throughout the 1980s and 1990s, to create learning environments that allowed children to learn about themselves and to develop affection, intimacy and social skills. This has contributed to the socialisation of hedonistic and largely peaceful people, capable of harmonious co-existence and equipped with a realistic and well-informed life-navigation system.

Most people, and the immense majority of the young, thus possess a social radar and self-navigation system that works more or less well. And everybody is looking for human kindness, harmony and cooperation rather than systematically pursuing vengeance or aggression.

The household and wider emotional networks are often conscious of the role of this learning environment and work hard to create it. They know themselves to be fragile and work on their shortcomings. Paying attention to one's relationship so that it lasts, raising one's children well so they find happiness, their place in society and self-realisation, taking care of networks of friends – all these aims form part of a greater ideal which people go to great lengths to achieve and which encourage particular forms of social savoir-faire which they continually refine. They are also a source of meaning. A large proportion of men and women between the ages of 30 and 40 whom we interview tell us how important it is to them that their relationship with their partner lasts, and how hard they work to achieve this. They say that harmonious relationships within the household seem to warrant more time and greater efforts than politics, the church or even work. The education of their children often seems to be an absolute priority. Both in America and in Europe, people have come to the conclusion that if they don't personally take their children's education in hand, then things may turn out badly. In France, people say they will devote less time to work so as to have *more time* at home to educate their children better, whilst in America in particular, people are looking to spend *more quality time* with their children.

The type of education that people try to provide for their offspring is quite particular. It is rather different from the education that they themselves received and radically different from that which their parents received. It is becoming clearer that nowadays the majority of parents seek to 'open their children's minds to dialogue, trust and communication of their deepest feelings', to 'teach them about life', to offer them 'tenderness and affection' and to 'share emotions with them'. In the vast majority of cases, even in the United States, they utterly dismiss 'the rule of authority without explanation'. They also sideline principles in favour of a navigation system that can intuitively adapt itself to situations which are always unique. A constantly increasing proportion of people think that in order to raise a young child well, it is more important to have physical contact, games and cuddles, than to explain to them how to behave. This type of family, even when it is fragmented or hard to define, is a loving family.

Another very important learning environment for young people is provided by networks of friends, especially when these networks are not entirely divorced from the family network. In Sweden and France, this begins in the nursery and continues at play-school, where children have the opportunity to experience social environments other than the household, to interact more or less among equals, to experiment with leadership dynamics and to manage the crises provoked by feelings of sympathy and antipathy. Most people who turned twenty in the year 2000 had been involved in friendship networks since their earliest childhood. In such networks, they had often formed intense emotional bonds that complemented or supported the ties that bound them to their relatives. They had also learnt how to operate in an informal society with alternating leadership roles. Drawing on their emotionally positive experiences among both friends and family, they had come to the conclusion that one can have a multi-faceted personality which allows one to operate equally comfortably in different social environments.

The education system's failure to adapt. Our society declares that it loves its children, but in stark contrast to the subtle contribution of their emotional micro-networks, children have a tough time at school. How the education system is organised differs from one country to the next, but there are certain key characteristics that we find to be more or less present in practically every case.

Those in authority in Europe and North America seem not to have fully realised that a child's education is a holistic process encompassing family, friends, school, television, leisure activities and holidays and the whole local environment. In most Western countries, many schools remain cut off from real life. There is no consensus among teachers, educational establishments, families and the local community as to which things should be forbidden and how to inculcate students with the desired ethos. Teachers and parents are more often mistrusting and at loggerheads than cooperating.

The primary and secondary schools that young people attended throughout the 1980s and 1990s were to a certain extent influenced by generational change among both pupils and staff. Relationship dynamics were not what they had been in previous decades. But, for the most part, there was a failure to develop the sort of relationships that would suit the evolving personalities of both pupils and staff. Many teachers had lost their authority without managing to retain a degree of influence with their pupils. Students often felt that their teachers failed to respect them and so responded with disrespect. The school system suffered from a general lack of confidence in itself.

In most Western countries, schooling is still very far from having adapted itself to the new situation. In contrast to play-schools, primary and secondary schools stress intellectual learning and neglect emotional learning: emotional and personal development, as well as social and general life skills. The education system's modus operandi is still marked by ideas that date back to before the Second Modernity – hierarchy, bureaucracy, constraint, competition and standardised curricula. Not only has the school system failed to take into account the diversity of personality types and forms of intelligence, but the teaching it offers has not evolved to meet the changing mentality of young people and it is hardly ever able to keep them interested. It often seems a strange and cold place, not to mention a boring one.

Because they are realistic and smart, many students conform to the strictures of school life. The more competitive or talented among them, as well as those who receive plentiful support from their families, have learnt to make the necessary effort and to manage the stress. Most, though, end up with a profoundly ambivalent idea of adult society and came to mistrust it. This ambivalence and mistrust are reinforced by the media, by children's observations of their parents and by their early experiences of the world of work. During interviews with students, we regularly see the germs of future discontent and future dissidence.

The three main youth personality traits in the year 2000. Most young people who turned twenty towards the end of the 20th century seem to have emerged from their education with three dominant traits that will mark their generation. These traits will help them make their way in society, will reinforce the modernity of society and will probably shake it up and speed up its transformation.

The importance of warm, affectionate relationships. Their emotions, encouraged and constantly stimulated from early childhood onwards, are intense and central to their lives. They look for this intensity and take pleasure in cultivating their emotions. The exchange of authentic emotions with others who are capable of sharing them is essential for them. They are highly aware of the importance of intimacy. Though they are capable of aggression, violence and even hatred, they are primarily focused on the search for warm, affectionate relationships, for authentic emotional dialogue and for the little pleasures that bring happiness.

Their social radar and their ability to navigate social situations are even better than those of their parents. Early on in life, they established an ongoing emotional dialogue with their parents and then their friends. They also had to deal with sensitive life problems in an uncertain and open-ended social environment and this forced them to adapt and to improvise. They grew up in a social micro-fabric of family and friends that was affectionate, heterarchical, tolerant, flexible, lacking in clearly-defined boundaries and where nothing was completely guaranteed or taken for granted. For the most part, this was a stimulating environment where they developed the capacity to empathise with, and to anticipate, others, where they acquired a therapeutic and strategic sensibility, where they trained themselves to foil attempts by others to assert authority over them and to recognise when it was acceptable for people to assume transient leadership roles, and finally where they learnt to take the initiative and to take the lead themselves.

Their relationship to society and to the prevailing system is unclear. Most of them feel comfortable in the micro-society of household and friends in which they live. They are viscerally attached to it. But they feel themselves to be somehow outsiders in the world of institutions and organisations. They vote less than their elders and distance themselves from political parties and they have no particular desire to work for large companies or for the state. They have little time for political or economic leaders, whom they often despise.

Instead they tend to fall back upon their own little world and there they try to create a comfortable life for themselves. However, if circumstances seemed favourable, they can equally become involved in subversive movements.

In 2000, Sociovision Cofremca carried out research among young adults living in Berlin, London, Milan and Paris. This showed that by the time they leave school, they tend to have an ambivalent and often disapproving or confrontational attitude towards wider society. Without entirely sharing its ethos and whilst maintaining their own 'secret gardens', some are determined to do what they must to carve themselves out a comfortable and happy place within this wider society. And they are reasonably well equipped to do so. Most, however, maintain some distance between themselves and society. They may get involved in groups that seek to break with society or even, in some cases, challenge it. And there is a small minority of true subversives.

Conformity and deviance: their mutual interaction leads people to self-regulate

Life gives rise to a new system of social control. Older systems of self-discipline, cohesion and homogeneity have gradually broken up. Christian notions of sin and hell, the acceptance of suffering as a route to heaven, the taste for sacrifice, as well as ideas of shame and modesty were all powerful tools of self-discipline. The state's monopoly of legitimate violence was scarcely contested, except by anarchists. The traditions, rules and conventions imposed by formal hierarchical authority were accepted as self-evident and this kept most people on the straight and narrow without any need for coercion. The same can be said for people's internalisation of a demanding father figure. Likewise, the relative repression of drives and emotions helped to inculcate reasonable behaviour. In the First Modernity, the bewitching act of consumption and the collectivisation of desire through hierarchical mimicry led most to work hard and to consume ever more, which was what the economy needed. Work was organised according to the requirements of mass production and large-scale bureaucratic firms poured their workers into a mould and prevented their minds from wandering. Even though the cunning and the powerful could find ways around it, the rule of law was self-evident and most had a certain respect for it.

The collapse of these older systems, which had helped to manage the relatively smooth running of society, has not led to complete chaos. It simply gives the impression of disorder to those who are most attached to older social forms.

In fact, without our contemporaries fully realising it, a new type of social control has emerged. It comes not from on high but from all over and emerges from the complex interplay of influences within networks, collectives and sociosystems that we are all part of and which help us to decide what it would be wise to do or to not do. This newly permissive and tolerant society produces mechanisms of self-regulation that allow it to leave people and their collectives a good deal of autonomy and room for improvisation and initiative. At the same time, these mechanisms also encourage people to conform just enough for society to maintain its cohesion. This conformity comes from mutual influence and self-control, not from coercion, so that it is autonomy itself that produces and sustains social harmony.

Processes that tend to produce self-control and tolerance. Our research throughout the 1980s and 1990s showed that affectionate families, intimate social networks and other forms of collective are concerned with the happiness and self-realisation of their members and so they become permissive and tolerant. Their members feel that they can bend the rules (if only slightly) and they create their own norms. But they have no wish to lose the things they hold dear: the affection of others in their collective and their social ties. These things are indispensable to them, and at the same time more unpredictable and less guaranteed than they once were. It is crucial for them to hold on to these ties, to take care of them and to further deepen them. To do so, they need to discipline themselves. And so we see enormous numbers of intraceptive and socially capable individuals who, to a certain extent, adapt their behaviour so as to increase the depth and the harmony of their micro-ties of family and friendship.

And yet, these people still want to feel they have freedom of movement and to be able to stand back from collectives when they become too restrictive. These collectives also know that they must remain tolerant if they are to keep hold of their members.

Relationships between (as well as within) collectives work in similar ways. Up to a certain point, they tolerate difference so as to maintain the synergies and alliances that matter to them. They communicate amongst themselves and they influence one another. Each element can influence the system and can be influenced by the system in turn. Together, they drive society and cooperate in the self-organisation of wider and wider systems.

People's eye for the future helps strengthen these regulatory processes. If these modern and grounded individuals have desires and ambitions that they hope, one day, to achieve, then they do what they must to avoid behaving in socially unacceptable ways and thereby spoiling their chances. It is this that gives rise to the strikingly mature realism and pragmatism of today's youth, so different from that of the generation of 1968. Harmonious emotional integration into the household and the concentric circles that surround it contributes to wider social order and favours the softer, more informal regulation of the new society that is now emerging.

The magnetic attraction and repulsion, the 'synergies' and 'allergies' and self-regulation that characterise these sociosystems are facilitated by advances in communication technology and by our greater capacity to communicate effectively, helped by counselling and psychotherapy and by increasing opportunities to meet like-minded people via the Internet. They are further encouraged by the accumulation of awareness that enhances people's social and interpersonal radar and by the culture of authenticity that they have developed. They have learnt to relate intuitively to others and to reveal enough of themselves, their real selves, to allow others to relate intuitively to them. Thanks to these skills, we become better and better at adapting ourselves to others. These are human adaptations that work like reflexes and without our necessarily being conscious of them. So, in the course of the 1990s and in the most modern parts of the world, a threshold was crossed. Thereafter, sociosystems took on a predominant role. Society became much more profoundly self-regulating.

Recent developments in work and consumer patterns contribute to these self-regulatory processes. Consumption used to be, above all, about one person or household and how he, she or it could be influenced by mass media, mass distribution and by the pyramidical structure of fashion, modernity and conspicuous consumption that advertisers had learnt to exploit. Now it is integrated into complex and influential networks of rumour and word of mouth and for the exchange of advice, products and services between people.

The same phenomenon can be observed in our working lives when they take on more modern contours. Though less bureaucratic, less rigid and less hierarchical, work still helps to maintain social cohesion and harmony. It makes more and more use of people's initiative, flexibility and independence. When one observes ordinary people whose working lives have already taken on such contours, it is obvious that work reinforces their ability to be attentive to others, to adapt to them and to come up with practical solutions. These new ways of working encourage them to become positive, albeit extremely individual, contributors to harmonious and innovative interpersonal dynamics.

Improvements in the way we manage deviance. In modern societies, it has not only become hard to define what constitutes deviant or abnormal behaviour, but the reality of social deviance is changing and evolving. It is hard to define because what is deviant for one person is entirely acceptable to another. And it is evolving because behaviour that might ten years ago have been thought deviant, is now acceptable, and vice-versa.

Activities which are both illegal and condemned by many are nonetheless tolerated by significant sections of the population. For example: the possession and use of soft drugs, the practice of assisted suicide or euthanasia, using public transport without paying, shoplifting, working in the black market economy and tax-evasion. And in most cases, people who engage in such activities feel no guilt or remorse. Their actions in no way go against their personal moral code and often seem acceptable not only to their friends and family, but also to a more or less significant proportion of the population.

Over the last twenty or so years, Western society has witnessed considerable changes in what is considered acceptable or unacceptable. These changes are driven by clear modernising processes, such as the increased respect for freedom and personal integrity. Violence directed against people by other individuals, and even more so by the authorities, is increasingly considered unacceptable: paedophilia, rape, assault, disturbing people's peaceful lives or their small pleasure, human rights abuses, etc. At the same time, there is a growing tolerance of deviations from the norm, so long as these do not impinge upon others. For instance, most sexual practices that were once frowned upon are now acceptable in the eyes of the law and of public opinion. Homosexual communities have formed pressure groups, held demonstrations, fought for recognition and forced changes in the law.

This type of change illustrates the workings of informal grass-roots regulation, inspired by ordinary people. Today's conformity comes from mutual interaction and self-control rather than from norms imposed from on high. In the same vein, some forms of autonomy, which might in a particular time and place be considered intolerably deviant, feed into social change and its shaping trends.

It is clear that people, civil society, schools, the media and the public authorities contribute to these changes. It seems as if our societies are trying to build a minimal consensus about those few forms of deviance that will be deemed intolerable. This self-regulation works well, but unevenly. At times it is too liberal and at times lacking in consistency. It allows certain forms of deviancy and violence that are utterly unacceptable to the vast majority of people to flourish. Were these to increase, they might lead to the establishment of multiple counter-cultures in a state of permanent conflict. But at times this self-regulation is also too authoritarian. Thus, vocal minorities and overwhelming majorities try to impose supposedly politically correct rules and practices, which many find stifling. The failure to listen to a particular 'tribe' and to take into account its points of view can drive its members to distraction and eventually to violence.

The intertwining of multiple, non-binding social ties favours looser regulations

Old antagonisms have faded away – those that divided nation-states, geo-political blocs, the Protestant and Catholic churches, colonisers and colonised, communism and capitalism, different social classes, neighbouring villages and feuding families... Instead, recent decades have seen the emergence of intertwined and subtly varying dimensions of difference. These are typical of a form of modernity that focuses on customs, culture and meaning.

The organisational model of this still inchoate society is fairly simple but tends to create complexity. Modern people are attached to their autonomy and so are wary of placing all their eggs in one basket. They try to engage with different networks, groups and social movements. This results in an intertwining of social ties which establishes bridgeheads between different collectives and reduces the risk of rupture and conflict between them.

As each person knits his or her own network of social ties, so complexity increases. In their efforts to network, people follow their own preferences and spur of the moment impulses and they look for exactly shared interests. They feel themselves to be permanently or temporarily connected to, or estranged from, different people and collectives. Analysis of the social and emotional profile of the generation aged between 18 and 30 in the year 2000 shows us young people who live their lives as more or less unique and evolving individuals, each of whom knits his or her own network of collective ties and who prizes the possibility of altering this network as and when they see fit and for reasons both deep and superficial. As events arise and provoke different emotions, so people's connection to different groups strengthens or weakens. One day, it may be a question of how to spend one's free time, the next day, of how to educate one's child and, perhaps the day after, of the future of climate change.

People's emotional affiliation, or their affiliation to a given group or social movement, operates in just the same way as their affiliation to personal networks: the autonomous individual is always central. People choose their collectives carefully and it is these moments of choice that breathe life into them.

The combination of different individual choices and preferences leads both to great diversity and to a constant reshuffling of the social tiles. It allows multiple synergies to emerge, develop and grow in complexity. Out of these synergies and out of the multiplicity of social ties, are born intertwined and entangled groups within groups.

Complexity builds bridges between collectives. The fact that everybody seems to have a foot in several collectives favours the development of an intertwined and imbricated social fabric that militates against long-term splits and divisions between collectives. And so it fosters cooperation and social harmony. Everybody, in their own way, goes about knitting their own network of social ties. They don't meet the same people – or even the same sorts of people – in the different situations and collectives where they socialise. And so they maintain bridges between different movements that might otherwise split apart.

People can express themselves differently in different environments, whilst remaining the same person. They can draw on a wide range of socially acceptable roles and can comfortably move from one to the other. In this way they develop multi-faceted personalities and avoid being poured into a collective mould.

This sociological process that encourages intertwining social ties and informal regulations also reinforces one of modern people's central personality traits – their preference for peace rather than war, their tendency to break off relationships rather than allow conflict to develop. Most of the people we interviewed prefer to deepen their ties with the collectives they like rather than fight against those they find unpleasant. Throughout the 1990s, we explored people's mental maps of the social networks to which they belonged and discovered many more instances of positive relations or a complete lack of relations than of hostile relationships. What is more, when antagonisms do arise, they tend to remain small-scale. They don't consume all of a person's energy. Competition or struggle may result, but this will ideally be non-violent.

Self-control and intertwining ties feed into one another and contribute to social harmony and cohesion. Processes that generate self-control and those that maintain intertwined social relations are mutually reinforcing.

People self-regulate and participate in tolerant collectives and sociosystems. Similarly, collectives and sociosystems self-regulate and participate in wider systems which are also tolerant.

The widespread tendency to privilege the search for synergies and, where allergies are encountered, to prefer rupture to conflict, leads to the construction of wider and wider systems of collectives that successively encompass one another.

So long as tension, unhappiness and obligatory contact between allergic people or collectives remain within reasonable bounds, then these micro-sociosystems tend to find enough points of synergy to maintain positive relations with wider collectives. In turn, these collectives find enough points of synergy to maintain relations with yet wider groups. Ultimately, we could see the emergence of an unstable equilibrium where all the different collectives and groups had enough points of synergy to maintain harmonious relations with the whole of a tolerant society.

A moderate neo-spiritual reawakening

The neo-spiritualist resurgence of the last thirty years brings with it the possibility for new religions to emerge. For the most part, the emotions stirred up by altered states of consciousness are moderated by reflection and the search for harmony and a peaceful standpoint. In the vast majority of cases in Europe, these emotions, once tempered, can be seen to provide people with inner equilibrium and peace of mind. Our societies lean very much towards open and tolerant forms of spirituality. It may be that the search for spirituality will remain a private and personal matter. Or it may be that we shall see the development of a spiritual, philosophical and religious alternative that gels with modern sensibilities and has the power to unite hundreds of millions of people in a nebulous, hedonistic and humanistic consensus. Or it may be that neuroscience, biology and ethology will come up with an explanation of mind and consciousness that is sufficiently new and sufficiently convincing to win most people's support and to temper people's potential missionary or confrontational zeal.

Processes that provoke violence and antagonism

Our societies are concerned with antagonism and violence which they see spreading in their midst like a cancer.

Contemporary society retains certain archaic forms of violence (such as crimes of passion) and, at the same time, has invented a whole range of new ones. Youth crime is particularly striking. From simple insults to extortion, gang-rape and murder, violence is present on the streets, in sports stadiums and in schools. Children and teenagers kill one another. Of course, the extreme violence of a handful of youths makes headlines in the United States, but it is not unknown in Japan and Europe. Hackers spread harmful computer viruses. Since the 1980s, juvenile delinquency has been on the rise everywhere in Europe. Dogs are trained to terrorise and to kill. Rival sports fans attack and kill one another. In Britain and in Northern Europe, hooliganism and urban violence are rife. There are also a few extremely violent sects. These may direct their violence against themselves, as with the Solar Temple in Switzerland, France or Canada, or, like Aum Shinrikyo in Japan, they may attack society. Ecologists and pro-life militants carry out commando missions. Ethnic groups clash with one another. Networks of fundamentalist Islamists terrorise parts of the world, whilst simultaneously delighting other parts who consider themselves victims of oppression. New divisions are emerging, based on people's interpretations of what is right and what is meaningful. Crowds demonstrate against neo-liberal globalisation or the Anglo-American invasion of Iraq.

These phenomena are, however, limited in scope. European and American anti-establishment demonstrators are, for the most part, peaceful and cooperate with the authorities so as to reduce the risk of outbreaks of violence. Terrorist networks and sects that preach radical dissidence only appeal to an extremely small proportion of modern society. And interpersonal violence, shocking as it may be, remains limited. The people who commit truly violent acts probably make up less than 1% of the overall population of the most modern countries. They are more likely to be youths than mature adults, but to take the example of France, they are still only 5% of the most violent age group (13 to 19 year olds). And with age, most of them mellow.

Given all this, can we conclude that it will not be overly difficult to limit and restrict these social pathologies? And can we perhaps look forward to a general evolution towards peace and harmony in modern society, as well as towards greater autonomy and increased opportunities for personal and collective fulfilment? We must, I think, be wary of jumping too hastily to this conclusion. Though antagonism and violence are still limited, they are troubling precisely because they are no accidents of history. Instead, they emerge from the intimate processes of society. They could yet increase and turn people's dreams of social harmony sour.

There are situations where the processes of self-control, social synergy and the peaceful interwining of social ties are pushed aside in favour of aggressive, self-feeding spirals of violence. Initially balanced interactive systems degenerate and this leads to concatenating chains of aggression, social exclusion, antagonism, hatred and violence. People and populations that are strongly attached to peace and harmony find themselves caught up in tension and conflict that they would have preferred to avoid.

Triggers of social schism, deviance and aggression

Ambivalence lies at the very heart of people's existence. The Vitalists who appeared throughout the course of the 1980s and 1990s are not insensible to the lure of violence, even if they prefer peaceful and affectionate relations and relationships. If the situation calls for it, they can be skilful and redoubtable fighters. This is clear from our portrait of the Vitalists in Chapter 4.

There are several factors that may encourage people either temporarily or more permanently to abandon their preference for peace and affection.

Stress. Our interviewees clearly distinguish between positive and negative stress. Negative stress is experienced as physical and psychic pain, bodily or mental strain, and as an anxiety that unsettles digestion, sleep and breathing patterns. This stress disturbs their happiness, destroys their peace of mind and may ruin their health. Stress seems to have become one of the archetypal pathologies of our era. Medical research supports the view that stress, if not properly managed, is far from being a trifling problem. If it persists, such intense stress can be dangerous for the sufferer. It increases susceptibility to depression, inflammatory illnesses and allergic reactions and can weaken the immune system. It may also lead to suicidal or violent behaviour.

By changing their goals or by organising their life in a different way, some people manage to escape stress. Many others are worn down in the struggle. Cofremca's research in France suggests that Vitalists are often the most stressed people in society, or at least the most affected by stress. In interviews with representative samples of the French population about the sorts of ideas they had had in recent weeks, Vitalists were the most likely to mention suicide.

Exclusion. The feeling of being excluded is particularly painful. Some people feel cast aside, unfairly treated, irredeemably poor in a rich society, unhappy in a happy one, or thirsty for freedom and self-realisation in a society that suffocates them. Temporarily or more permanently, they may lose all hope of being part of things. They feel alienated and rejected. They have a deep-seated feeling of injustice, and perhaps of resentment and hatred. They can be tempted to 'take up arms' against society: individual revolt in some cases, collective uprising in others.

Often from underprivileged backgrounds, out of work, with no access to sports facilities, with little or nothing to do, they may live off petty crime and have no more links to wider society than those offered by their television screens or the occasional trip to a stylish neighbourhood. They have no opportunity to build up multiple social ties. Even their mental links to wider groups or society at large are extremely weak. They may turn to crimes like shoplifting (trying to even things up for themselves) or go down the path of antisocial behaviour, vandalism or urban guerrilla tactics (as a way of getting revenge). They band together with others who are more or less like them, either through chance encounters or because they live on the same estate. This gives rise to small groups or networks who may clash with other groups or, alternatively, attack the symbols of wider, dominant society.

Psychological problems. Major psychological traumas are not uncommon. Education; genes; lack of social skills; loss of an important social relationship or link; quasi-autists who haven't yet found the right psychotherapist, neospiritual exercise or antidepressant to help them reintegrate into affectionate social networks – there are many possible reasons for the problem. Individuals whose personality or environment affords them little protection may be incapable of facing up to the complexities, uncertainties and aggression of modern life and can be crippled by stress.

In the United States, cases of unipolar depression (clinical depression) have increased tenfold since the end of the Second World War. Today, 7% of Americans suffer from this problem and many resort to chemical solutions. The same is true of France, whose per capita consumption of tranquillisers, anti-depressants and other neuroleptics is said to be one of the highest in the world. But just what it means to make use of these substances is unclear. It might be a symptom of mental imbalance or a sign of one's striving after peace of mind and taking control of one's own problems.

Educational problems. People's education and upbringing (including their schooling, socialisation and exposure to television and the Internet) can sometimes turn them into predators or unstable individuals – people whom society considers somehow ill. They are a threat to social harmony. A small minority of young people lived through unpleasant and adverse experiences whilst they were growing up in the 1990s. These experiences led them to be dominated by predatory and aggressive emotions and motivations, such as hatred and rage. This sort of upbringing can also produce directionless adults who are poorly equipped to find happiness in a complex and uncertain society. These people lack the smart life-navigation skills common to most of their peers.

They are often young people living in poor neighbourhoods, members of outcast communities whose families (often immigrants) are either absent, or themselves in trouble, or unable to counteract the nefarious influence of gangs of antisocial youths. Not without good reason, these problems are often attributed to poverty, aggressive and violent intra-household relations, ghettoisation, unemployment and immigration, as well as problems with education and broken families.

School drop-outs are commonly from underprivileged backgrounds, often with illiterate and unemployed parents who are incapable of dealing with the situation and have neither the ability, the culture nor the authority that might allow them to help their children and to oversee their behaviour and their school-work. Poor students often have low self-esteem and may suffer from lasting feelings of failure and social exclusion. In such cases, the teacher-student relationship turns into a power struggle. The student learns how to fight, rather than how to communicate and adapt to others. This combative stance then colours all his or her subsequent relations with parents, the police and other authority figures.

This phenomenon is not restricted to the poor and dispossessed, but extends to middle class youth. They may have a degree of financial security, but are incapable of finding any emotional happiness in their immediate social circle. They are often people who failed at school, aren't especially close to their families, who aren't involved in a stable, long-term relationship and have no particular prospects in life. They are drowning in boredom and spilling over with resentment. Aggressive and inclined to drink, they look for fights and sometimes even kill.

We are beginning to understand and take into account the idea that the brain is permanently marked by its life experiences. It tends to re-feel, re-see and re-think things it has previously felt, seen or thought. Physical aggression, sexual abuse or a lack of love can set a child on the wrong track. The mother-child relationship can seriously affect later, adult behaviour. It seems pretty much certain that a lack of emotional dialogue from childhood onwards, and abusive or conflictual families, can mark those children who experience them with a predominant feeling of fear and of having been abandoned, as well as producing in them aggressive, violent and predatory drives. These family experiences prevent the development of an effective interpersonal and social radar and life-navigation system. They are all the more damaging because schools are only rarely able to overcome the sort of educational failure that gives rise to such personalities. If these people increase in number, they will pose a threat to social harmony.

The lack of warm and affectionate social networks. The lonely, who lack emotional support networks or whose homes are in permanent turmoil, have few opportunities to make up for the frustration and stress inflicted upon them by a still unbalanced society. If they reach a certain point of unhappiness, they may just disconnect.

When new networks fail to step quickly and effectively into the breach left by old attachments, solitude looms. It may become one of the plagues of our society. Today, it varies widely from country to country. Drawing on a study by Sociovision, we can make some international comparisons: 10% of Germans, around 20% of Spaniards, French, Italians and Swedes and more than 25% of the English and Americans say that they feel lonely and see very few people. These are disturbing figures. [40]

Households are also struggling. Couples who are sexually or personally incompatible face serious difficulties. People have trouble dealing with infidelity. Conflicts spiral out of control even among couples who would like to stay together. The culture of parents and that of their children's peergroups may be violently at odds. Parents have lost authority and respect in the eyes of their children. Parents despair as they see their children turn out badly. Unwanted pregnancies occur. Households break up in pain and conflict. Children are tortured. In some households, there is constant fighting. But these struggling households are only a tiny minority. Asked in 1995 about the atmosphere in their household, more than 80% of the French described it as warm and less than 2% described it as a scene of permanent conflict. Even if some respondents are making the most of a bad situation, this is still an impressive figure. And France is probably not exceptional in this.

Outrage. For some Vitalists, it is difficult to tolerate the accumulation of frustration and stress, the lack of participation and, above all, the impression that they can't do anything about the meaninglessness they experience. Put in situations where they are not listened to or even heard, where they feel powerless to change things that directly concern them or have to submit to illegitimate and meaningless authority, modern people suffer. They try to make themselves heard. And if they don't manage, they are overwhelmed by outrage. They may become dissident and subversive.

---

40   *GlocalConsult*, 2000.

Revelation. It sometimes happens that emotional people, who are open to occult powers, sensitive to contemporary spiritual messages and whose rational control is limited, undergo a revelation. They are spoken to or touched by some vengeful God or by aliens or by some guru or another. They may wish to save their souls or protect the human race and planet Earth from imminent disaster. They respond to the message they hear even if it isolates them from most of their peers. They draw closer to people like them, there finding a warm refuge and perhaps an aggressive platform from which to attack an evil, godless society. They may join a sect. They may be convinced to take up arms against wider society or against a particular enemy. More numerous in the United States than in Europe, these spiritual warriors have nevertheless remained a relatively rare phenomenon. Contemporary society is, however, pretty much defenceless against this type of attack.

Processes that lead to isolates and antagonism

Isolates. Modern society is a sort of social soup, made up of people, networks, collectives and special-interest groups, all of which are intimately intertwined and interacting. But the soup can grow lumpy and were these lumps to multiply, the nature of our society could fundamentally change.

So long as society remains happy and relaxed and leaves people enough freedom and autonomy, then the system of multiple belonging and multiple identifications described above can prosper. This system guarantees the existence of cross-cutting ties and bridges. It keeps social boundaries vague, informal and, above all, porous. It also helps make people open to others. Sometimes, though, a particular social fracture can overwhelm these bridgeheads and sweep them away. The outcome is isolates: closed communities cut off from the outside: ghettos, gangs, sects, foreign bodies that act like pathogens on organic society. These closed communities, though, are safe havens, harbours in the storm for people in need of support.

Fear and the feeling of rejection cause people to withdraw and shut down and this, in turn, leads others to reject them. People who feel close to one another but rejected by society tend to strengthen their ties with each other and weaken those that link them to other forms of collective. Together they create multidimensional communities that serve as the principal and then the only nodal point for their members. This cohesion reinforces their rejection by society. Finally relations between the soup and the lump become purely defiant and hostile.

Extremely tense situations or the feeling of being rejected, misunderstood or abandoned by society can drive people to seek either shelter or a base for aggression against society, and often both at once. Instead of looking for opportunities for osmosis, resonance, kindred spirits and participation, they shut themselves off, seeking one place of belonging to the exclusion of all others. Gathered together, such people form hermetically sealed units.

We interviewed men and women who had undergone a profound religious experience and had then shut themselves off in a group that shared their views. We met extremist ecologists who had set themselves as a group the onerous task of saving the planet. We saw depressed and directionless individuals who wanted only one thing: to abandon their autonomy and entrust their wellbeing to a sect. Others, especially in sink estates, felt so rejected by wider society that they were prepared to turn against it violently, with whatever allies they could find. The personal trajectory of Khaled Kelkal, a French terrorist shot dead in 1995, is typical of the negative chain reactions that we often came across. As a young man, he had maintained multiple social ties and identifications: he was French, Arab, from the suburbs[41], a Lyonnais, unemployed, a bit of a gangster and generally fairly modern. By the end, he was only a Muslim and at war.

This phenomenon can touch cultural and ethnic groups just as much as it touches sects, gangs or groups of ideological extremists. It generates violence and raises levels of social tension. It undermines society's hedonism. It often introduces an alien sociology that favours brute force, machismo and hierarchical or feudal social relations.

This natural process of mutual exclusion is particularly dangerous when it is articulated around territorial divisions. People who feel shut off from the majority of the population tend to shun wider society. This is how ghettos are formed. Ghettos for the rich and, especially, for the poor. The problem is particularly serious in the United States and in France, where poor minority groups find themselves ethnically or culturally stereotyped, unemployed, on social welfare and rejected. They feel excluded and have ended up living on grim, run-down estates. And so American city-centres and European suburbs have seen the emergence of profoundly alien, aggressive, macho and violent cultures where brute force reigns. It's hard to say whether this situation can be turned around.

Once ghettos have formed, they are hard to penetrate and harder yet to break up. Attempts to do so are often seen as acts of aggression by the authorities and so the vicious circle continues.

---

41   The suburbs in most French cities tend to contain the poorest and most deprived estates and neighbourhoods, while in some other countries these latter will tend to be found in the decaying city centre.

In many Western countries, poorly integrated immigrants are a constant source of low-level dissidence. They are often unemployed and haven't the money to take part in a modern, consumer lifestyle. They have little hope of joining the middle classes, are crammed together in run-down estates and their cultural and religious background is often different from that of local populations. They are often a starting-point for ghetto-formation and constitute a permanent challenge to wider society.

Antagonistic structures. In modern society, some interactions between individuals will always result in divisions. Whenever one has an 'allergic' reaction to someone else, there is a tendency to avoid further contact, which serves to initiate such divisions. This process normally happens easily enough, but some of these divisions can harden and become more entrenched. For example:

Conflicts of interest. A local population can be split over plans to build a tunnel, an incinerator or a factory – which might bring employment and pollution to the area.

Conflicts of identity. Most modern people, collectives and institutions have a number of changing, fluid and merging identities. Sometimes one of these identities can be strongly energised or provoked, leading to a violent reaction which can, in turn, provoke a reflex reaction elsewhere. This can extend even to whole countries. The patriotic/evangelical reaction of the state and of some individual Americans to the attacks of 9/11 provoked a hostile reflex reaction based on identity in the Arab/Muslim world.

Religious conflicts. Conflicts of identity that have a religious dimension are particularly dangerous.

Territorial conflicts. When groups and collectives that are culturally allergic to one another are forced to live in close physical proximity, it can be extremely dangerous. In the 1990s we interviewed a good many unemployed, white French and German citizens who were exasperated at being surrounded by immigrants and who became aggressively nationalistic. In Germany, racist gangs hunted foreigners in the streets and set fire to their homes and meeting places.

Conflicts of meaning. These are not unusual. Hardcore ecologists and people seeking to defend a traditional hunting culture can clash, as can advocates and opponents of censorship on the Internet. But disagreements are not just those between libertarians and conservatives; modern people are often divided amongst themselves over euthanasia, abortion, adoption by same sex couples, genetic engineering, etc. Most of these issues touch on what gives our lives meaning and have enormous emotional significance.

Escalating violence. When tensions mount, we often see an escalation of violence. In the '90s it was not unusual to see violent police intervention provoking retaliation and escalating violence from young people in deprived city areas where the police were often afraid to go.

The shortcomings of this society in transition provoke unrest

While small businesses, large companies, public sector organisations and states have changed over recent decades, they have done so less quickly and less profoundly than have ordinary people. The former have often clung to old structures, stances and practices and the resulting gap is irksome to modern people. In the next three chapters, we will look at the efforts that business and the authorities have made to compensate and catch up.

People respond to these perceived shortcomings in different ways. Many seek to leave the fray and to shape for themselves a life that suits them better. In so doing, their actions lead to a more general change across society. Others join mouvances, networks and other organisations that are trying to change society or develop new forms and practices of citizenship. Yet others (or sometimes these same people driven to act out of exasperation) become openly and sometimes violently subversive. This further increases the levels of tension in society and undermines existing, informal regulatory systems.

The structures of daily life. In most modern countries, the social and even the legal atmosphere is generally becoming more permissive and tolerant. But government remains authoritarian in its approach. In their daily life, people meet bureaucratic constraints and authoritarian rules and regulations at every step. Most states have not yet learnt how to hold a dialogue with their citizens. Politics are still characterised by ideology and a confrontational approach, which alienates the public. They don't feel genuinely represented by their elected officials. Rather they often feel more like objects than real people, with little chance to exercise their initiative or room for manoeuvre left to them. At times, this leads them to take matters into their own hands through protests, demonstrations and robust direct action.

The pressures and constraints on their time, overly busy schedules and the way that their work spills over into their free time, troubles people more and more. These things have eroded the small pleasures of daily life and helped to increase levels of tension and frustration. People feel the need to have more time for themselves and for their families and friends and social networks. The way that society as a whole, public transport and work are organised does not help. In 2000, just over half of the Americans and Germans, and more than three-quarters of the French and Swedes interviewed by Sociovision said they would rather have a job that gave them more free time than a job to which they felt deeply committed.

The constraints of work. Plenty of those who are self-employed or working in small companies or in the voluntary sector feel that their work offers them room for personal growth, the opportunity to exercise their initiative, a sense of meaning and the feeling of being valued as human beings. But in large companies and the civil service, a clear minority of employees feel this way. Here, the majority complain that they feel paralysed by their managers and by the bureaucracies in which they work. They feel they are treated like pawns. They don't complain too loudly because of losing their jobs but many become gradually less involved in their work and explore their creative sides at home, amongst friends and in their cultural, sports and leisure activities.

There are plenty of such people. A 1990 Cofremca survey revealed that Vitalists made up 47% of all employees and that nearly two thirds of this group felt frustrated in their work. After 1990 the situation grew even worse.

The growing use of PCs at work has been one of the great revolutions of the 1980s and '90s. Middle managers and employees believed that they would bring with them greater autonomy and subsequent developments proved them right: for a while they helped to deliver increased flexibility, room for manoeuvre and scope for employees to use their own initiative. They made many companies less monolithic, better at internal communication and generally more attractive places for Vitalists to work. But a number of senior executives and consultants, once they had begun to understand and master the intricacies of the new computer and telecommunications technologies, tried to use them to recentralise, to tighten controls over staff and reduce the scope for employees to exercise individual initiative. This, in turn, has caused renewed problems and stress for the workforce.

At the start of the 21st century, in America as in Europe, many employees and middle managers dream of working for themselves, in a start-up business, for a consultancy or for any business where they might feel more like human beings than hired mercenaries.

Mass consumption doesn't suit Vitalists well. They like highly customised products and services which meet their individual needs very precisely and which don't at any point leave them feeling used or cheated. During the 1990s, Sociovision would repeatedly remind its corporate clients that they must come up with solutions to this demand for customisation and convenience because any shortcomings in this respect could be extremely damaging to them as manufacturers or suppliers.

Computers, whether in the factory or the office, could help in this respect to tailor products and services to meet the individual needs of Vitalist consumers. But commercial pressures mean that many service sector companies, from travel agents to hotels and insurance have actually begun to offer a poorer level of service to customers.

Vitalists flourish where there is interaction and dialogue. New computer and communication technologies make it possible for companies to stay in close and almost constant contact with their customers, identifying and resolving their complaints and trying to ensure their total satisfaction. But many businesses have resisted this opportunity, imbued as they are with outdated mental models of authority and influence rather than dialogue. Their customers often feel that their privacy is being invaded, that they are being talked down to and manipulated. Vitalists, of course, continue to consume, but this experience has put them on their guard and made them distrustful and hostile towards most businesses and the marketplace as a whole.

Dissidence. The gap between modern people and the new values that they are tentatively reaching towards, on the one hand, and the pre-existing values of institutionalised society on the other, is wide and getting wider. The sense of meaninglessness often inspired by shopping, work, politics and government fosters growing levels of resentment towards business, the authorities and 'the system'. People fail to understand why they cannot find the products and services they want; why so much human energy and potential is left to go to waste; why unemployment is so widespread; why schools remain so bureaucratic, so seemingly focussed on the needs of teachers rather than students and so out of touch with young people; why government and business leaders fail to take the environment seriously; why the international community is unable to resolve the geopolitical problems that confront it; why human beings the world over continue to be crushed and wretched and women continue to be oppressed by men.

As a result, for many, the state seems to be little better than a parasite. Conventional society seems to them to be 'bad and ugly' and they seek to distance themselves from the mainstream. Their dissidence takes many forms and, even when it is genuinely subversive, still tends to be peaceful, unless they find themselves provoked into violence. But at the start of the 21st century, their dissidence is manifesting itself in an increasing number of violent and aggressive ways.

The pseudo-moral clothing often assumed by dissidence tends to legitimise actions that are either illegal or held to be immoral. And we have already seen how modern people admit to behaviour like tax evasion, shoplifting and tax avoidance without guilt or remorse.

The climate of dissidence also feeds the development of a 'neo-barbarian' culture, which manifests itself as greedy selfishness, crude hedonism, brutality, the desire to shock and the systematic subversion of what is held to be politically correct. Our observers across Europe and North America have witnessed an increase in all these kinds of anti-social behaviour, which could herald the end of a process of socialisation that encouraged people throughout the 1980s and 1990s to seek harmonious and gentle relations with others.

Disgust and a climate of dissidence fuel large-scale but ephemeral waves of emotion and popular protests. At the death of Princess Diana, enormous crowds demonstrated their modernity in the face of an establishment that seemed unaware of the human dimension to that event. The same thing happened with the 'Marche blanche' in Brussels and the demonstrations against the American war in Iraq. Some of these waves of emotion could bring about permanent rifts that would themselves cause further antagonism.

Humanist groups organise mass demonstrations, which can be violent on the edges, against the economic and financial forces of globalisation or against a company that treats its staff in a way that they see as shameful.

Rage against a society in which one feels an outsider or in which one cannot be heard can lead to violence. It can inspire gangs, hooligans, direct action groups and even terrorist cells. It motivates many computer hackers and those who create and disseminate computer viruses, as well as environmental activists who destroy GM crops. In the USA, a growing number of hate groups (often linked via the Internet) have emerged and united young middle class people, often racists, filled with a nameless spleen and unsure of their own identity. More than 500 white supremacist groups have been counted. Mafias are themselves dissident and marginalised socio-economies, which are spreading well beyond the borders of their country of origin and acquiring alarming power.

Since the closing years of the 20th century, observers across Europe and North America have reported a renewed outburst of dissidence. The response that this has elicited from the authorities and from mainstream society has sometimes been one of compromise and sometimes a combative one. The former has tended to lead to an overall modernising adjustment, while the latter has tended to cause an escalation of aggression.

A system for maintaining and repairing looser regulations

Many of our contemporaries are inspired to act by empathy, a viscerally-felt humanism and the wish to help reduce distress and conflict. They do so on their own, in their daily lives and in the micro-sociosystems in which they are involved. They do so also in collaboration with others, in local networks or as part of vast mouvances or international organisations. For all of them, the intention is clearly therapeutic: they are trying to help individuals or society at large; and they are guided by an intuitive sense of which social processes bring happiness and wellbeing and which don't; which promote peaceful and harmonious relations and which don't. Taken in the round, these individual and collective actions encourage the self-organisation of a **powerful immune and repair system** that treats suffering and seeks to prevent or counteract damaging, self-perpetuating social processes.

Cultivating happiness, preventing distress

As early as the 1930s, people were beginning to insist on the practice of marrying for love, which substituted personal choice for social propriety and increased the likelihood of a couple achieving a satisfactory, erotico-affective partnership. Later, they imposed the notion of the biodegradable couple and the practice of contraception on society and the legal system. In the course of a few decades, these new practices have helped people to lead happier lives and increased the numbers of children who are both wanted and brought up in a warm, loving environment. In several countries, like France and Sweden, women have managed to get creche systems and employment legislation in place to allow young mothers to choose a balance between motherhood and work that suits them personally and helps maintain a positive emotional climate.

Society as a whole has encouraged warm and affectionate mothering. Health professionals, government and public agencies and, above all, the media offer advice and information to help mothers and, increasingly, fathers to build close, loving and emotionally communicative relationships with their children.

When relationships get into difficulty, all is not lost and friends, family and professional advisers increasingly offer their expertise to help these couples resolve their problems. There are more and more Internet dating sites and ways of meeting people. These help people to find partners and to build networks of friends.

Newly established support networks exist to help people overcome addictions, to help the victims of domestic violence and childhood abuse, the underprivileged and other victims of all sorts around the world. Social and economic innovators are setting up agencies to help get unemployed and disabled people back into work. Biodegradable organisations are emerging to challenge redundancies and lay-offs that throw families on hard times. NGOs are organising the struggle against abuses perpetrated by authoritarian governments or against companies that mistreat their staff or put at risk the environment that we will bequeath to our children.

Counteracting problems with education and upbringing

Problems with the education and upbringing of children and adolescents are widely held to be one of the biggest challenges facing us today. In North America and Europe the vast majority of young parents pay enormous attention to bringing up their children well. But society is getting involved at a wider level. Here and there, social entrepreneurs are launching new initiatives: they are trying to identify these problems early, to put them right or to undo the damage that they cause. In both continents, local authorities are also taking steps to help. Associations and networks are appearing that are designed, for example, to help children who are struggling at school, to teach reading skills, to treat emotional problems, to deal with drug addiction, to provide leisure facilities for young people with nothing to do, to organise sports activities and competitions, to provide holidays for disadvantaged children and to rehabilitate young offenders. We have seen mothers living in deprived areas undertaking initiatives to set up a dialogue with local schools, the police and the local authorities to help protect their children from the destructive spiral of neighbourhood violence.

Other associations are trying to improve sex education in the home, at school, in the media and elsewhere, so that children will be better prepared to enter into happy relationships and a rewarding family life. Their aims include reducing the number of unwanted pregnancies, helping young people to learn about the emotional, erotic and technical aspects of love-making and relationships and helping them to understand the different expectations of men and women.

Public opinion in all Western countries has only fairly recently understood how destructive sexual abuse in the family and in school can be and our societies are now hunting down paedophiles.

Reducing violence and anti-social behaviour

It is only since the 1990s that individual citizens in any significant number have become involved in trying to reduce levels of violence and anti-social behaviour. Before then, it was seen to be the exclusive job of the authorities: maintaining law and order in the eyes of the right and a more forgiving social policy for those on the left. Today, more and more people see the struggle to reduce violence and disorder as one that involves society as a whole, calls for a careful and sophisticated response and requires the involvement of individuals. Vitalists, whilst remaining humanist and tolerant, are also keen to see the sociosystems in which they are involved – including society worldwide – working harmoniously and helping them to achieve their potential. This desire grew in importance during the 1990s as violence and anti-social behaviour became more common and more troublesome. In order to 're-civilise' society, they called for harsher penalties from the courts and the establishment of law and order, without abandoning their constant search for greater autonomy and respect for individuals. A good number of them got personally involved in trying to make this happen. In run-down neighbourhoods, residents overcame their tendency not to get involved and began to work with young people to discourage their violent and anti-social behaviour or to stop drug dealing. Others decided to intervene when faced with violent incidents on public transport. Some shopping centres recruited young security staff from among the local population so they could talk easily to their peers. These men and women would rather engage in dialogue than resort to violence and often worked closely with the local police.

Young delinquents toy with the prospect of reintegration

Interventions of this sort often meet with a better response than one might have expected from the young city gangs at whom they are aimed. Both sides can, in this way, begin to sketch out a process for controlling violence. Our research in numerous city neighbourhoods has shown that many of these delinquent and violent young people don't feel entirely out of sync with the rest of modern society and don't want to be thought of in that way. In some ways, they are still very much part of it and we need to build on this sense of belonging. If we can, then it will offer a way for these young people to be reintegrated. For example, in France we have seen what are normally very aggressive gangs volunteering to help clean oil-polluted beaches.

* * *

Finding a way to retain looser regulations is one of the biggest challenges of our times. Our studies suggest that a virtuous circle is currently self-organising: one that emanates from the initiatives and cooperative efforts of ordinary people and that tends to encourage calm and integration. Society, as it becomes more alive, produces its own cures for its own ailments. A kind of immune system seeks to counteract the unhappiness, loss of vitality and meaningfulness and the causes of violence and hostility in society. This immune system has, no doubt, already had a significant influence in terms of calming things down and keeping violence at a tolerably low level. But it cannot, on its own, ensure peace and cohesion in the society that is presently emerging. For that to happen, the powers-that-be, governments and big business, instead of rubbing salt in society's wounds, will need to play their full part in establishing new forms of wiser and pacific governance.

Chapter 8
Business faces up to mutations in society

From the early 1970s onwards, those large companies that had strengthened their position by co-opting the trends and developments of the First Modernity were wrong-footed by the Second Modernity and especially by the re-emergence of self-organisation. Qualities that had once been their strengths became handicaps: hierarchy, top-down command structures, repetition, standardisation, bureaucracy, Taylorism, mass-marketing, imperialist, mechanistic and predatory approaches, and so on. Often without fully realising it, they were faced with the challenges of adapting to people and to a social fabric that had been transformed by the Second Modernity, and of reinventing capitalism. These were also major challenges for society at large.

Large, bureaucratic companies and civil society grow apart

The 1970s and 1980s: companies try to adapt, but not hard enough

In the 1970s and throughout the 1980s, many companies looked for ways to align themselves with the changes brought on by modernity, but they did so in piecemeal fashion and in the face of considerable internal resistance. By the 1990s, they still did not know how to make the most of the opportunities on offer in the Second Modernity.

I shared the enthusiasm of a few innovative MDs who had intuitively understood that they were helping to contribute to a more prosperous world and one which gave people more possibilities for personal development and fulfillment. Some of them struck gold and others copied them.

Volvo had a visionary CEO in the person of Per Gyllenhammer and, in 1974, the company foresaw the possibility of replacing production lines with autonomous, self-directed teams. Soon after, many companies began to speak of *human resources* instead of personnel. They recognised that people were in fact resources, which were often underused and which could be mobilised.

This led to an expansion of goal-oriented management and quality circles, along with efforts to reduce the lead weight of hierarchies and to increase the scope for autonomy and initiative.

Chief Executives like François Dalle at L'Oréal realised that companies were living organisms and that management needed to make use of informal networks. They encouraged such networks and the emergence of natural leaders. With the introduction of micro-communication systems, the internal communication pyramid of some companies began to turn into a conversation.

But it was evident that, in the late 1980s, companies were still not making use of their employees' full potential. In 1975, many people still dreamed of finding fulfilment in their work. By 1985, they wanted a job that gave them time to look for fulfilment elsewhere.

Marketing techniques were modernised, but were not radically transformed. In the 1970s and 1980s, quite a few managers and marketing teams dreamed of shaping their businesses so that they were completely in touch with consumer diversity and people's changing tastes and sensibilities. Some companies distanced themselves from abstract categories like 'our market', 'the consumer' or 'housewives under 50' and tried instead to get a grasp of real people in all their complexity. Some of them threw out the old techniques of influencing and manipulating people and instead tried to establish reciprocal dialogues. We witnessed growing interest in marketing tools that were both quantitative and sociologically and psychologically intelligent. Companies managed to identify groups of potential kindred spirits that might be open to their products. Others managed to integrate some of the paradoxes of modernity. Benetton, for example, showed themselves to be capable of extreme versatility whilst maintaining a clear, long-term identity. Nokia managed to be both high-tech and high-touch[42]. Some companies learned to release their products to coincide with shifts or U-turns in consumer sensibilities (for example, the move away from conspicuous consumption discussed in Chapter 3).

That said, by the late 1980s, dialogue based micro-marketing had still not been invented and few companies had managed to develop a real symbiosis with their consumers. Market analysts noticed that consumers were losing interest, and companies reacted with more advertising or price-wars. In the most modern countries, advertising companies had run out of ideas, and

---

42   Dealing with a human being (the personal touch) rather than with a computer screen or voice response system. The term was coined by John Naisbitt in his book *Megatrends*.

so they turned to emerging markets where capitalist competition was still relatively new or where mass-marketing techniques could still win over huge numbers of consumers.

In the wake of the oil crisis, many people realised that they had entered an era of uncertainty when it was no longer possible to make long-term projections and predictions. Management teams had to learn how to navigate in the fog. Royal Dutch Shell was a pioneer in this respect. In the early 1970s, inspired by André Bénard and Pierre Wack, the Anglo-Dutch oil giant developed a system of strategic scenario planning. Pierre Wack's innovative approach gradually won over the wider business community. In parallel, during the 1980s, many Western businesses made use of analyses of major socio-cultural trends to predict the threats and opportunities that lay in store for them.

Across the Western world, most management teams realised that people expected new things of companies. Before, they had only been interested in the economic and transactional aspects of business; now, they also had relational, societal, moral and ecological expectations. But most enterprises made few real changes and relied mainly on well-timed statements and declarations.

The 1990s: faced with short-term competition, companies tighten up

The spectacular success of Japanese companies in the 1970s had thrown down the gauntlet to their American and European counterparts and forced them to act. The competition from Japan had been seen as a long-term and potentially fatal threat to Western business. Japanese industry was turning out innovative and reliable cars, motorbikes and electronic equipment at apparently unbeatable prices. In the 1980s, Jacques Calvet, the boss of Peugeot-Citroën, saw no way to keep up with them and predicted that without tariff barriers the French car industry would vanish.

Further down the line, in the 1980s and 1990s, rapid globalisation and the spread of communications technology increased competition even more. This time, it was not just the Japanese. The competition came from all sides and something had to be done. This globalisation of competition was intensely demanding. At the same time, it was a blessing for more dynamic businesses. They were no longer so dependent on nation-states, whose sovereignty was limited to a particular territory. It gave them more bargaining power in their dealings with trades unions and provided them with an immigrant workforce that was happy to take on the jobs that resident nationals no longer wanted. These companies found a plentiful supply of cheap labour and docile new consumers in developing countries.

Medium- and long-term strategic planning was having trouble coming to terms with the new situation of uncertainty, and companies focused on short-term profitability. The combination of a few key aspects of the prevailing economic and financial climate helped to push companies down this path.

- American business models, which had traditionally tended to privilege short-term profitability, were widely admired in Europe. They had developed extremely precise and apparently reliable short-term accounting systems, which gave permission for some European companies to follow suit.

- Trade liberalisation made financial markets more mobile and increased their global reach.

- People wanted to make the most of unprecedented stock market performance and many bought stocks and shares for the first time.

- During the 1990s, the stock-market performance of traditional companies, unlike start-ups, was directly dependent on their short-term profits, or on analysts' predictions of them. At the same time, their ability to finance projects came to depend on their stock-market performance.

- Anglo-Saxon pension funds trying to optimise returns on their investment portfolios began to acquire considerable weight in the capital markets and on the boards of both American and European companies.

- American consultants flooded Europe. Many of them could only justify their extremely high fees by showing that their advice generated short-term profits that far outweighed the costs.

The combination of these phenomena increased the say of shareholders and reduced that of managers. Many shareholders were more interested in short-term stock-market performance than in companies' long-term viability. A slightly distorted form of capitalism emerged, which forced many companies to compete to optimise shareholder value. These companies were judged (and judged themselves) on their quarterly or even daily stock-market positions, which were themselves affected by their short-term profit announcements.

Under intense pressure and not yet having developed the sort of expertise that would have allowed them to benefit from the hidden potential of these modern employees and consumers, many companies chased after productivity gains and short-term profitability. They relied on mechanical and rational improvements in organisation or strategic planning, even if this damaged their working environment and their adaptation to their socio-economic ecosystem.

They designed better organisational systems and made use of new technologies (which often constrained personal freedom) to demand productivity gains from their employees. These rationalisations and harsher management techniques often overlooked the human element of business and increased stress. They could achieve the same productivity levels with a smaller workforce and so downsized massively. Living companies were ripped apart, stripped of their assets and put back together with complete disregard for the different work cultures of these hybrid entities. Huge companies were created, but they had no socio-human substrate. This process ignored history, the accumulation of knowledge and collective intelligence.

Nevertheless, these efforts paid off: the profits of listed companies quadrupled between 1982 and 2000. But there were also unwanted side effects. Competition over shareholder value shut many companies off from wider social, human and sometimes even economic reality. This prioritisation of short-term success went in the opposite direction to other, contemporary modernising processes, which stressed fulfillment, long-term vitality, the protection of the environment and a meaningful life.

People and big business grow apart

This separation had serious consequences. Companies became estranged from their workforces. As big business became seen as more and more morally reprehensible, so people began to challenge or reject it. These companies lost their capacity to navigate wisely and, in some cases, their very survival was threatened.

By the end of the 1990s, we and our fellow socio-cultural observers across the modern world noticed an increase in work-related stress and frustrations, often linked to the management practices of large companies and the public sector. More and more people felt unreasonably constrained and that their work was meaningless. They also began to behave in ways that were potentially harmful for business. They banded together to look out for one another and to work as little as possible, and resisted any attempts by management to change the way things worked. Alongside this, we witnessed a brain drain (of both young and established employees) away from big business and the public sector, and people dreamed of early retirement and 'finding themselves a more interesting job'.

A growing majority of employees thought that their best interests conflicted with those of their employer. This feeling spread to middle managers and even senior management. A dangerous gulf was beginning to emerge between shareholders and boards of directors, on the one hand, and the living company, on the other. This gap was reflected in opinion polls.

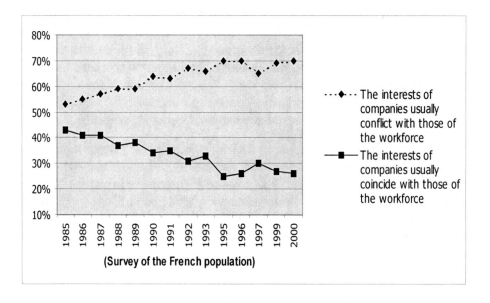

(Survey of the French population)

© copyright Sociovision

While public perception of big business worsened, people remained positive about smaller companies. This moral condemnation was evident in all of the most modern countries, but was particularly pronounced in the United States and least damning in Germany. In all Western countries, more than half, and sometimes even three-quarters, of people thought that big business did not serve the public interest.

Public opinion clearly understood the rupture between big business and its workforce. In France, for example, from 1985 on, the proportion of those who thought that the interests of business were usually at odds with those of the workforce grew each year.

People objected to many things. Most thought it was meaningless for companies to devote themselves to the pursuit of profit and ignore social harmony and employees' quality of life. Big business was accused of exploiting child labour in developing countries, carrying out animal-testing, polluting, firing people despite accumulating profits, neglecting the communities that surrounded them, lacking respect for their customers, and reducing the quality of the service they offered. Companies' efforts to convince employees and consumers that they had strong moral values were often dismissed as mere marketing ploys. Surveys showed that some of these campaigns did more harm than good to the companies concerned. The prevailing climate of mistrust was worsened by the growing number of corruption scandals involving big business and politicians.

It was often young people who challenged these companies. They knew how to tug at people's emotions and set waves of popular discontent in motion. A few charismatic leaders emerged. Their consummate skill in using the media and micro-communication tools made them all the more redoubtable enemies, especially as they rode a wave of public support for the underdog, for localised, not widespread, action and for social, not financial, concerns.

In this tense climate, social crises broke out. Ordinary people rose up against individual companies or business in general. Even if they were often orchestrated by NGOs or by improvised collectives riding public opinion, these were above all grassroots movements. They could be very localised or operate worldwide.

One of the most powerful companies on the planet, Royal Dutch Shell, had to bow down before a (misinformed) Greenpeace initiative and agree not to sink a disused oilrig in the open sea. Companies like Nike, Body Shop, Coca Cola, McDonald's and Danone, which were in some ways very modern, were faced with boycotts. Workers who had been fired engaged in acts that came close to terrorism. In Seattle, Gothenburg and Genoa, huge crowds demonstrated against globalisation and free trade. There were outbreaks of violence. They probably managed to make people think twice about these issues and undermine the apparent consensus. They forced the WTO to take things slowly and perhaps to change direction. And growing numbers of people, especially among the young, thought that our economic system would have to reinvent itself.

For some traditional companies, this became a question of survival. Cut off from a changing population and an ever more complex social fabric, these companies failed to come up with an adequate managerial response to the situation. They wore themselves out trying make rusty hierarchies function and trying to exercise authority over people who wanted self-determination. They were (and are) losing consumers at a time when it was (and is) ever more expensive to win over new ones.

Brilliant companies have made serious strategic errors. Apparently impregnable brands have suddenly collapsed. Emerging markets expand, companies rush in, there is cut-throat competition and then suddenly they contract. Traditional companies, long admired and held up as moral standard-bearers, are plunged into crisis and their reputations tarnished. Business leaders who were placed on pedestals are knocked off them in the space of a few weeks.

These often dramatic events have played a part in regulating socio-economic change. They have made many business leaders and establishment figures step back and take a look at their practices. They have encouraged companies to try to make the most of their ecological context and human resources. They may have paved the way for better relations between large, traditional companies and modern society.

If business leaders and establishment figures from the worlds of economics and finance ignore these problems and challenges, and if they fail to come up with appropriate responses to them, then they could get worse and the gulf between business and some ordinary people could widen. Stress and discontent could run riot. If big business neglects the human element, then the new socio-economy (built on informality and individual initiative) will develop in ways that undermine it: ever more serious internal conflicts and social crises will chip away at its foundations. This sort of conflict could go on for decades.

It is worth taking a look at history. In the 19th century, business practices led to the emergence of a revolutionary proletariat which was at the core of a philosophy that virulently opposed market models, fostered the development of radical trades unions and violent strikes, and in some countries even culminated in a centralised, economic counter-model and the dictatorship of the proletariat. It took trades unionism, Fordism and the triumph of consumer culture to reintegrate the proletariat into wider society. It is not impossible that this story might repeat itself in different ways.

A new socio-economy struggles to find its place

New economic and social agents have emerged. They are quite different from the companies, associations, political parties and trades unions that had been set up in the late 19th and early 20th centuries. They have woven new relationships between themselves and between themselves and their environment, sketching out a new socio-economy that we need to take a closer look at, because little by little it may change our world. For the moment, though, it is struggling to find its place in a transitional society that does not always welcome it with open arms.

Outside the old economic order, work is being done, activities organised and formal or informal associations and companies are being created. Regulation takes place outside official market structures. People's lives go in new directions. Volunteers devote themselves to civic and charitable work. Ideas that hit the spot can make people millionaires almost overnight. Young entrepreneurs emigrate and grow rich elsewhere. The brightest students from the most prestigious business schools shun old-style macro-companies. No one is sure how long certain forms of copyright will last. Cash-in-hand work and the informal economy have boomed in an unprecedented way. All European and North American countries have, to a greater or lesser extent, been affected by this explosion of life: a new economy is struggling to emerge.

This new economy began to appear in the 1980s and 1990s, carving out a place for itself among the structures, rules and constraints of the old economy and the Welfare State and taking advantage of their weaknesses. It has created jobs for large numbers of people, be they employees, consultants, temporary workers, volunteers or the self-employed. This new economy is everywhere but certain sectors have been particularly affected: health, education, leisure, culture, communication, spirituality, consultancy, environmental protection, commerce, new technologies, social-action networks and charities, etc. Most of these new organisations remain small and fragile and their influence has only been felt because they are part of a wider system. A few others, like Microsoft, Nokia, Greenpeace and Médecins sans Frontières, quickly acquired real power.

This is more a socio-economy than an economy

There are companies, associations, types of freelance employment, networks and types of organisation for which we still have no terminology. Ambiguity is everywhere. The new socio-economy takes on a multiplicity of shapes that

Chapter 8

challenge classical divisions. Many new businesses are clearly capitalist and some of them have done very well for themselves on Wall Street or on the main European stock exchanges. But others, whilst being no less market-oriented, seem to be looking outside conventional capitalist structures for their inspiration. This is true of most major consultancy groups. Yet others are less concerned with profit. Many of these are freelance groups, often in liberal professions, often more or less micro-enterprises, but also involved in the informal economy. Many are private traders who are inventing new forms of business in small boutiques, public spaces or on the Internet.

What we used to call the charitable or voluntary sector has still not entirely reinvented itself, but is larger and more dynamic than ever.[43] It is centred around meaningfulness and creates a space for learning, involvement and exchange, with opportunities for physical, mental, artistic or spiritual development, opportunities to be in a group and to learn from one another. Be they clearly defined formal organisations or ephemeral groups, all these entities depend on their members' motivation, time, energy, creativity and money. If they become big enough, then the language of bureaucracy calls them NGOs. Some (like Amnesty International or Christian Science) are powerful enough to stand up to and influence both big business and the state. They may have significant financial resources, but their ability to mobilise volunteers and enthuse their members redoubles their impact. A sort of market in volunteers, gifts and personal involvement is emerging.

Virtual organisations emerge when different types of businesses, associations, and individuals enter into relationships that give rise to larger entities, but ones which have no legal existence. These new socio-economic agents are also sociosystems. They often struggle to find their place in a society whose legal forms have still not adapted to their existence. They can remain informal so long as this informality is draped in some sort of formal cloth that makes them acceptable. There are also clearly illegal agents involved in the new socio-economy: people doing undeclared work, drug networks and various mafia-like groups. And interactive systems are springing up that work like markets, but which eschew money and avoid state regulation. Some examples are information-sharing networks, LETS (Local Exchange Trading Systems) and online file-sharing sites like Napster.

This new economy is then not so much an economy as a socio-economy. The boundaries between society and the economy have been broken down, and

43   See Sue R. *La Richesse des Hommes: Vers l'Economie Quaternaire*, Paris: Odile Jacob, 1997.

this socio-economy seems to produce as much meaning as money and as much human energy as matter. If we speak of added value, then we should also speak of added meaning and of added energy.

This socio-economy has probably ushered in a new era. Economic historians distinguish between different stages of economic development. Wealth creation initially depends on the primary sector (agriculture and mining) and this employs most of the population. Later, the secondary sector (industry) and the tertiary sector (services) generate wealth and employment. Now, in the late 20th and early 21st century we are witnessing the emergence of a quaternary sector, which also revolves around services, but different ones. It is more than likely that, just as before, this transformation will affect the economy as a whole. History shows that, until now, the emergence of a new sector has always encouraged existing sectors to change. Agriculture, for instance, was mechanised and industrialised. Now it is being integrated into the information revolution and is increasingly affected by biotechnology. Industry has been affected by services, information technology and by knowledge management.

The new socio-economy is still at an embryonic stage of development and its structures are still unclear. However, some of its dominant traits allow us to speculate about these structures.

Shedding light on the sociology of this new socio-economy

In October 1999, GBN[44] organised a conference in New York that allowed members of our network and participating business leaders to get a better idea of the extraordinary vitality of this new socio-economy. Fifty or so start-up companies had been selected: Internet businesses, civic organisations, communications technology consultants, commercial spaces, health spas, community media groups, continuous education institutions, etc. We had the opportunity to analyse them and talk to their founders and leaders. I personally analysed ten of them and compared my observations with those of my colleagues. Later, I measured these against the results of a French survey carried out a year later by Sociovision.[45] This survey looked at innovators who were leaders of, or participants in, a team that was guiding a new

---

44   Global Business Network, a Californian organisation dedicated to future planning and scenario building, which heads a worldwide network of perceptive observers.

45   *Les entreprenautes. Nouvelle économie, nouvelle société.* Paris: Sociovision Cofremca, 2001.

company or organisation. Sociovision called them *entreprenautes*, because they were both entrepreneurial and comfortable with the Internet. A few common characteristics emerged.

Entreprenautes from both France and New York embodied in their business activities the kinds of mentality and desire that Sociovision had seen taking shape amongst young people in the 1990s. In Germany, France, Italy and Great Britain, young people had often expressed a desire to do their own thing, to create a job that they enjoyed, to escape the constraints of the public sector and big business, to explore new areas, and to live meaningful lives. With the development of the new economy, we finally felt that yesterday's mutants had managed to carve out a space for themselves in society and to establish themselves or to change the way that business was conducted.

The new companies and organisations we looked at had all been born out of a vision. These projects were always built on a complex plan or conception that brought together multiple elements in a meaningful whole. There was an idea of a particular product, solution or service that seemed meaningful for the people who launched, produced and distributed it. This motivated them. But these ideas were also meaningful for potential customers who, in certain situations, felt drawn to them. They involved numerous different types of existing or potential knowledge and skills, which had to be combined in order for the product or solution to come into being and find its ecosystem. Innovative organisations discovered or borrowed these types of knowledge, often from the field of cutting-edge technology, and then combined them. Through a process of trial and error, they then developed the skills needed to commercialise them.

People involved in these new adventures were mainly motivated by pleasure, personal development and the search for meaning. Despite what many people thought, they were not primarily in it for the money. This is obvious for non-commercial *entreprenautes*, but it is almost as true for those involved in market-oriented start-ups. For them, money was no longer as symbolically charged as it had previously been. They neither rejected nor idolised it.

Members of these teams threw themselves into their work and did not count the hours spent. But they were not workaholics. Both they and management shared the belief that everybody has the right to a good life and that there has to be a balance between work and private life. At times, they dedicated themselves entirely to work and at others, when it did not matter so much, they eased off.

These businesses and organisations were living, responsive organisms. Their leaders realised this and chalked much of their success up to:

- flexibility, improvisation, informality, adaptability, etc. Where traditional managers would have seen chaos, they saw not only effectiveness, but also fun.

- the importance accorded to each member's individual personality. Most of these *entreprenautes* thought it was more effective to build on individuals' personalities and abilities than to try to shape them.

- treating each separate case on its own merits. They were less attentive to groups as a whole than to each of the people and entities they comprised. They looked for specific and sometimes innovative adaptations rather than for repetition.

- the way they dealt with mistakes. Everybody was constantly learning and the company was too. In this new socio-economy, short-term failure was not a problem. Making mistakes was par for the course – people learned from it.

- the decisive importance of relationship. When choosing where to locate the business or organisation, which R&D avenues to pursue, and who and how to employ, they focused on the decision's impact on relationship networks.

These organisations were largely non-hierarchical and non-bureaucratic. The layout and atmosphere of the offices we saw in New York gave no sign of hierarchy or conventional order. Managers were leaders or facilitators whose enthusiasm and direction were transmitted to the rest of the group. These qualities were appreciated across the board. People aimed for informality and a relaxed approach in their behaviour, their clothing and their offices. This was more about responding to events, improvising and inventing than organising and planning.

These budding companies and organisations did not talk down to their clients or their audience. They tried to develop dialogue and conversation. They did not see themselves as being at war or in conflict with others. They felt as if they were part of a partnership network, shifting their alliances according to the needs of the situation. They were open to the outside, where they established relations that pursued complementarity and synergy. This way of working often created complex webs and clusters of relationships: cells combining to create organs that can, in turn, form organisms. Unlike its predecessors, this new socio-economy was less based on zero-sum games (with winners and losers) than on positive-sum games (where there can be many winners).

IT networks allowed for new types of relationships between members, customers and partners, where everybody could interact with everybody else. Each individual's wishes and desires could be directly transmitted to the production or distribution company. This radically changed consumption, distribution and marketing and information campaigns. Where use was made of the Internet, these interactions and mutual adjustments could be multiplied almost indefinitely and for very little money. Our interviewees claimed that these new tools allowed for informal development and freed them from geographic constraints. Without them, they would have been unable to self-organise, develop and slot into their ecosystems, which were often planet-wide, even if the companies themselves were small. Without them, they would also have been unable to connect rapidly and to mobilise people, knowledge and skills when they needed to.

Most of the new companies and not-for-profit organisations we analysed in New York, or encountered in Europe or California, subtly combined self-organisation and self-regulation with smart and inspirational leadership. Although actively sought after, self-organisation and self-regulation were nonetheless carefully managed: sometimes welcomed with open arms and in other cases confined to particular areas of the business. The leadership had a strategic vision and a sensitive and highly reactive strategic and management approach. The people who drove these organisations were gradually learning how to make smart interventions. They developed a set of self-organisational skills and knowledge that formed the basis of a modern way of going about business. In the Second Modernity, this sort of organisation and management promotes and encourages vitality.

Vitality also came from the surrounding environment. The more start-ups there were, the more new ones were begun. The new socio-economy naturally created pockets, or perhaps nodules or clusters, of fertility based on geography or business sector.

Resistance to the new socio-economy

In most Western countries, the legal, economic, financial, social and fiscal apparatus did not make life easy for these new socio-economic entities. New companies and innovators struggled to find their place in a social world whose laws and regulations had been designed for a different age. The Internet was not yet free, reliable or fast enough. Many projects were either stalled or aborted because legal structures and the habits and values of investors and backers, conservative trades unionism and state bureaucracy stifled or hampered them. Across the Western world, the new socio-economy was struggling to get established.

Nor was it yet clear how to finance the sort of social projects that would sit well with the Second Modernity. Civil society and charitable organisations had great difficulty finding sources of finance, especially in countries like France where the public sector had traditionally been suspicious of them. The contradiction between the new socio-economy and the bureaucratic Welfare State that had emerged in the mid-20th century was central to this.

In the 1990s, the stock market's irrational exuberance pushed the share price of many start-ups through the roof, regardless of their actual profitability. Accordingly, many new companies were poorly managed and went to the wall when the markets got cold feet and abandoned them.

Despite these difficulties, the perspective is not bleak. New networks and non-commercial organisations are still emerging and flourishing and they now seem to have a better relationship with the state. And many of the start-ups that survived the collapse of the stock market bubble have made a new start.

Towards the living company in a living environment

The ideal for large companies would be to find a way of fully incorporating the ethos of modernity, whilst still competing well in the short term with business rivals. This would be a way of ensuring their future vitality.

If enough companies followed this path and were successful, then others would follow suit. In a few decades, the entire socio-economic system might change. The institutions that oversee and regulate companies and capitalism would then adjust to the new situation. Each new company that adapted would benefit and, at the same time, would contribute to the sustainable and harmonious development of the whole.

We are not yet there, but some things do seem to be moving in this direction. And, in any case, I believe in methodological optimism because it increases our chances of avoiding worst-case scenarios. With this in mind, we can look at some of the initiatives undertaken by large companies.

Paying attention to life sciences and technology

The old paradigm of imperialist companies driven by mechanistic rationality is losing ground and, little by little. a new paradigm is emerging and spreading through management circles in Europe and America. Some boards of directors have finally understood and begun to behave as if their companies were living organisms. They are less in thrall to the idea of winning and achieving power in the short-term, and more focused on short-term vitality and medium- and long-term health. They have become more modest. They have realised that power and coercion are not always the best tools at their disposal, and that they have to deal with forms of organic complexity that their intuition sometimes usefully clarifies for them. Beyond this new pragmatism, their ideas and theories of action are changing. It is no longer surprising to hear people use biological terms like ecosystems, natural selection and symbiosis. Those who have internalised this biological paradigm see companies as living organisms that compete and cooperate with others in a complex and constantly evolving ecosystem, which feeds and is fed by them and within which they can develop symbioses. They are aware that these living entities have their own particular dynamics, which they can perhaps take advantage of.

In this context, they closely follow developments in life sciences and technology. From molecular and cellular biology to sociology and neuroscience, the life sciences offer new models that these people can feed off. Advances in the life sciences synergise with the radical changes in people, in the social fabric and in businesses that are currently taking place. They foster the discovery of new ways of organising people and of steering a business and the invention of new products and production techniques. We even find our moral values changed by them.

Making the most of single-storey sociosystems

Some business leaders have realised that many discrete sociosystems affect the development of their companies and are attempting to identify and understand their dynamics. They wonder how to nullify or reduce the influence of apparently negative ones and how to build on or make the most of positive ones. They are fine-tuning their understanding and paying attention to internal systems, external systems and systems that combine the two.

Internal systems. Changes taking place in wider society have penetrated big business. Staff at all levels have been affected by modernity and brought its tropisms and attitudes into the workplace. Their new ways of going about things have challenged traditional structures, norms and regulations. Even those companies that have fought the hardest to preserve their old norms and culture have been unable to avoid change.

Employees have become more intraceptive and more independent-minded; they are on the lookout for connections and meaning and they give free rein to their intuition. These people have not simply shrugged and accepted the constraints of their allotted role in the organisation. They have sought out new contacts and work models and have found them not by looking upwards but by turning to their peers. They have linked up informally with colleagues here and there and set up new networks. 'Flatter' sociosystems have emerged. With the help of information technology, they have multiplied and grown denser, changing the structure and life of companies. Everyone has seen decisions ignored and this has undermined hierarchies and made them less tangible, even for those people who remain strongly attached to them. Heterarchical society has reached inside business, and swept up in its wake even the most conservative managers and staff. The informal structure is increasingly different from the official one.

In the 1980s, we saw pioneering American and European business leaders trying to accommodate and take advantage of this movement. They thought it could be beneficial for their companies. Today, there are more of them and they are more perceptive. They have realised that a multiplicity of sociosystems within a company is probably a sign of vitality, but also that some of them inhibit development, whilst others promote it.

Managers and consultants try to develop businesses practices that feed off these sociosystems. Their intuitions seem to have led them in five distinct directions. They may try to encourage multiple sociosystems, by providing opportunities for short-circuiting official channels; they might, for instance, have installed decentralised fax and photocopying machines, created a company intranet or put cafeterias in all their buildings and encouraged employees to use them. They may promote informal, cross-functional or cross-departmental processes that stimulate creativity and consensus-building. They may invent semi-formal structures or rules that make use of living sociosystems. They may use existing, informal sociosystems as communication channels that keep managers in the loop and allow them to leak certain types of information. They may encourage leadership qualities in people competing for particular internal posts. This increases the power of those employees who understand the dynamics of a system, who can feel for the synergistic opportunities and problems of a given situation and who know how to act at precisely the right moment.

External systems. These emerge amongst a company's customers and stakeholders. Many marketing executives now feel that it is not enough to think about consumers as individuals looking for a life that suits them. They also have to think about the sociosystems in which they are involved. They have understood that modern consumers are involved in complex webs of relationships. They can no longer be conceived of as belonging to one overarching group (like working mothers or the over-50s) or to a pyramidical sociosystem (like the traditional A, B, C, D categorisation), but as individuals involved in single-storey sociosystems. Each person is not only individual, but also unstable, because people are involved in diverse systems and situations that have their own logic and that bring out different facets of their personality.

These sociosystems are highly resistant to advertising and economists are often unable to predict or explain fluctuations in levels of consumption. Accordingly, patterns of consumption have a life of their own and are less susceptible to influence and control by business, though market leaders try to understand what is happening in these systems, to anticipate the changes they produce and to begin a dialogue with them in an effort to take advantage of them.

As Alvin Toffler predicted, consumers have become producers of that which they consume. They spend hours on the Internet. Equally, much of their free time is taken up with forms of activity and exchange for which they do not have to consume. Gatherings of rollerbladers or mountain bikers, for example, can last a whole weekend without buying very much. Modern people attribute 'added meaning' to the products they really want: their computers, video games, mobile phones and yoga classes. They spend their holidays in the countryside, buying local produce and avoiding official hotels and restaurants. They also trade with one another and lend each other money, thereby sidelining the commercial sector. Companies that try to synergise with modernity realise that there is a serious risk that consumers will increasingly avoid conventional market channels. They wonder how they can slow this process down, divert it or take advantage of it.

They are also looking for communication techniques that make use of living social networks. Modern people are co-creators of their own communication networks. The Internet has spread like wildfire, whilst traditional forms of mass communication no longer work as well as they once did. Modern people tend to trust their natural environment more than the world of marketing when it comes to making consumer choices. They have been manipulated before and, having learned their lesson, are disenchanted and at the same time better integrated into local networks. They are more likely to listen to the word on the street and the advice of friends than to advertising campaigns.

Systems that mediate between the internal and the external. Business leaders who pioneered a biological way of looking at the organisation in its broader context, were also interested in the discrete sociosystems that employees, customers and stakeholders developed at the intersection of the company and its environment. (Pursuing the biological metaphor, I shall use the terms 'environment' and 'ecosystem' here, to describe the physical, commercial, competitive, socio-economic and human or stakeholder context in which businesses find themselves.)

When employee dissatisfaction is no longer limited to people's individual situations, but extends to an entire sociosystem and affects local and family environments, the result can be social crisis. It is better to anticipate and prevent such processes than to try to fix them.

But employees and customers also create sociosystems that are good for business. Surveys we carried out in France in 1995 helped a number of companies to focus on, and try to benefit from, sociosystems that they had often previously failed to notice. They either wanted to identify these systems and encourage them, or instead to adopt a sort of bio-mimetic approach and study their emergence so as to deliberately reproduce them. As we looked at employee behaviour in many companies and public sector organisations, we were struck by the increasing number of cases in which personnel spontaneously adapted to customers and their needs. This adjustment had not been decided upon by management, but was the product of the employee's intuitive understanding of the customer's needs in a particular situation. This affected many sectors: airline staff, bank tellers, managers of a large IT company interacting with client companies, postal workers, and so on. We observed these people at work and asked them about those times when it seemed to them that their work had a little more meaning than usual. One after the other, and in their own way, they told the same story. Faced with a customer where things did not seem to be going well, the employee had suddenly realised what was going on and found some way to adapt and make a breakthrough. In each case, this moment of truth had achieved something important for the customer, for the company and for their relationship. It had brought some sense of meaning to their work.

As companies and their employees adapted to their customers, so they also adjusted to suit their environment. A self-regulating, and even self-organising, system sprang into action. Unplanned events and encounters like those described above helped to improve a company's adaptation to its ecosystem. They helped it to overcome one of the major challenges of the time: how to function like an organism instead of a machine and, in so doing, become a bio-enterprise.

This kind of innovation has spread, with companies spontaneously adapting to their customers' needs without management intervention. But sometimes more perceptive managers notice these adaptive encounters and events. They see how they might help the company and draw people's attention to these new opportunities. And sometimes they even send the message back up the hierarchy, awakening the interest of strategic management teams and giving them the idea of orchestrating such initiatives on a wider scale.

Nowadays, companies are trying to systematise this practice, which allows businesses and their environments to adapt to one another and to develop synergies.

Looking for renewable vitality

Problems of longevity, remaining competitive and sustaining vitality are now publicly debated. A study carried out by Shell some years ago, and since revived, usefully illustrates this. In the early 1980s, Shell's management, driven by Pierre Wack's scenario planning, became interested in why so many companies failed. A third of the companies featured in Fortune magazine's 500 leading companies of 1970 had disappeared by 1983. They had been taken over, merged or broken apart. In order to understand why these companies had prematurely failed and why a handful of others were so astonishingly long-lived, Shell organised a study looking at how forty or so companies founded more than 200 years before had been able to survive radical changes in their social and economic environment and sustain their vitality.

Arie de Geus, who had spent his entire career with Shell and occupied senior positions within the group, first published an article in the *Harvard Business Review* and then a book, in 1997, which analysed the study's results and the lessons Shell had learned from them.[46] The study showed that large companies fail when 'the prevailing thinking and language of management are too narrowly based on the prevailing thinking and language of economics'. And the author added, 'To put it another way: companies die because their managers focus on the economic activity of producing goods and services,

---

46   de Geus A. *The Living Company: Growth, Learning and Longevity in Business*. Boston, MA: Harvard Business School Press, 1997.

and they forget that their organization's true nature is that of a community of humans.' The study showed that companies adapted for survival tended to share four main characteristics:

- they were sensitive to their environment and knew how to learn and adapt to change
- they were cohesive, had a strong sense of identity and were able to mobilise their employees as well as customers and suppliers
- they were tolerant of difference and novelty. They cultivated difference and were able to develop synergies with others
- and finally, and this is where economic considerations come into play (although not in the now omnipresent idea of short-term maximisation of shareholder value), they were financially prudent and conservative and so always had sufficient funds to put their strategies into action.

The book appeared at a time when large parts of the business community were ready to listen to its message. This is even truer today, when a turbulent financial market and errors of judgement by businesses and consultants are making people think about new forms of management. Many companies are also realising that ten or twenty years spent focusing on their short-term profits have put them in a situation where their very survival is threatened, even if they are still extremely profitable.

The learning company

In the early 21st century, companies are like living organisms whose environment has changed and who must adapt to this change if they are to survive. They have to manage their development in a hyper-complex ecosystem, whilst simultaneously taking into account

- short- and long-term perspectives
- profitability and vitality
- economics and finance, the health and happiness of their staff, social harmony and the global ecosystem.

This is no easy task. Which practices, structures, institutions, skills and ways of being they will need to guide their development are still not clear. There is no straightforward template for survival that can be taught or found in a book. This is why I think we need to pay attention to the simple biological idea of learning.

To this end, a few dozen multinationals, some of which are major players, have created an informal mutual support network. Both on their own and together they are learning the necessary expertise and ways of being. They modestly consider themselves to be learning companies.[47] They help one another to progress. They believe that they have to get to know this unfamiliar environment and acquire the structures, culture and business reflexes that will allow them to steer a way through it. These companies focus on perfecting and intensifying their knowledge of themselves and their environment. They develop complex feedback networks that connect them to their vital organs, to people, to their partners, their markets and to society. They are beginning to pay attention not only to familiar economic and technical issues, but also to socio-human realities. They are becoming ethnographers of themselves, their environment and shifting modernities. They are contributing to the knowledge and technologies of complexity. However, even if they are smart, they can't integrate this new expertise if they remain rigid and uniform. So they develop flexible, shifting and complex structures that welcome novelty and favour self-organisation and spontaneity. They are learning how to transform their business culture. They are diversifying so as to make the most of the different opportunities that their changing environment throws up.

The challenge of transforming large companies, which are still monolithic, standardised and obsessed with this quarter's profits, into learning companies that are attentive to socio-human and ecological issues is enormous. If it had to be done all at once, then nobody would even think about it. But these changes lead onto one another and have a cumulative effect. This is not necessarily a conscious learning process. Often, new adaptations emerge and develop without anybody fully realising it. But conscious learning is more fruitful. Where it occurs, then information becomes knowledge and reflex reactions become expertise that can be taught and not just imitated.

It is not enough to learn new ways of organising, conceiving and enacting strategy, management and marketing. Part of the challenge is to invent new forms of capitalism. English, American, French and German forms of capitalism all work differently. But they are all based on legal company frameworks that were, for the most part, drawn up more than a hundred years ago. Companies have explicitly set out to look for new structures that will allow them to escape from the tyranny of short-term profitability. This new capitalism still needs to be invented, but it will doubtless involve

___
47   Many books have looked at this approach. See Senge P. *The Fifth Discipline*. New York: Currency/ Doubleday, 1990.

power, influence and information structures that work in such a way that companies will have an incentive to take into account profitability, care for the environment and concerns about the individual and society.

If the traditional large companies that go down this learning route manage to increase their vitality, their efficiency and their profit margins, then others will follow. In that case, the hiatus between the new socio-economy and the old economy will be softened. Big business will get back in touch with society, will recover its lost legitimacy and influence and will contribute to society's internal balance and harmony. If we want both profits and the actualisation of our latent potential for human fulfillment and social harmony, then we have to encourage the learning approach adopted by these pioneer companies.

For the time being, however, short-term visions and share prices still weigh heavily in the balance. The battle is not yet won.

Chapter 9
Hopes for smarter societal governance

At this point in the early 21st century, most modern societies – and, in fact, the world as a whole – lack good governance. The situation looks bleak. Frustrated and marginalised sections of the population are turning into closed and aggressive communities. Even in the most democratic countries, the political superstructure is cut off from people and living society. It is poorly regulated and widely mistrusted. Those people who challenge the system are becoming more radical. The commercial economy is also still artificially cut off from the rest of society and from the environment. It lacks both internal and external regulation, wastes enormous amounts of creativity and energy, excludes some people and ravages the biosphere. Mounting violence pits people, 'isolates' and ethnic and faith communities against one another. States take part in this crescendo of violence. The United States, in particular, wages war on terrorism whilst reinforcing the very processes that give rise to it. Those in power short-sightedly turn people against the ruling elite, and the Third World against the First. The major threats to our planet go ignored and the global process of modernisation goes unmanaged. This leads to increasing inequality and increasingly intractable problems. In the end, the result could be destructive hostility.

I will now look at the challenges, impasses and steps towards creating smarter – let us say wiser – systems of governance that would fit comfortably with, and work efficiently within, modern society. Here, I focus on the governance of modern nation-states, and in the next chapter on global governance.

We have seen how the collapse of social norms and of the power of statutory authorities has not led to chaos or to an explosion of violence. Western society dreams of peace and harmony and is capable of creating them, but not always capable enough. The emerging social fabric is characterised by peaceful relations and looser regulation and this has generated autonomy, independence and opportunities for happiness and self-development for both individuals and networks, as well as large numbers of non-hierarchical sociosystems and a sort of vibrant cohesiveness. We might dream that this process would go on and on until a flourishing, hedonistic society emerged.

But the reality is less rosy. The spontaneous intervention of large numbers of new civic entrepreneurs has failed to prevent the emergence of processes leading to tension, division, antisocial behaviour and violence. These are limited phenomena, but they have steadily increased over recent years and government's clumsy attempts to resolve them often make matters worse. Our modern societies need wiser governance, which their political regimes and states are unable to provide. We are making some progress in this direction, but there's still a long way to go.

The Western statist and democratic model has been wrong-footed by modernising processes and slow to adapt. There is now a gulf between an incredibly vibrant civil society, which has already changed enormously, and states, governments and institutionalised political life, which have all failed to keep up.

Modernity and the political system are out of sync

Western political systems all share certain characteristics that are simply at odds with the type of society that is emerging. Citizens feel divorced from, or even hostile towards, the political system and government loses its effectiveness.

Territorial power politics

The states that emerged in the 19th and 20th centuries pursued power politics and territorial security. This approach no longer represents the goals and motivations of modern citizens, neither is it suited to the tightly interwoven social and geographical architecture that is emerging, nor to changing technology and weaponry. Modern citizens want an approach that sets out to build a material and relational environment that offers more opportunities for happiness and fulfilment and would like to get rid of the remaining pockets of unhappiness. They want an approach that stimulates the human and economic vitality of the different groupings within society. And they want an approach that protects people and minorities, wherever they may be, and tries to find forms of planetary regulation that guarantee our security and the possibility of sustainable development for humankind.

Cold and non-participative representative democracy

The democratic regimes that emerged in the 19th century and were improved throughout the 20th were representative in nature. Major decisions were taken by elected representatives. At the time, this form of democracy mobilised the masses, but it no longer manages to engage its citizens. It leads to ineffective government and a sense of democratic deficit.

Modern citizens feel that their representatives, who have been chosen by party bureaucracies or by party activists, fail to represent them properly. People, especially the young, vote less and less. For them, it is not enough to be represented. They want a form of democracy that establishes closer relations between people and their representatives and allows people, organisations and sociosystems to participate in actions and developments that concern them.

Democratic systems based on majority law and one-size-fits-all politics

Democratic systems based on majority government instituted the belief that power belonged to the majority, rather than to a monarch or a minority. This constituted a decisive step forward for democracy. Today, however, modern people find it shocking and undemocratic that the majority should impose its will on minorities and equally shocking that it imposes certain forms of socially acceptable behaviour on eccentrics who are not harming anyone. People want protection for minorities and harmless eccentrics.

The state learned to govern by drawing up laws that applied to everybody, everywhere, and made such laws a central criterion of justice and democracy. But in complex and overlapping living societies, such generalist approaches are often counter-productive. This is why one-size-fits-all politics should give way to an approach that is both global and particular. In order to predict and to adapt their response to the needs of each individual situation (at a particular time and on a particular date), politics has to organise itself in such a way as to be close to the ground and able to understand particular concerns, whilst simultaneously being able to see the wider context. It has to create decentralised structures where dialogue between all members on an equal footing is possible. It has to be creative and flexible and adapt its actions to the specific reality of each situation and to the opportunities and threats it contains.

A sovereign and constraining state

History made the state sovereign over its national territory. The state acquired a monopoly on legitimised violence and used its police, and occasionally its army, to keep the peace. It alone was supposed to embody the public interest and it insisted on having the last word.

In the Second Modernity, all this was called into question. Modern people are no longer inclined to bend their knee to authority unless they deem it legitimate, relevant and appropriate. Besides, the social fabric is now made up of networks and sociosystems; it reacts in its own way and can produce negative outcomes. Too much red tape nullifies economic and citizen initiative. In a modern context, attempts by government to assert its authority often provoke divisions and unrest, waste energy and damage cohesiveness. The old state still contains coercive and repressive elements, which can exacerbate processes that produce violence and antagonism. Surveys carried out in France provide numerous examples of cases where the state's arrogance increases citizens' discontent and vice versa.

The idea of the public interest, which was once clear, is now becoming blurred. Across the modern world the state is losing its legitimacy. Rather than embodying the public interest, it often seems to embody that of the party in power, or of civil servants, or of the political class in general, or... that of Texan oil barons. The nation is no longer the principal point of reference. People tend to evaluate the common good according to their own interests: one's family, one's locality, one's company, humanity, the ecosystem. On top of this, many local, self-organised collectives and NGOs have their own vision of the public interest.

Faced with divisive problems, the state can sometimes be tempted to enact its sovereignty and unilaterally impose its conception of the public interest, without engaging in extended public consultation, without having looked for potential compromise and without making sure of the strength of its legitimacy. This can reinforce existing antagonisms, which can then be hard to break down.

In order to regain their effectiveness, states and other power structures have to learn how to use what Joseph Nye calls 'soft power'. The doyen of Harvard's Kennedy Business School has shown that in a context where the power to mobilise others or to get one's way has become more important than the power to constrain, even the world's most militarily and economically powerful nation is no longer all-powerful.[48] It is caught up in networks of states and their interactions. It is faced with non-state actors and sociosystems that grow more powerful by the day.

This soft power requires modesty. Michel Crozier long ago highlighted this necessary change.[49] The new state and its representatives need to understand

---

48   Nye J. *The Paradox of American Power: Why the World's Only Superpower Can't Go It Alone.* Oxford: Oxford University Press, 2002.

49   See, for example, Crozier M. *État Modeste, État Moderne.* Paris: Fayard, 1987.

that they are not all-powerful, and that they cannot just do as they see fit. They must enter into a dialogue with their citizens on an equal footing. Only then will people trust them.

This soft power is also a smarter and wiser sort of power. Governments that learned how to make use of it would give themselves the tools they needed to understand the processes that, at various different levels, regulate the course of events. They could attune themselves to the dynamics of these processes and perhaps influence them.

It is hard to imagine governments being able to dispense entirely with the threat of violence. But, in order to gel with modern society's capacity to be peaceable, they need to wield it sparingly and only when they are sure that such violence both seems legitimate to most people and likely to be effective. In such cases, informed constraint could help to maintain peace and calm.

By the same token, ill-considered violence risks appearing illegitimate. It raises social tension and can lead to escalating violence, which if multiplied, might lead society in the direction of intense and sustained conflict – in other words, in precisely the opposite direction to that pursued by most modern societies in the last few decades of the 20th century.

A paternalistic and legalistic state

In the mid-20th century, Western states became paternalistic. They set out to look after their citizens. However, this approach is counter-productive in a society where most problems are resolved through self-organisation and self-regulation and where people have developed sufficiently far to feel that they are their own masters. The ideal modern government would try to make sure that autonomous individuals took responsibility for their actions, but would at the same time offer a brotherly hand to those who were unable to do so.

When disasters occur, governments often look for somebody to blame. In a hyper-complex and rapidly changing society, this approach may satisfy the masses, but it is counter-productive. A better tactic is to identify the different factors that upset the system and then try to learn from them.

Bureaucratic, technocratic and partisan power

Governments and local authorities in the West have tended to make decisions and laws based on expert advice and technical analysis, or on opposing party political ideologies. Rather than trying to achieve goals, they have focused on following the rules. These practices disheartened Vitalists and were rarely effective when applied to complex, living societies.

Political parties have played up their differences rather than trying to overcome them and so govern more effectively. This division of the political spectrum into formal, often bureaucratic, and ideologically rigid political parties has been ill-adapted to the way modern society works. It has tended to transform representatives into professional politicians who are often more dependent on party structures than on their electors. It has also tended to focus debate on party political divisions born of ancient struggles, rather than on responses to change. It has created antagonism not alliance. Vitalists often feel that these bureaucratic, technocratic and partisan practices are meaningless. If they are to be accepted and so become effective, then those in power have to be therapists, catalysts and visionaries.

One of their principal functions would be **therapeutic**. Modern people's idea of the collective good involves notions of harmony and of making the most of different kinds of potential. Our increasingly disordered society demands both order and freedom. It does not want geometry or bureaucracy, but a living order. And not any old living order, which might be pathological or feverish, but a healthy one that harnesses potential. The government of the future needs to allow people to create their own happiness, whilst intervening in processes that lead to closed communities, social division and violence. It needs to be neither too controlling, nor too laissez faire, and it needs to stimulate the vitality of people and social and economic groups and to discourage sterile processes. It should manage change and undertake the inevitable institutional changes without provoking conflict.

Most of the time, this would be a **catalysing** form of government. By intervening in limited ways, government could encourage desirable forms of change and prevent undesirable ones. Catalysing political practice would involve adopting or integrating the natural structures of the living ensembles it wanted to change, and exploring the potential synergies between government and latent social dynamics.

In times of change and uncertainty, prediction and planning become almost impossible. But there can be no smart management without visions **of the future**. But these visions have to be freed from partisan blinkers and strategic intuition has to be nourished. They also have to be flexible and pragmatic, so as to adapt to change in the real world.

Hesitant but significant steps towards modernity

During the 1990s, modernisation accelerated in three different directions. States moved towards more participative forms of democracy, ordinary people took the initiative, and the authorities began to evolve towards wiser governance.

States move towards more participative forms of democracy

Local and central government began to realise that it had to listen to the electorate and try to engage in dialogue. This conviction was not universally shared, but it was gaining ground. It inspired **new administrative approaches**. Some of bureaucracy's rougher edges were rubbed off. Civil servants had to understand that their users were citizens and customers. Services were adapted to users' needs and user satisfaction surveys were carried out. Some countries went further, changing, for example, the opening hours of offices serving the public to suit their customers. This reduced tension and in some cases created virtuous circles: civil servants began to see their users as real people and this led them to new discoveries. They started to understand their customers and then to get a feel for the hidden potential of different situations. Intermediaries and mediators became important. Sometimes this was little more than a superficial gesture to alleviate tensions, but sometimes it was indicative of real efforts to bridge differences and move towards cooperative action.

Governments tried to reduce bureaucracy in the public sector and the civil service by encouraging them to enter into a mutually regulated interaction with their environment. If a school or post office, for example, interacts with its clients on a daily basis and on an equal footing, then it will adapt. Instead of blindly following protocol, it will look for solutions to real problems. The first, and easiest, step in this process took the form of impact studies and the evaluation of results. The next step, which hardly anyone took, involved getting the relevant people to enter into the kind of interaction I have just described.

On a national level, it is difficult for governments to listen to their citizens, and even more difficult to organise real dialogue. Most citizens, and especially the young, do not make things any easier for them. They often have nothing to say to politicians; they despise them and turn their attention elsewhere. If they do get involved in public life, then they do so in ways that are radically different from those of professional politicians.

It takes exceptional circumstances or particularly charismatic leaders for professional politicians and ordinary people to develop a shared language and shared emotions. Referenda or the direct election of heads of state can sometimes be opportunities for people and the authorities to come into a sort of emotional symbiosis. But such symbiosis is rare, because the questions raised in referenda or the political options on offer are normally pre-selected by those in power. Occasionally, national leaders manage to ride a wave of public emotion and to channel it – as Tony Blair did on the death of Princess Diana. In a similar way, on the day after 9/11, George Bush shared the American people's surge of horror and patriotism. These are not unprecedented phenomena, but modern people, on the lookout for emotional participation, are particularly susceptible to such events.

A politician's personal style and savoir-faire are crucial catalysts for public debate. Some politicians can make people realise how particular debates affect their everyday lives, and simultaneously make people aware that they are open to dialogue (which encourages people to participate) and project their personal leadership capacities. President Clinton, for example, spent time participating in local debates on important questions, like pensions. He managed to inform people, be objective and avoid advancing particular political propositions, thereby keeping the debate open. 'It's up to you to decide.' These debates were often televised on local networks and discussed on the Internet.

Few politicians are capable of this. They find it hard to shrug off their authoritarianism and enter a debate without having a preconceived idea that they want to get across. Outdated ideas of a politician's role prevent them from being catalysts of consensus. And so, these debates are often little more than media circuses, modernised versions of old forms of political marketing, rather than open dialogues that try to build consensus. They are often little more than attempts to ease the passage of decisions that have already been taken or to revamp a political career.

The spread of the Internet has given politicians an opportunity to engage more closely with citizens and to try out new kinds of debate. Political leaders' websites and online forums are not yet a new democratic institution, but they do provide them with useful information about citizens' sensibilities and serve as an ideal learning opportunity.

In the United States and in many northern European countries, **public consultation exercises** were carried out in the 1990s. They aimed to link policy to people's informed reactions, rather than relying on experts or political parties. So far, these have been just tentative steps, not a full-blown revolution. They were attempts to give participants a chance to step back from ideological clichés. In 1996, *La Lettre de la Cofremca* analysed several of these experiments.[50] They were carried out by governments or organisations for reasons of public interest:

- Denmark was a forerunner and has been organising 'consensus conferences' that contribute to public policy development since 1989. These involve citizens, experts and the media, and in some cases, are open to the public. This formula was adopted by the Netherlands in 1993, by Great Britain in 1994, and then pretty much everywhere else.

- Deliberative polls lie half-way between consensus conferences and traditional opinion polls. The first such survey was carried out in the UK on behalf of *The Independent* and *Channel Four* in 1994. It looked at the causes of crime and potential responses. The United States followed suit in 1996, focusing on the central themes of the presidential campaign.

- South Africa went one step further, innovating on a major scale in a time of institutional crisis. This innovation drew on Royal Dutch Shell's approach to strategic scenario planning. In the run-up to the first universal elections at the end of Apartheid (1994), members of the African National Congress, business and trades union leaders, local government officials and academics met to discuss future scenarios for South African society. These forums were widely discussed in the country at large and allowed many leaders and citizens to think about possible strategies and to develop a shared language that helped contribute to the country's peaceful democratic transition.

Innovation can come from local government. In most countries, citizens are much more favourably disposed towards local authorities than to central government, parliament and even judges. At the same time, most governments have felt that many contemporary problems are easier to identify and deal with at a local level, where the authorities are closer to the ground.

Cities have grown in vitality and become more alive. Power has tended to be devolved to the regions. In Europe, regions and cities seem destined to play a role in wider networks of power and most countries in the European Union are engaged in this kind of decentralisation.

---

50   No. 43, December 1996.

Local and regional government finds it easier to engage in dialogue with citizens and organisations on an equal footing. In small towns and villages, people have face-to-face relationships with their representatives and there are often strong traditions of dialogue and cooperation. In large cities and suburbs, the link between government and the people is less straightforward, but efforts are being made. Mayors and city councils are trying to build links with non-state organisations, stimulate their emergence and finance their development. They employ mediators and community organisers. People are looking for ways forward, for the right structures and for forms of cooperation, and sometimes they find them. Local and regional authorities and their national partners also engage in benchmarking to identify practices and institutions that really work.

For the optimist, these innovations can be read as an index of new, smarter societal navigation. Dialogue and interaction can create alliances that influence the course of events. The authorities play their role, sometimes as actors and sometimes as directors. To be effective, they recognise their limitations and they adopt learning stances in the face of obstacles to progress. But this is not a single, smooth transition. Many mayors are openly sceptical about residents' associations and people's active participation in local life.

In December 2000, the CIA released a report drawing the US government's attention to the challenge of **improving governance by encouraging interaction with non-state actors**.[51] It highlighted this new awareness. The report was a collaborative undertaking that looked at potential global scenarios in 2015. It suggested that states will still play a dominant role (at both a national and international level), but they will have less and less control over flows of information, technology, disease, populations, arms, and legal and illegal financial transactions. They will have to work alongside non-state entities who will wield increasing power and influence. Multinationals, micro-companies and business networks will continue to develop. The not-for-profit sector will not only grow, but will discover its new-found power and act more aggressively. It will participate in the shaping and implementation of policy, either as a partner, or as a competitor. The report also highlights the increasing importance of criminal networks and ethnic and faith groups. The authors of the report believe that states will have to improve and refine their

---

51   *Global Trends 2015: A Dialogue About the Future With Non-Government Experts,* December 2000. This report was prepared by the National Intelligence Council and approved for publication by the National Foreign Intelligence Board, under the authority of the Director of Central Intelligence.

governance and will have to learn to collaborate with non-state actors. They believe that the American government, along with other democracies, is well placed to acquire this expertise.

Ordinary people take the initiative

In the face of governments and authorities that are increasingly open to dialogue, ordinary people are also getting involved. People and civil society have decided to take their place at the democratic table, but they are not always welcomed by the authorities.

In previous chapters, we saw how citizens have involved themselves in all sorts of **civic activities**, from the local to the global level. They often intervene in social life in the name of the public interest. In so doing they take on positions of public responsibility abandoned by the state and they lobby the authorities to act in meaningful ways. Over the last twenty years, governments and other political bodies have reacted ambivalently to this growing movement. They have tried to protect their territory, so to speak, but at the same time they have developed links with this movement and profit from it.

Citizens' organisations and civic networks are fundamentally new, lack traditions and easily adapt to a changing society. As they lack power, they have to be resourceful. They look for ways to influence people and states. They are learning by trial and error. Charities have increasing financial resources, but they are beginning to realise that it is not enough to just throw money at a problem. They are trying to understand how systems really function and look for opportunities to act more effectively. They use levers and pivots and subtle manoeuvres to maximise the impact of their financial and human activities and actions.

Governments and local authorities are still partly enmeshed in a bureaucratic, technocratic and production-oriented mindset, which is largely impervious to public influence. The absence of lively, but directed, participative democracy leads to the emergence of **wildcat direct democracy**. When people feel strongly about something but are not listened to, then they look for ways to circumvent institutions. They demonstrate, take to the streets, sign petitions or throw petrol bombs. Across Europe and North America young people who feel sidelined vent their anger on symbols of authority, which they deface or vandalise. In China, Japan and the United States, sects defy the authorities either peacefully or violently. Even terrorism can be seen as an extreme form of wildcat direct democracy. It is a way for people who feel rejected to make themselves heard. Some national and international leaders are getting the message. They try to treat the root cause of a problem rather than relying exclusively on military or security-oriented responses. From Seattle to Paris, via Hong Kong, huge peaceful demonstrations can affect the decisions of major institutions.

In particular situations, when grass-roots initiatives find fertile ground in public opinion, then **biodegradable organisations** emerge to orchestrate wildcat direct democracy. This often occurs at the local level when a public project runs into the entrenched interests or sensibilities of a section of the population. People protest and a collective emerges to embody their protest. In France, for example, most nationwide social and political movements and strikes since the late 1980s have been led not by unions or parties, but by biodegradable organisations. Parents' groups calling for a greater choice of schools, secondary school students protesting against university entrance exams, hunters objecting to new hunting laws, nurses, train drivers, truckers, teachers, tax collectors, the police, doctors and many others. They all feel poorly treated or misunderstood and rise up against what is probably the most rigid, centralised, authoritarian and invasive state in the Western world. Their demands are often supported by a wide public semi-consensus. Squads of activists tear up experimental fields of GM crops. Workers who are being laid off threaten to blow up their factory. Young rioters burn cars and attack police stations.

These violent social storms blow up quickly, but so far have not proved devastating. It is as if many of the people who participate have remained attached to measured action, trying to keep things from getting out of hand and so prevent irreparable damage. We should not, however, rule out the possibility that one day one of these storms will simply sweep away the existing edifice of power and authority, unless we manage to civilise wildcat direct democracy.

A new **digital democracy** is also beginning to emerge. New communication technologies have led to the proliferation of sociosystems and to the increasing power of civil society. The spread of the Internet and of mobile phones goes hand in hand with people's desire for dialogue and participation. Citizens who share common concerns can now gather online and engage in debate. People share and develop ideas in online forums. Different networks identify one another, assess each other and sometimes form alliances. It is now vastly easier for groups to mobilise their members and engage in action. Technology favours the creation of virtual civic communities that use petitions and manifestos to launch real campaigns. Digital networks bypass traditional political channels and influence the authorities. In a crisis, these networks make protestors much more efficient. In France, for example, the student demonstrations of 1995 owed much to the use of websites. The Indonesian revolution in spring 1998 was the first revolution where the Internet played an important part and was, without doubt, one of the elements that contributed to President Suharto's rapid downfall. Overall, the Internet will very likely help to catalyse the development of a new type of citizen and the self-organisation of new forms of citizenship, helping to combine the humanism of the Left and the economic vitality of the Right.

Some movement towards wiser governance

Good leaders have always had to understand people's emotions and how their actions and behaviour are intimately interconnected, to intuitively grasp the dynamics of a situation and the course of history and to understand the living web of interactions concealed by the mask of the realities one wants to change. In the 21st century, the increasing complexity of society and growing numbers of self-organisations mean that now more than ever, leaders need to have both a cognitive and an intuitive understanding of the art of governance and above all an ability to identify, and make use of, windows of opportunity.

However, over the course of the 20th century, these abilities withered rather than flourished. They were stifled by dogmatic political ideologies and by a mechanistic, bureaucratic and technocratic mindset. In the early 21st century, the selection and training of political and administrative personnel in many modern countries still has a legal, technical and economic bias, when what we need are intuitive, creative and innovative people who listen to other people and to society and can analyse the whole as well as its constituent parts. The organisation of governments and the public sector remains for the most part hierarchical, lumbering and initiative-stifling, whereas flexibility, diversity, responsiveness and local awareness are what is called for. This makes for an environment that is far from ideal for the development of wiser forms of social governance that would keep society as healthy as possible.

That said, during the 1990s, public sector developments in many countries seem to have helped to prepare the ground for wiser social governance. They began to distance themselves from the traditional right/left divide. National and local authorities shifted their position on violence. Better protection was offered to minority groups and personal freedoms. Finally, a political culture based on visions of the future began to develop.

Moving beyond the right/left divide. It is hard to shake off the often sclerotic ideologies of the last two hundred years. They act like blinkers that focus attention on yesterday's problems and distract us from the problems of today and tomorrow. They lead some sections of the population to hold onto what they have got rather than encouraging them to look for modernising reforms. They promote antagonism rather than alliances and they encourage politicians to try to convince or indoctrinate the electorate, rather than helping them to open their eyes.

A few leaders have understood this, while the people at large often feel that a political system based on adversarial parties is poorly adapted to a changing society. This is most obvious in Great Britain and the United States. Tony Blair and Bill Clinton owed much of their popularity to the way they distanced themselves from traditional party programmes. Tony Blair radically transformed the Labour party. He did not reject the Thatcherite heritage and he knew how to take the pulse of modernity, seize the opportunities it offered and avoid the dangers. He taught people to understand modernity. In the same way, Bill Clinton abandoned many of the Democrats' previous projects and incorporated parts of the Republican programme. He modernised the American system of government by reducing the role of the federal government and passing a number of laws that promoted justice and social harmony. In Germany, Gerhard Schröder probably took heart from their success and presented himself as the champion of the new centre when he was elected in 1998.

In France, by contrast, partisan politics remains firmly entrenched. The left and the right oppose each other out of principle. Political parties often put forward exaggeratedly partisan manifestos and if they win, they feel more or less obliged to follow them, rather than taking a fresh look at real problems and challenges. If they fail to stick to them, then the political press (which is out of touch with modern sensibilities) calls them to order. And this despite the fact that the electorate has repeatedly confused the situation by voting for a right-wing president and left-wing government, or vice versa, or by showing its appreciation for apparently non-partisan governments.

We have reached a point where modernity has produced values centred on peace and harmony, on achieving human potential, human rights and the protection of the environment. Governments may be tempted to try to identify themselves with modernity and its values so as to strengthen their electoral support and to gather support for a reformist programme. However, Western societies have not transformed these values into a motivational myth like they did between the 1920s and the 1960s, or like people in China are doing today. The rigidity of the right/left divide prevents them from forming a coherent whole.

Towards a therapeutic approach to violence. For a long time, European governments have hesitated between tolerance (society makes people violent) and repression (people themselves are to blame), and failed to attend to the processes that produce social exclusion and violence. These are processes that take root in families, gangs and rough neighbourhoods and that are too distant for central governments to understand. They operate more or less independently of wider socio-economic action and are closely linked to local circumstances. Governments have neglected problems of education and upbringing and, in Europe, have failed to integrate immigrant communities. Where efforts have been made, they have often been too little too late, when the damage is already considerable.

In the 1990s, some local authorities and civic groups faced up to the problem of violence without worrying about whether they were mixing up traditionally left-wing attitudes (prevention, rehabilitation) and traditionally right-wing ones (repression). They took an honest approach to their successes and failures. How to obtain the best short- and long-term results? Which situations require unequivocal punishment and which situations call for tolerance? Many of them began to adopt new policies for lowering tension in their fight against violence: policies that combined prevention and rehabilitation as well as repression.

Protection of minorities and personal freedoms. During the 1990s, many minorities fought for and won the right to express and enact their unique identity. These minorities were groups united by ideas, ways of life, moral precepts, religion or ethnicity. People became more liberal and the law often followed suit. Throughout Europe and North America, racial minorities received legal protection, homosexuals no longer had to hide their sexual orientation and practical and technological advances helped to make life easier for disabled people. People's individual freedoms were increased. Abortion was legalised. In the Netherlands, euthanasia was legalised and soft drugs decriminalised. In Great Britain, France and Germany, Muslim and Buddhist minorities were free to build mosques and temples.

However, both France and Germany continued to persecute sects, and there were also signs of increasing intolerance. In the United States, political correctness was taken to extremes. Citizens felt that the increase in red tape at both the national and European level limited their freedom. The ideal of 'live and let live' was far from universally shared. And throughout the world, vocal minorities who assumed they were in the majority, or were convinced of their moral superiority, tried to impose their traditional or religious values on others. In many domains and in many countries, the majority still reigns supreme. Later on we will look at how international agreements protect citizens from their own governments. Modern society needs national and international government to protect people and minorities.

A political culture based on visions of the future. Visions of the future have, in some cases, helped governments to move in the right direction. The Netherlands saw potential problems with the welfare state model and, as early as 1982, social partners opened negotiations over how best to adapt it to changing socio-economic conditions. More recently, whilst still US Vice President, Al Gore set out to sell the idea of a wonderful technological future to the American people, opening their eyes as he did so. In many countries, visions of geopolitical and military change have led to intelligent military reorganisation. The UN and the scientific community have warned nation-states of the dangers of blindly pursuing our current industrial and agricultural models. Tony Blair had a global vision of the future and tried to make Great Britain a pioneer of modernisation.

For the most part, though, governments lacked vision in the 1990s. Few of them foresaw the emergence of urban ghettos, international mafia organisations and terrorist networks, and they intervened too late to prevent their development. They failed to adapt our institutions to increasing life-spans, failed to reduce industrial and agricultural pollution and failed to avert the financial crises caused by economic globalisation.

Nation-states' analytical and predictive tools were ill adapted to the uncertainty of modernity. Over the last century, most states had improved their short-term economic prediction and analysis models. However, they had limited understanding of the medium and the long-term, and tended to adopt approaches based either on ideological voluntarism or on the continued development of current trends. Most governments just dealt with current affairs or, in times of crisis, simply tried to manage the most pressing concerns. When they did reform, they did so for ideological or demagogical reasons. They contented themselves with pleasing their electors, activists or militant lobby groups.

In government circles, it is hard to conceive of a different world, and harder still to take such ideas into account. Even now, this mental inflexibility is still widespread. For instance, many reports and articles published in 2000 and 2001, as well as CIA briefings, stressed the risk of major Islamic terrorist attacks in the United States. But this was not enough. It took a real catastrophe to change the American government's agenda and concerns.

That said, political perspectives are gradually changing. This is not always obvious from one year to the next, but most contemporary governments take a very different stance from that of their predecessors in 1980. Both the left and the right seem to have realised that the world is changing. Most of them have at least a vague idea of the gathering socio-economic, ecological, health-related and geopolitical challenges they will have to face. There is a growing sense of urgency. Almost all of them talk about modernising their countries. Often they still use outmoded political language, be it socialist or liberal, but they can act in ways that contradict their discourse if they have to. They seem to be aware that modernity requires new approaches.

The proliferation of strategy groups and futurology has doubtless contributed to this change, and that of civic associations and NGOs perhaps even more so. These latter organisations often seem to be limited by their narrow and one-dimensional concerns. In most cases, they were created in response to particular issues – e.g. ecology, human rights, helping the poor, protection of environmental diversity, social reintegration of young tearaways, and so on. In some cases, this initial goal became ossified, focusing their attention on one particular threat and giving them a limited and inflexible vision of the future. Nevertheless, together, the diversity of their concerns creates a positive system of change and of constant evaluation of future risks and opportunities. These civic associations and NGOs collaborated with and challenged a wide variety of organisations, public and private think tanks, the scientific community, governments, the press, churches and many others. This helped them to detect problems early and to gain increasing momentum. Their cooperation gathered pace throughout the 1990s and contributed to the many vague visions of the future that characterise our society and that governments have to bear in mind.

It may be that in China, America and Europe, we have begun to develop a 'radar system' tuned to the future, to replace bureaucrats with blue-sky thinkers, and to break away from fixed ideologies. But this is a slow and gradual process.

A living society and the politico-administrative system co-exist, but do not really communicate

A profound mutual incomprehension now characterises relationships between people and the political establishment. The steps taken towards dialogue and social governance in the 1990s were too timid to really change this and failed to prevent growing public resentment.

Citizens abandon institutional politics

From the late 1970s onwards, it was clear to us that people in European and North American were quietly drifting away from institutional politics. As one French idiom would have it, they were abandoning 'politician's politics' (*la politique politicienne*). Over the next two decades, they continued to distance themselves from political and administrative elites, political parties and governments, which they deemed incapable of dealing with contemporary problems. In most Western countries, opinion polls showed that parents actively hoped their children would not enter politics. People voted less and, if they did get involved, it was in civic or charitable associations that supposedly lay outside mainstream politics. In the late 1990s, their gradual desertion of politics often segued into outright dissidence.

In Europe and North America, people's opinion of governments worsened. Almost everywhere, polls showed that the majority of people thought that states and large companies (unlike local authorities and small companies) failed to act in the public interest.

In 1999, Sociovision carried out ethnological field research looking at young adults in Berlin, London, Milan and Paris, which showed that these changes were becoming more pronounced. Young people felt remote from national politics. Some of our interviewees had political leanings, but none of them belonged to political parties or unions. For them, politics was a vaguely pitiful business. Many of them mentioned the ineffectiveness of governments, especially in Milan and Berlin. They were largely unaffected by traditional right/left divides. They had little time for national leaders and political parties, but respected groups like Amnesty International or Médecins sans Frontières. Some of them strongly identified with the Dalai Lama or José Bové, a French peasant activist fighting against multinationals and poor quality food. They thought that politicians and activists had claimed politics for themselves. When profoundly shocked or frustrated, these young adults, like many modern people, are capable of signing petitions, rising up and taking to the streets. Some of them were more or less actively involved in alternative political networks.

Judges' attacks on political leaders contributed to the climate of suspicion. In some contexts, judges, people and the popular press were united in their anger. They shrugged off their respect for authority and political leaders ceased to be untouchable. The press joined the attack because scandal sells and because some journalists like to play judge and juror. Judges, meanwhile, wanted to avenge themselves on the politicians who had previously intimidated them. This was dressed up in a discourse of meaningfulness and morality. The judges' attacks began with the *mani puliti* operation in Italy, where it decimated the political class and ruined its reputation. It then spread to other European countries, especially France, where it did similar damage. It also weakened the American presidency. Had it not been for his popularity in the opinion polls, Bill Clinton would probably have been stripped of office. Public perception of these judicial attacks undermined the state's legitimacy and ruined the political class's reputation, but the justice system was also tarnished.

Professional politicians are out of step

Politicians complain about people's lack of concern for the *res publica* and their flagging sense of public service and duty. They fail to see citizens' engagement in civil society organisations as 'real' politics. They even wonder whether such activity is properly democratic.

Most of them either are or feel misinformed about the direction society is taking. Reformists lament their inability to find ways to make things change. When my colleagues or I have had the opportunity to speak with heads of state, prime ministers and ministers, we have found that they were all disappointed at their perceived inability to influence things in the way they had hoped. Of course, they tend to receive a distorted view of society. In many European countries, especially France, they resolutely focus on opinion polls, which give them an idea of short-term fluctuations in public opinion and a rationalist and normative vision of the population. Heads of polling agencies complain that they do not even try to understand what lies underneath opinion poll results. Their regular contact with paid-up party members (i.e. people who are not only in their camp but who are actually interested in politician's politics), distorts their intuitive understanding of the electorate as a whole. And finally, they read the press and watch the television, which echo their own prejudices about people and society. They lack the desire, the conceptual frameworks and the subtle observational and analytical models they need to develop a simultaneously precise and wide-ranging awareness of citizens' potential and momentum, their tendencies and their habits, as well as the potential and momentum of new collective entities and sociosystems.

Television and the press deepen the divide between people and politicians

Television and the press are failing to connect the people with those in power. Specialist journalists adopt the political vision of professional politicians. They have similar interests, the same sets of references and use similar language. They are deeply involved in their quarrels and their ideological differences, and take pleasure in each low blow or snide attack – in short, they live in the same world. Their articles and their reports are faithful reproductions of a political world that most ordinary people find profoundly strange and which, although it may amuse them, they have no desire to take part in. And so journalists involuntarily feed people's rejection of the political class and discourage them from getting involved.

In several Western democracies, journalists and politicians collude in maintaining an artificial left/right divide. This system often restricts debate to traditional party political positions, which are out of step with modernising processes. It paralyses attempts to make modernity understood and distances modern people from their politicians.

Television, with its 'spitting image' puppets and impressionists, deliberately mocks the pointless and ridiculous aspects of professional politics. In the United States, and especially in Great Britain, the press delves into politicians' private lives and sometimes destroys their careers.

At the same time, the mass media give a distorted vision of ordinary people's concerns and their lived reality. Sociovision and its partners regularly notice huge discrepancies between public feeling and the media representation of it. The media like to foreground dramas, sorrows and conflict and they paint a bleak picture of reality. Sometimes, they give a faithful representation of public feeling (like on Princess Diana's death or after 9/11), but most of the time they caricature and exaggerate it. They often give the establishment's point of view, instead of that of ordinary people. This discrepancy is hard to overcome. Television and the press are still lumbering mass-media organisations, and so largely incapable of participating in a society based on networks. Society has outpaced them. Political journalists feel closer to the establishment than to ordinary people, and this affects their reporting. And so, despite watching television and reading the press daily, politicians are incapable of improving their intuitive understanding of society.

New media are emerging online. This is often serious and professional journalism that has nothing to do with the gossip and rumours that are so widespread elsewhere on the Internet. This electronic press has a more intimate relationship with ordinary people and is less part of the establishment than the written press or the television. It is more often aligned with public sensibility. It can better act as an intermediary between the public and the establishment. There are signs of such change in the United States – new media like *Salon*, *Slate* and others. Thanks to its constant interaction with its audience, this press is more in tune with its public than the mass media. It picks up on topics that people care about and that they actually discuss. Its journalists are more distant from the establishment. This provides an alternative to the classic triptych of political figures / mass media / and citizen-spectators and perhaps represents resurgent public interest in political debate.

Innovation or eruption

The lack of communication between people and the political class maintains the gulf that isolates institutions and institutional practices from living society. It slows down processes of change. National societies are global systems that need effective feedback between ordinary people and their leaders. Society lacks governance. Anything could happen. Even the most authoritarian governments are not immune to a sudden upheaval. If change is not well managed then it can provoke long-term and serious antagonism.

Without doubt, the majority of ordinary people (be they wrapped up in their close circle of family and friends or engaged in alternative politics) still put up with these discrepancies. They feel ignored and do not understand their leaders. But they tolerate this so long as it does not personally affect them and so long as they manage to hang onto their own personal sense of well-being. However, growing numbers of people are becoming active dissidents who behave antisocially and engage in wildcat direct democracy and extremist politics.

The political class benefits from maintaining this system of mutual incomprehension. It insulates it from social pressure and allows the revolving doors of elected representatives, activists and journalists to keep on turning for a while yet. But it also makes government ineffective. Deaf to the voice of the people, political leaders navigate in the dark and lose their bearings and ability to effect change. Throughout the 1990s, most governments simply modernised their bureaucracy and technocracy and remained seemingly ineffective, hesitant and baffled by the complexity of the challenges they faced. Often their clumsiness closed opportunities down rather than opening them up. In Europe, they ran up against unemployment, uncontrollable and unpredictable financial flows and the imperative of reforming the welfare state. In Europe and North America, there emerged new forms of poverty, social divisions and violence, and the pressing need to reinvent education and the process of socialising young people became apparent.

The challenge is to invent institutions and institutional practices that synergise with the society of ordinary people.

Humanity has invented the state several times over. The first states only emerged five or six thousand years ago in Mesopotamia, Egypt, the Indus Valley, the Yellow River basin, and more recently in Peru and then in Central America.[52] These states all emerged independently of one another, as if something drove humanity to invent the state. Norbert Elias has shown how, after the Middle Ages, the centuries-old Western civilisational process led to the creation of the modern state with its monopoly of violence.[53] Driven by the West, the world divided itself up into nations, each of which was governed by a state. In the 20th century, these states tried to control everything, including economic life and, in some communist countries, political, social and cultural life as well. Then, after the Second World War, the West invented the welfare state. All these states were authoritarian and hierarchical.

Today, Western societies have discovered a new vitality. They spontaneously self-organise in interdependent and heterarchical, rather than hierarchical, ways. They dream of autonomy, independence and self-fulfilment, of peace and harmony, and are capable of creating these things, but not always capable enough. If we hope to live up to their expectations and extend the modernising and humanising innovations of the 20th century, then we urgently need to invent a wiser, strategic and therapeutic state – one with more finely-tuned navigational skills and one that will be able act heterarchically and integrate a system of social governance that includes ordinary people and a variety of organisations (civic, economic, philosophical, spiritual, etc.).

The changes we will see over the next few decades could be either progressive or brutal, peaceful or violent. If states are too slow to adapt to modernity, to find partners in civil society, to cooperate with them, and to invent and impose incentive, surveillance, arbitration and regulatory structures, then the seriousness of the threats and crises we face may lead to chaos or to the rapid self-organisation of radically new systems.

Whether they know it or not, national societies are competing to create smarter and wiser societal governance. This competition involves the authorities, businesses, associations of all sorts, political parties, the trades unions and all the other key elements of civil society in each country.

The most rigid societies may experience real crisis before they manage to modernise, unless they are helped out by leaders who intuitively understand

---

52   Harris M. *Cannibals and Kings.* New York: Random House, 1977.

53   Elias 1939.

modernity and can make the most of windows of opportunity. Perhaps they will only change when they are forced to, caught up in the wake of other, more successful societies.

Innovations that work will be copied. Although it may well be that different nations will follow different paths, as in the 1920s and 1930s. For example, Europe, the United States and China may each develop their own model, only to find twenty or thirty years later that they have ended up with very similar systems of governance.

Chapter 10
Planetary governance tries to find its way

The current system of warrior and sovereign states, which we inherited from the Treaty of Westphalia (1648), is on its last legs. In the first half of the 20th century, it gave rise to two world wars that laid waste to Europe. After the second of these, the world was divided into two opposing blocs, each of which developed a nuclear deterrent. This froze East-West relations for 45 years and exported that conflict to the margins of two empires. The collapse of communism and the implosion of the Soviet Bloc freed up global relations and accelerated globalisation.

Improved communication and weapons technology, along with political decisions to liberalise international economic and financial transactions, has tended to unify the world and increase intercommunication. Globalisation has made the world smaller and made countries and continents dependent on one another.

The last few decades have seen an explosion in cheap travel, which has benefited Westerners, Asians and Russians, among others. Global telephone networks and the Internet have allowed people to communicate in real time. Radio and television are beamed across the planet, keeping people up to date on the latest events and innovations wherever they occur. These updates are almost instantaneous. We *live* simultaneity.

Many companies, even smaller ones, now operate in a competitive global marketplace.

Large, well-equipped armies operate tens of thousands of kilometres from their bases. New and deadly weaponry (be it biological, chemical or nuclear) can now be accessed by small, non-state groups, which could inflict serious damage on even the most powerful nations.

The world is trying to construct a **new architecture and new rules of the game.** Modernising processes combine with economic and geopolitical forces and equilibria to influence this effort, which has taken several important steps since the early 1990s.

The decline of the nation-state and the search for new forms of global governance

In the 20th century, the world was divided into nations and blocs. Traditional civilisational and religious divides partially transcended the nation, but seldom explicitly. These structures are now being overturned. Contemporary socio-cultural dynamics favour complex sets of overlapping interconnections and heterarchical structures, rather than simple divisions. It seems unlikely that the developments of the last twenty or thirty years will give rise to a global super-state, but rather to a much more complex concord of formal and informal legal measures that implicate a multitude of participants.

The weakening of the nation-state

National identity is not only losing its importance, but it has become less harshly divisive. Nations are no longer fundamentally warlike and aggressive. They have become the locus of a shared culture, way of life and visions of existence – almost like the groups of kindred spirits discussed in Chapter 6. This is most marked in Europe. The French, British, German and Spanish nations, for example, are no longer clear-cut entities based on a flag, frontiers and interests that need to be defended. Instead, they are frameworks for collective existence which may be economically dynamic or lagging behind, politically innovative or inflexible, but which are, above all, places one feels attached to and cultural spaces in which one feels at home.

New forms of local or regional identity have emerged, some of which are reinforced by cultural nostalgia or ethnic and religious communities. Often people are more attached to regional or ethnic cultures than they are to national ones. In most European countries, regional 'nationalisms' are emerging and in the United States, people's rejection of the federal has increased since the early 1990s. When people's desire for autonomy is frustrated, they may identify even more strongly with their region or ethnic group and even become violent. In such cases, groups of kindred spirits become isolates. That said, the ties that bind us to a region or locality, like their national equivalents, tend to be loose and changeable. For modern people, it is less a matter of birth than of choice. Many of our interviewees have a foot in several regions and do not necessarily feel attached to the village, town or city they were born in, or where they live, but to the ones they love, whose culture they admire, where their family is from, or where they have a second home. In the vast majority of cases, people's identification with a national or local culture is no barrier to their participation in other cultures, be they geographically rooted or not. Many of our interviewees have a sense of belonging to fluctuating emotional and cultural spheres that overlap and intersect with one another. They are at ease with multiple affiliations and, unlike their predecessors, they do not see these different affiliations as contradictory, but as complementary or synergetic.

At the same time, continents, civilisations, membership of the human race or global citizenship can all provoke feelings of attachment in people, although normally in a muted way. Many of the Europeans and Americans we interview let slip, sooner or later, the suggestion that they feel first and foremost an attachment to the rest of the human race rather than to a particular place or state. The planet and Homo sapiens have become an integral part of the mental cartography of modern people. They see other people's suffering on the television. In Europe at least, people are aware of our biological co-evolution – that we are all part of wider processes. In America and Europe, people are suspicious of biotechnology, climate change and new viruses that threaten both human beings and the planet as a whole.

The modernising process also favours planetary structures whose constituent elements are not hierarchically ordered, but which are interdependent and heterarchical. Many modern people feel that the world is one system. Our actions can affect people on the other side of the planet. They want to understand planetary systems, are concerned with physical and biological impacts on the biosphere, and increasingly concerned with socio-human harmony: social ecology. The actions of people and companies affect the air, water, food, climate and our health, as well as future generations' quality of life. Poverty, famine and cultural destruction contribute to migration flows and feed people's resentment, which may lead to conflict. Westerners have a new approach to the world and they put pressure on their governments to act. Steps are being taken. Planetary society is beginning to function like a self-regulating system.

Global civil society and NGOs grow in importance

Different groups are competing for power and influence. During the last three decades of the 20th century, the modernising process overturned the distribution of power within society. Some traditional powerhouses were weakened (nation-states, governments, the mass media, traditional churches), whilst others grew in strength; either because they were close to the ground (like local associations, towns and regions) or because they were free to act on a global scale (multinationals, NGOs, charitable organisations, new religions and supra-national institutions) or because they were in tune with modernity (like some of the above, as well as judges, the micromedia and small companies). Ordinary people's networks, movements and organisations gave rise to a global civil society that can increasingly affect the course of events.

NGOs, or rather the indistinct mass of organisations spawned by civil society, play an increasingly important role. Some of these are small-scale and operate at a local level, whilst others are looking to become major global players. Although it is doubtless incomplete, the Yearbook of International Organizations indicated that the number of NGOs operating in more than one country leapt from 6,000 in 1990 to 26,000 by the turn of the century.[54] In 1985, the Worldwide Fund for Nature had fewer than 600,000 members; this has since grown to more than 5 million. The number of private foundations went from 22,000 in 1980 to 55,000 in the year 2000.[55] Each year, they spend more than 23 billion dollars, which represents an increase of 700% since 1980. And they are increasingly present on the international scene.

The global development of NGOs like Greenpeace, CARE, Médecins sans Frontières, the Worldwide Fund for Nature, Attac and Amnesty International, to name but a few, has helped to restructure global power systems. They can now push large companies around and even influence national and international governments and institutions. As early as 1992, it was NGOs that forced governments to reach an international agreement on carbon dioxide emissions at the Earth Summit in Rio. In 1995, protestors stole the limelight at the World Bank's fiftieth anniversary celebrations and forced it to re-evaluate its aims and methods. In 1998, NGOs played a major part in preventing the ratification of a multilateral investment agreement recommended by the OEEC. Along with Princess Diana, they fought for a ban on anti-personnel landmines. And in 1999 they made a mockery of the WTO meeting in Seattle, contributing to its failure.

In Seattle, people and their NGOs were better organised than the organisers and had more effective channels of communication than the official delegations had. They made better use of modern communication technology. They showed they could cross partisan divides and build improbable coalitions, as when industrial trade unions keen to hang onto polluting production plants teamed up with environmental organisations. It is increasingly clear that some NGOs can call on experts who are better informed than civil servants or government advisors. More adept governments and international institutions realise that they must cooperate with NGOs.

---

54   *The Economist*, December 11, 1999.

55   *Newsweek*, February 4, 2002.

NGOs have a remarkable capacity to create complex, interlinked and crosscutting networks. Constantly connected by Internet and telephone, lacking formal structures or centralised leaders, these NGOs function like a swarm of bees and represent a formidable challenge to existing bureaucratic power structures. After the failure of the WTO summit in Seattle, people realised that civil society could sometimes have the final say.

The relative importance of states, companies, associations and NGOs will depend on how well they manage to develop synergies with ordinary people and with civil society. These latter constitute the environmental niche in which they compete for survival. Traditional authorities, states and companies, if they are locked in hierarchical postures and structures and unable to make the most of people's new attributes, will lose ground.

Fluid networks of states emerge and adapt

Created in the mid-20th century, the UN was the product of a period when the victors of the Second World War rewrote the rulebook and when sovereign states still retained their legitimacy and vitality. It included only states and accorded them all equal weight, regardless of the size of their population or their military, economic and moral strength. One state: one vote. It has found it hard to enforce its decisions and its legitimacy is increasingly challenged.

The UN and its sister organisations are more open to civil society than are nation-states. The UN, UNESCO and others involve NGO experts and de facto civil society representatives in their planning and activities. This openness to civil society is probably in large part due to the fact that international organisations are less seats of power than sites of negotiation. In the UN, no state is sovereign; instead, it has to enter into discussion with others. It costs the UN nothing to let other interested parties join the debate. It is a space in which states can learn new forms of dialogue.

What is needed and what is trying to emerge is an organisation capable of creating a wide enough consensus to legitimise military intervention against dictators, rogue states and terrorist networks.

However powerful it may be, it is hard for any state to act independently of a network of other states. For as long as nation-states have existed, they have been sovereign, but also involved in networks. They exchange ambassadors, make agreements, forge alliances, put pressure on one another, and make war. In the second half of the 20th century, they tended to form blocs: the West, communist countries, the Third World. In the 1990s, however, informal networks of states became increasingly important. These were flexible and overlapping networks that rearranged themselves in the light of changing circumstances. States learned how to share power. Even extremely powerful countries discovered that their influence over people and events was less dependent on traditional territorial sovereignty or brute force than on their ability to build a consensus. Perhaps they had learned from the lesson of two world wars and the Cold War. Or perhaps better informed, more risk-conscious and, therefore, wiser governments were better able to play the complex game of competition and cooperation, which took global concerns into account and simultaneously allowed them to avoid serious conflict. They were equipped with rapid global information systems. The presidents and prime ministers of the major powers were frequently in touch with other leaders. They assessed their personalities, interpreted their reactions and second-guessed their strategies. This direct communication improved their intuition and reduced the risks of serious misinterpretation. Most states were involved in networks of interdependence. The least involved became known as 'rogue states'.

Economic globalisation also evolved: no longer just a system of economic and financial exchange largely tilted in favour of industrialised countries. The network of states listened to the protests of civil society. It was, above all, the growing effectiveness of concerted action by less developed countries that forced it to change. These countries too had learned. They understood better the subtle mechanisms of exchange and of international economic and financial regulation. Driven by India, Brazil and South Africa, they challenged both Western governments and Western activists. Unlike the latter, they were in favour of free trade, but wanted to rewrite the rulebook in their favour. These countries no longer formed an ideological (anti-colonialist) bloc, as in the time of Nehru, Tito and Nasser. They were less a rigid and stable camp than an evolving network of alliances. Their leaders met with one another, talked, worked together and tried to build partial or global consensus. They also managed to play Europe and America off against one another in order to achieve their ends.

Progress in the sphere of Individual and Human Rights

One of the most striking signs of the emergence of a new humanist moral system was the acceleration of the process that weakened state sovereignty in favour of individual and human rights. It was one of the major achievements of the 1990s. It was understood that people needed protecting from those in power, and especially from the state. This principle affected national and international law. International tribunals now protect ordinary people from states' infringement of their human rights. Citizens often successfully challenge their states in the European Court of Justice. The principle of concerted humanitarian intervention in a state's sovereign territory is increasingly accepted. Crimes against humanity have become imprescriptible (not subject to a statute of limitations) and an international court has been set up to deal with them. Following on from the tribunals set up to deal with the former Yugoslavia and Rwanda, 125 countries (but not the USA) signed the Treaty of Rome on 17th July 1998, which created an international criminal court. A sort of natural law that was not derived from God or the state, but from people, was imposed upon states. This new law chipped away at the corporatist system that had united states against their people and allowed retired dictators to live out their lives in peace. This acceleration affected not only Europe, but the entire world and particularly states that were too weak to inspire fear in others: Chile, Malaysia and Serbia.

'People's justice' began to impose itself and even developed its own system of enforcement. The international community, or part of it, or just one representative state claimed the right to intervene in other sovereign countries so as to protect their people against ruthless leaders. In such cases, military action was coordinated by the UN or more surprisingly, in Kosovo, by NATO, or even by the dominant power – the United States. Intervention was becoming legitimised.

Europe invents new forms of governance

Europe, birthplace of the nation-state and its wars, is now perhaps engaged in moving beyond it. Not so long ago, Europe virtually committed collective suicide in two world wars. This tragic period is now behind us. After fifty years of rapprochement, it is now unthinkable for Western European nations to go to war. Europe has invented an international sphere of peace.

Other, more civilised means of regulating conflict are emerging. By dint of discussion and handshakes, Europe is creating new forms of non-centralised government whose major decisions (except in extreme cases) emerge out of cooperation and regulation rather than being imposed by a centralised and sovereign authority. They are well adapted to a world made up of networks, which privileges human beings and the collectives they form.

What is more, the European community's efforts to be open and to build wide-ranging international partnerships is a sign of improving techniques of non-military diplomacy that might even spread to the rest of the world. This is perhaps the beginning of a decisive step towards the elimination of international violence, something that chimes with modern people' desire for peace and harmony. Europe can legitimately dream of exporting this new and still inchoate mode of governance across the globe. Given the size of the demonstrations against the Iraq war, it might be tempted to allocate itself the civilising mission of bringing about world peace.

The modernising process goes global

Since the late 1980s, democracy has made progress in several parts of the world. Contrary to George Orwell's expectations, dictators never managed to control their citizens' thoughts. Most dictators are overthrown by non-violent protests. Some of the Asian revolutions of the late 1980s were successful: the Philippines, Thailand, South Korea, and Bangladesh. Others were not: Burma and China (Tiananmen). In 1989, the citizens of Eastern Europe followed their lead: in two years, 350 million Europeans were liberated almost without a struggle. In 1994, South Africa ended apartheid. In 2000, Indonesia overthrew Suharto and Serbia did the same to Milošević.

As Sociovision and its partners began to gather data on socio-cultural change in China, India, Russia, the Middle East, Latin America and elsewhere, our hypothesis that the modernising process is contagious was confirmed. It is now firmly implanted in Western society and has spread to other societies and civilizations, which both imitate their Euro-American predecessors and invent their own ways of life. Everywhere, the process tends to emancipate and vitalise people and encourage the self-organisation of a network-based social fabric. If we are simultaneously able to galvanise this process and use it as a springboard, then we will have a much better chance of making the 21st century a peaceful one.

Sociovision's new research suggests that the same learning processes and the same changes that took place in Europe and America are now occurring elsewhere. But the process does not follow the same series of regular steps that it took in the West. Sometimes it skips a stage. Whilst the precursor states had to invent their future at every step, other people and societies have the advantage of Western products, technology and experience. They can go much faster.

As a result, the clear sequence of First and Second Modernity that we saw in the West becomes confused elsewhere. Out of this whirlpool emerge socio-cultural innovations that sometimes take the world by storm.

New laboratories of modernity

Invented in the West, the race to consume has already affected the behaviour of large numbers of ex-Soviets, as well as a significant proportion of Asians. The presence of desirable products and prestigious brands stimulates people's appetite and drives them to keep up with their neighbours, just as it did in Western Europe fifty years earlier. However, sections of these populations are already developing immunity to such stimuli and are beginning to think about self-expression, self-realisation and meaningfulness. This leads them to adopt a critical stance towards forms of consumption that characterise the early stages of modernity.

We first observed this combination in Russia. It struck us even in the first life histories of people who had received a higher education that we collected in Moscow in 1990. People combined a hedonistic and consumerist voracity, typical of the First Modernity, with well advanced practices of personal development, self-analysis and self-improvement and a search for meaningfulness – all things which had not emerged in the West until the Second Modernity. These life histories showed that in both Western and Soviet society, people's need for meaning was born of disappointment, although not the same disappointment. In the West, people felt conned by the race to consume. In Russia, there was a gradual realisation, developed over countless conversations accompanied by bottles of vodka and apple tarts, that they had been gulled by the reigning ideology and by the idea that Russia was one of the world's guiding lights. Here, the temptations of rabid consumerism confronted people who were already very aware of both themselves and their inner worlds, and so who were more able to avoid them. Unlike in Europe and North America, these temptations did not completely intoxicate people and they did not make up for the lack of meaningfulness.

In China, consumption has grown massively and, at the same time, people have won some autonomy. Sexual taboos have fallen away and people are experimenting in the same way as Westerners did when they grew tired of consumption. Love marriage, divorce, cohabitation and contraception are all increasingly common. Educated young women are choosing to remain single and free to select their partners. People aim to have a happy relationship. Latent human potential is being realised; people are more in tune with themselves, smarter, more concerned with meaningfulness and less easy to manipulate. Socio-political conditioning is being relaxed; work communities and neighbourhood communities, which used to allow the party to observe and control people's lives, are losing their importance; they have become more like service or mutual help networks that provide new opportunities for even greater independence and autonomy.

New intercommunication tools are rapidly spreading throughout China. They synergise with a society whose cultural traditions mean that it is naturally inclined to develop family and social networks. They spread faster than in some Western countries, where they are slowed down by what is left of hierarchical and centralised organisations or by the weight of investment in older technology.

In most parts of the world where modernity has arrived more recently, networked PCs, the Internet and mobile phones have arrived at the same time as the products and brands typical of societies of mass consumption. These technologies undermine mass-structures, strengthen interpersonal relations and autonomy and encourage the development of a network-based social fabric. China, Korea, India, Russia and Eastern Europe are already well advanced in this process. Although this process develops more or less rapidly and in slightly different ways depending on the culture of the countries in question, it seems to be universal.

This creates a double overlap that Western countries never experienced:

1. Phenomena that are typical of well-developed Modernities appear at the same time as the enchantment of consumption.

2. Products, postures and attitudes that emerged in the West meet and interact with completely different civilisations. These new, original and varied combinations create the ideal conditions for innovation.

As a result, many countries that once lagged behind, as well as the deprived areas of French, German and English cities and suburbs, can become laboratories churning out innovations that may sweep the world and inspire the West. This is taking place at a time when the most modern Westerners are increasingly open to Chinese, Arabic, Celtic and many other cultures. It is tempting to suggest that what started out as a Western civilising process is becoming a global and inter-cultural co-production.

A process that is well under way, but that could still be reversed

A series of multiple, overlapping factors drive the development of modernity in non-Western countries, making it an incredibly powerful phenomenon. Even though governments sometimes play a major role in initiating and accelerating the modernising process, as in China, it is always ordinary people who carry it forward. Their enthusiasm makes it likely to succeed. Modernity infiltrates society through multiple channels.

Governments. Since Deng Xiaoping, the Chinese authorities have encouraged private wealth accumulation and the race to consume. The government artificially stimulates household consumption and people's desire for refrigerators, clothes, televisions, motorbikes, cars, processed foods, etc.

Information. The public, and especially the young, have access to a wealth of information about the modern world. Governments are relinquishing control of television, although at different speeds in different places. It shows the West, modern lifestyles and Western politics; it awakens or reinforces people's desires, makes them think and activates latent human potential. The Internet has joined radio and television. Those who can are sucked into the race to consume and to acquire status symbols.

A myth of modernity. In many of these countries, just like in France in the 1950s and 1960s, a myth of modernity has established itself. The idea, for instance, that it is good for China to modernise has come to dominate. This is no way affects people's pride in being Chinese, and so they want to be modern, but they are looking for Chinese forms of modernity.

The use of technology and appliances that emerged in a changing Euro-American society have helped their new users to have experiences that free up their feelings and emotions and promote independence and heterarchical networks. These include such things as household appliances, motorbikes, mobile phones, the contraceptive pill and neuroleptic medicines. The Internet has also begun to change the way in which many young people from developing countries live their lives.

In the West, peoples' struggle for emancipation had been one of the most powerful drivers of the modernising process. In that search for emancipation they threw themselves into consumerism and demanded new information and communication technology. These new habits and technologies in turn strengthened their autonomy and their ability to form networks. In other cultures like China, people's growing independence and autonomy has resulted less from the struggle to emancipate themselves and more from the daily practice of consumerism and the use of these new interpersonal communication technologies.

Women played a primary role in spreading new ways of life. They were and remain both the principal vectors and the principal beneficiaries of Western socio-cultural change. With the help of the media, women's liberation reached the rest of the world – not just South and East Asia, but also the Arab world. Across the world, women transmitted individualising and personalising forms of socio-cultural change that also undermined authority.

The phenomenon is so marked that it has already destabilised demographers' predictions: the population of non-Western countries (including those who are still economically underdeveloped) is growing much more slowly than predicted, largely because women have begun to escape from traditional models, to behave independently and to control their fertility. Even in the most rigorously Islamic countries, women are modernising.

A predisposition towards personal emancipation. It seems that emancipation and happiness are somehow irresistible. Humans are quite capable of building hierarchical societies, making the most of superior force and submitting to coercion. But they undoubtedly have a tendency to favour personal emancipation when it is not too dangerous. They probably have a genetically determined drive to strive for freedom in certain contexts. Men and women can survive oppression, but when they see that other people have slipped the shackles of constraint and grinding poverty, and they realise that they could do the same, then they begin to dream of freedom and start to act. Across the world, large parts of the population are drawn towards everyday freedoms as well as democratic ideals.

Modernity really began to affect the entire planet in the 1990s, but it will not necessarily be adopted overnight. Some changes will take generations. And there will be resistance. This may be strong, but probably less strong than the modernising process itself.

Modernity undermines despotism and breaks down the traditional social fabric and traditional paradigms. Despotism and conservative social forces fight against this invasion. In many cases though, authoritarian leaders try to promote certain aspects of modernity, even though they are aware that modernity forms an indivisible whole. Once it has been awoken, telecommunication is just as hard to control as spiritualist networks and the process of emancipation. Authoritarian powers will probably be unable to resist the dynamic of emancipation and the viral spread of technology.

In tense situations, forms of religious fundamentalism sometimes manage to erect effective barricades. In the early 21st century, Islamic fundamentalism has met modernity head on and seemed to present a perfectly united front.

However, even where resistance is strongest (in some Islamic countries or among certain immigrant communities in the UK, France and Germany), change is under way. Women are struggling for freedom, birth rates are falling and a middle-class is emerging.

In the early 1980s, Cofremca charted socio-cultural change in the Lebanon. This showed that even rigorously Muslim families, which were highly critical of and aggressive towards modernity, had adopted a wide range of very modern postures and habits of which they were probably scarcely conscious. These had to do with the daily life of the household and children and the ways in which they lived in their homes; those families that had the means tried to give each child a separate room, thereby offering them some autonomy. They had begun to move towards modernity. More recently, the same evolution has been particularly marked among Iranian youth. And surveys carried out in Saudi Arabia show that, even there, women and their households are following the path of modernisation.[56]

Given these observations, it seems to me that the Muslim world and the West are unlikely to experience the sort of clash of civilisations discussed by Samuel Huntington.[57] It could only happen if the West paved the way for it by committing repeated blunders.

Stimulating challenges

At the start of the 21st century, the planet and the human race face a series of grave challenges that threaten our societies and civilisations and the survival of the human species.

Environmental equilibrium (at the level of climate, air, water, energy and biodiversity) is threatened by human activity and by the disruption of complex physical systems with which we are still unfamiliar. Vital resources (like food, water and energy) are running out. Our methods of production and industrial organisation are clearly not sustainable. Collectively, we need to find answers to these threats and apply them coherently.

Modern life and technology encourage the emergence and worldwide transmission of resistant microbes, new viruses and new vectors of infection. Other epidemics will probably take up where AIDS and CJD leave off. Humanity is thus presented with an unprecedented public health problem, in the face of which all countries need to work together.

---

56   The survey was carried out by Reachmass in 2003 and analysed by Sociovision's Daniel Weber. *Unveiling Modernity among Saudi Arabian Women*, The Sociovision International Observer, No. 3, September 2003.

57   Huntington S. *The clash of civilizations and the remaking of world order*. New York: Simon and Schuster, 1996.

Across the planet and within some countries, socio-economic imbalances are now vast. Extreme poverty rubs shoulders with unprecedented wealth. In the early 21st century, the inhabitants of the world's poorest countries (almost one and a half billion people) live in a state of absolute poverty, and their numbers are increasing. A globalised civil society aware of this situation would be unable to tolerate the situation for long. If we have to rely on egotistical nation-states to reduce economic imbalance and regulate migratory flows, then we run the risk of seeing an increase in tension, especially in certain sensitive regions of the world.

The challenge of terrorism is local, national and global. The terrorism of rough estates, of ethnic groups and of fundamentalist Islam can all join up in complex networks. Modern weapons technology gives these small networks the capacity to inflict massive amounts of damage. This threat should encourage us to coordinate our anti-terrorist activities and set up a global police force.

Be they originally Sicilian, Russian, Chinese or more heterogeneous, mafia networks are making use of new technologies to spread their sphere of influence more widely. They can escape the authorities so long as different countries are unable to act in concert. In the absence of some degree of global governance, it would not be unthinkable for the mafia and corruption networks to become one of the world's major powerhouses.

The resurgence of warrior religions presents us with another threat. Modernity favours a culture of emotions and a neo-spiritualist re-awakening. The shock of modernity, poverty and a sense of rejection encourage revolt and the search for communitarian identities. These factors combine to strengthen the development of hard-line communities brandishing religious banners. Cultural and ideological camps might split along religious lines. In the early years of the 21st century, religious extremism has grown in strength and its different variants (Islamic, Hindu, Jewish and Christian) have spurred one another on. But perhaps a pacifist and secular form of social governance, once created, could prevent this process, which is already under way, from spiralling out of control.

Whether they are ecological, epidemiological or socio-economic, whether they arise from terrorist, mafia or religious groups, these threats are both global and local. Growing awareness on the part of civil society and the world's governments of just how serious these multiple threats really are increases the pressure on us to create some form of coordinated planetary government. It encourages us to establish local and global early-warning, analysis and joint-action systems. It encourages civil collectives to emerge and to intervene. It encourages states to engage in dialogue with a variety of NGOs, to build consensus with other states and to look for ways to endow inter-state organisations with effective and legally sanctioned means of military intervention.

We need to see the emergence of a form of participative and innovative global governance that can bring peace. The processes described earlier in this chapter all tend to act in its favour: the decline of the nation-state, the growing involvement of other, non-state entities and regulatory systems, the spread of the civilising process across the world and the global nature of the challenges we face. But the special pleading and narrow self-interest of local and national groups are still powerful. Nothing is yet certain.

The United States: a source of uncertainty

At the time of writing, the USA was the principal source of uncertainty. America's awareness of its military superiority, as well as its economic strength and vitality, leads it to underestimate the real importance of networks of states and of global civil society. As a consequence, the US continues to act like a sovereign and bellicose state. Perhaps it is ambitious beyond its means. It feels sovereign and is looking for another state or another territorial entity that it can think of as its enemy. In the mid-1990s, conservative think tanks dreamed up dramatic scenarios in which China played this role. Today, the American administration has turned its attention to the states that make up the so-called axis of evil, to Iraq and the rest of the Islamic world. In reality, however, the enemy is likely to be much more nebulous than that and it is no easy task to say who is a friend and who is an enemy.

On the 11th September 2001, America was attacked on its own soil and reacted patriotically. George W. Bush and the neo-conservatives made use of this. The most conservative elements of the American elite abandoned their dream of an isolationist America and began to support the idea of an American empire that would use its military muscle to pacify the world and bring about Good.

However, things are not so straightforward. America's potentially imperialist approach is unlikely to give rise to a *pax americana* to which the rest of the world will peacefully subscribe. Neither humanists, nor nationalists, nor Islamists will accept it without a struggle. A worldwide network of states and NGOs would probably spring up to protect the planet from American hegemony. Moreover, America's military superiority, wealth and economic strength are probably insufficient to allow it to organise, discipline and pacify a recalcitrant world. In today's world, hard power is probably only decisive if it is backed up by soft power.

The neo-conservative camp is much better organised and much more active in the United States that in any other modern country. And it has considerable influence over large parts of the media. But it is not in the majority. Even though this wave of patriotism has blurred the range of public opinion, there is nothing to suggest that it has fundamentally altered the course of American socio-cultural change. The personal positions of most Americans and North-West Europeans remain profoundly marked by the civilisational process described in this book. Since the late 1960s, Americans have taken great steps forward in terms of their personal autonomy, vitality and capacity to find happiness and meaning and live their lives in wiser ways. And the social fabric in both America and Europe has been radically transformed by the proliferation of single-storey networks and sociosystems, which it is hard to influence. Beyond a certain point, it is probably the American population itself that would reject further authoritarian measures and further wars.

The war in Iraq has damaged confidence in America and split Europe down the middle. It has also reduced the UN's influence. It might yet prove to be a turning point that sends history off in the direction of increasing tension and antagonism.

So far, however, all is not lost. There is also an optimistic scenario. Faced with a series of setbacks, America might elect informed and capable leaders before the end of the decade. They, along with Europe and others, might then try to build a vast consensus that would allow us to move towards forms of planetary governance that confront the challenges faced by both humanity and the planet.

Conclusion
The challenge of our times:
building wiser governance

In a few short decades, hundreds of millions of Westerners (the majority of the populations in question) have undergone a profound anthropological change and this has provoked equally radical change in the social fabric. They have developed more direct, less mediated contact with their physical senses, their emotions and their intuitions and this has allowed them to access their own inner worlds and those of other people, as well as to become more autonomous and better able to live their personal and family lives in smarter and wiser ways. They have begun to develop new representations of the world, which are centred around living people and a new, predominantly humanist, moral system. A new social fabric has woven itself into existence. This is made up of networks and overlapping, single-storey sociosystems that are extremely resistant to hierarchy and to constraints imposed from on high.

Westerners are changing more and more. By integrating their different faculties – sensory, emotional, intuitive, cognitive – and improving their sense and understanding of how they and others operate, they are learning each day from their moments of satisfaction and disappointment and living in ways that take into account their physical and social environment. They have not all reached the same stage of development. For instance, some of them watch reality TV shows and use them to better understand their own emotional and sexual responses, while others read cutting-edge neurobiology texts and consider the implications for their own lives. But they are all involved in a learning process, even if it is not always consciously chosen.

At the same time, the life sciences have entered a period of very rapid progress. They will soon reach a better understanding of the way that people live their lives and operate in society. Our understanding of ourselves – an intuitive understanding garnered from daily experience as well as from our scientific knowledge – is growing and seems likely to take major steps forward. Because of this, we are individually and collectively becoming better equipped to face what will, no doubt, be significant challenges.

In the last third of the 20th century, the architecture and functioning of societies in the West have changed in astonishing ways. Although hierarchical authority and social norms have broken down, and although the self-determination displayed by individuals and collectives has massively increased, these societies have managed to regulate themselves in such a way as to create peace, order and harmony. The social fabric that has self-organized promotes personal development and gives people opportunities for emotional and mental happiness, without harming the functioning and effectiveness of the whole. The result is a society that loves peace and harmony and that, in the main, manages to produce them. Nevertheless, serious deviancy and violence are still present. Although these are very limited, if not negligible when compared to the horrors of the two world wars, our peaceful society is troubled by them, and is looking for ways to manage them.

It seems, in spite of everything, that Western man's long, humanist quest for personal emancipation and happiness could give rise to a society that guarantees liberty and self-realisation for individuals, as well as peaceful and effective self-regulation for the collective. If this promise is realised in the 21st century, then the last few decades will look like the beginning of a new era.

But nothing could be less certain. In the future, our current era may come to look like a temporary oasis of happiness. Perhaps we have already left this happy age behind. In North America and Europe, unresolved problems mean that increasing numbers of men and women, and especially the young, feel rejected and castrated, and cut off from society. This leads to dissidence and violence. Growing numbers of people feel embittered and are turning to protest. We see alienation, urban violence, terrorism, frontal challenges to those in power and the emergence of warring religions. If we do not manage to deal rapidly with a number of major social divisions and rising tension, then they may crystallize. The authorities may be tempted to take a hard line, and in so doing, provoke equally hard-line reactions. In such circumstances, it would be difficult to return to a situation where tensions were lower. We have to act now, if it is not already too late. **If our societies are to build on and develop the predominantly peaceful trends of the late 20th century, then they urgently need wiser systems of governance.**

We can only speak of the future in terms of tendencies and scenarios. There is no room for firm forecasts or predictions. Broadly speaking, there are three main sets of scenarios:

- In the most catastrophic of these, the world splits once more into a small number of hostile blocs, which may or may not be associated with particular territories. These blocs might be formed around powerful and authoritarian states attached to their sovereignty, religions or old and new philosophies, or traditional civilisations.

They could drag the world into a new round of potentially destructive conflict that might also raise tensions within the different blocs.

- Scenarios that envisage a 'New Middle-Ages' are more interesting. They combine the Middle Ages and the New Age. The world is divided and much of it is prey to disorder and violence, but there are islands, archipelagos and networks of fulfilment, harmony and peace.

- In other scenarios, the modernising process realises its humanistic potential. Civic entrepreneurs become more active and more audacious. Inspired leaders manage to catalyse transformative energy. Traditionally monolithic and authoritarian companies engage in a modernist learning process. In most countries, the authorities loosen their bureaucratic regulation, develop policies that allow most people to find happiness and fulfilment, and talk on an equal footing with other stakeholders, like public authorities, companies and civil society. The result, at different levels, would be a balanced and wiser form of social governance. The modernising process would flourish in the West and affect the rest of the planet. The Third Modernity would lead us towards humanistic and tolerant societies that were also peaceful and ordered. They would be well equipped to face the threats that hang over us in the 21st century.

Is it within our power to guide History down this peaceful and humanist path? Can we facilitate this major step along the path of progress of which modern people dream?

If the observations and analyses put forward in this book are sufficiently close to reality, then this project is no chimaera. Without wishing to underplay the strength of old habits or the powerful urge to resist, it is essentially a question of easing its emergence, of assisting at a birth. It is a matter of reinforcing and accelerating these deep-rooted trends that grew in strength throughout the 1990s – trends that are driven by ordinary people, innovators and forward-thinking elites. Everybody can contribute in their own way, be they ordinary citizens who want to participate, central or local government officers, employees, middle or senior managers, members of charities or NGOs, participants in modern mouvances, teachers, consultants, social innovators, entrepreneurs, parents, students, or simply people involved in family and friendship networks. Everybody can help or, if necessary, force the hand of those authorities and organisations that hinder the modernising process. Everybody, when faced with the temptation of combat and violence, can struggle to engage others in dialogue.

Rather than grand schemes dictated from above, it is cooperation at many levels and temporary alliances between well-intentioned individuals, groups and organisations that will be the most effective and useful midwives at this birth.

I cannot shake off the idea that we are at a crossroads. If it is an optical illusion, then at least it is a tenacious one.

I would like to read the book that my successors at Sociovision will doubtless write twenty or thirty years from now. Making use of improved techniques of sociological analysis, informed by work in the social sciences, they will tell us whether and how history has exploited the potential for humanism, tolerance and harmony that is latent in contemporary society, or, alternatively, whether and how we have been dragged into another century of violence, discord and division. And they will describe the winding path of history as it has led us towards progress or disaster. Or perhaps they will show that there is still everything to play for.

Afterword
Entering the Third Modernity

I finished work on this book in September 2003 and have just re-read it. The intervening five years have made it clear that the civilising process I tried to describe has continued to unfold along the lines I originally suggested, and has done so faster than ever. At the same time, we still cannot be sure of the eventual outcome.

Interconnections and inter-reactions of all kinds continue to feed into one another and create new dynamic systems. As people change, they transform society as a whole; this, in its turn, reinforces the changes that individuals are undergoing and contributes to the process of developing new social forms. Both individually and collectively we adopt new technologies whose application and use brings about further change. As parents change the way they are with their children, so those children grow and develop very differently from how they would have done a generation earlier. And they, in their turn, raise their own children differently. More and more leaders and innovators sense the directions in which these changes are heading; in response, they develop yet further innovations which are seized upon and further reinforce the process of change.

Since the beginning of the new century, ordinary people, emerging networks and organisations, as well as businesses and government, have tried a little harder to keep in step with this civilising and humanising process. So history is perhaps leaning towards a relatively harmonious version of the Third Modernity. A Modernity in which, both locally and globally, society is more aware of its current shape and of the changes it is undergoing, and more inclined to play an active part in shaping its own future. A Modernity in which a good number of ordinary people, innovators, think tanks and younger business and government leaders will cooperate implicitly to put in place wiser and more participative systems of governance, which will help to reduce the risk of conflict and violence. In short, a Modernity which might see humanity at large trying, in more self-aware ways, to take its own destiny in hand.

1) People increasingly demand peace and harmony

If you have read this book, you will have understood that, throughout the last third of the 20th century, ordinary people took active steps to reduce the levels of unhappiness, meaninglessness and violence around them. Right across the Western world, a growing number of individual initiatives, networks, NGOs and other organisations has given rise to a sort of informal social institution that is reducing unhappiness, injustice and the causes of violence in our societies. This system, which seeks to immunise against, prevent and repair damage to the social fabric, plays an essential role in ensuring the relatively peaceful equilibrium in which we live in the West. But the level of aggressive, anti-social behaviour is still too high for modern people in search of peace and harmony.

One new development emerged and gathered strength throughout the '90s: modern societies no longer hold back in the demands they make on the authorities for greater personal freedom; they also demand greater order and harmony and, even, more police. The authorities, whether at a national or a local level, are ill-prepared to respond to this demand, which can seem paradoxical. They have become a little more aware that they cannot primarily rely on authoritarian or violent measures, because these can serve to provoke further violence. Rather, they are trying to develop dissuasive systems and some early examples of this can already be seen. A profusion of automated speed control systems can be seen on the roads, with offenders prosecuted automatically. In the UK, CCTV cameras everywhere monitor people's behaviour in public places. In parallel, governments are learning to regulate those social processes which are most divisive, for example by increasing the number of schemes designed to integrate disadvantaged young people into wider society.

These trends are encouraging the development and installation of local, national and international public authorities that seek to act therapeutically. These new forms of governance are coming into being alongside the system of social immunisation, prevention and cure that I have just described, and they will know, when the time is ripe, how to invent new means of dissuasion or prevention.

2) Collective, systemic intelligence gathers weight and comes to influence the course of events

Since the beginning of the century, powerful waves of collective intelligence have helped to shape the changes that are taking place in societies and organisations.

To understand how these waves come about, we need to remember the revolution that, in the space of half a century, has transformed the personality of ordinary Europeans and Americans. Their understanding of the world is not what it was in 1950: daily life has taught them a broader, more systemic appreciation of the world around them and taught them to respond to events in more considered and autonomous ways.

Systemic appreciation. The resurgence of empathy has been the deciding factor. It began in the 1950s and led a growing number of people to perceive others not as objects but as living creatures, to understand them, to feel and anticipate the intricate nexus of actions and reactions which linked them to each other and, finally, to develop a global and systemic awareness of what was happening. An event or an action came to be seen as emerging from, and feeding back into, this nexus. In a clear break from traditional European culture, the vast majority of our contemporaries now tends to experience life not as a series of states and facts but as a network of systems and processes.

Autonomous responses. In parallel, ordinary people, men and women, young and old, rich and poor, are carving out more autonomy for themselves. They respond to things in their own ways. More and more people are breaking free of old prejudices and ways of thinking and deciding what they think for themselves. Faced with an event or a situation, their reactions are less guided than in the past by the fixed ideas of the social class, groups and camps to which they belong. Rather, their reactions are increasingly shaped by their own individual impressions and burgeoning awareness.

This transformation underpins a series of waves of collective intelligence. Those whose personalities have been radically transformed do not exist in isolation. Their empathy wires them in to the reactions and responses of others. Together, they come to understand how things work. They resonate with others to whom they draw close, even if only in passing. The sum of their individual responses is at the source of the numerous transient communities and emotional waves that we see emerging and resisting conventional classification and that are often able to change the whole course of events.

The American war in Iraq has inspired one such wave. People in several European countries – often in stark contrast to the positions taken by their governments and political leaders – felt very early on that the war threatened to destabilise a fragile system and to set the world on the road to disaster. This wave of feeling led to mass demonstrations and helped to change the way that people saw Tony Blair as well as contributing to the fall of the Spanish and Italian pro-war governments.

Some of these waves of collective intelligence take shape slowly, then suddenly become mainstream. So it is that the growing **awareness of**

threats to the environment has gained ground over the last few decades amongst ordinary people thinking for themselves, independently of the ideological stance taken by Green parties. These people's growing tendency to be aware of the systemic interconnectedness of things has made them more open and responsive to the advice of experts in the field and to news of dramatic droughts and floods, devastating hurricanes, hotter summers, glacial melting, the disappearance of bees and the destruction of coral reefs, rising oil prices and so on. But over the last few years, helped by Al Gore's film *An Inconvenient Truth* and the Stern Report, this environmental awareness has suddenly assumed new weight and importance in the West (and perhaps across a good proportion of the planet) and begun to play a significant part in influencing the behaviour of governments and companies.

There is growing **animosity towards predatory, uncaring and profit-driven businesses**. A good many companies and banks seem to be focused on short-term financial profits. This puts them at risk. A wave (and many smaller ripples) of collective intelligence have damaged their vitality and cohesiveness and undermined their public image. This threatens their stability in the event of a crisis. The whole capitalist system in its current form could be at risk.

Between 2004 and 2007, much of the French population from across the political spectrum came to share a **dream of an emerging society**. They sensed the arrival of a peaceful society that would prioritise happiness, be more humanist and less profit-driven, more participative and less hierarchical, and respectful of people, children and life and the environment as a whole. They had an embryonic idea of the future that included several possible scenarios. Society as they dreamt it seemed about to take root and flourish in contemporary France, but people generally felt that their leaders were trying to take them in a different direction. They were angry about this and wondered whether collectively they might not be strong enough to turn things round. This collective dream was more or less clearly identified by some major players on the political scene and they made use of it. In the presidential elections of 2007 this dream finally combined with the statements of several political leaders to undermine, perhaps permanently, a series of mental and social models that had paralysed French governance for several decades. It sidelined a generation of political leaders and weakened the whole apparatus of party politics. It shook the traditional system of theatrically contrived opposition between political camps, left and right, both of which were locked in outdated, adversarial positions. It reduced the influence of civil servants and the *'noblesse d'Etat'*[1]. It placed more women in positions of power and opened up the possibility of participative democracy.

This collective intelligence is, without doubt, an important aspect of the system of wiser governance that is being sought. It's a form of intelligence that is not just intellectual but encompasses physical sensations, emotion, intuition, empathy and intentionality. It is a systemic intelligence that decodes the meaning, direction and significance of a given situation and that tends towards action. As it strengthens, people become less guided by their prejudices and established ideological positions and arguments; they find themselves less imprisoned in any particular large-scale, socio-economic identity and less influenced by the propaganda and manipulative advertising of the powers that be. So, we are leaving behind a period that we might describe as a democracy of opinions and entering a democracy of impressions, feelings and personal strategies that can all coalesce. Collective intelligence can be seen as the equivalent in a bottom-up society of public opinion in a top-down society. Public opinion is largely shaped by the authorities, influential organisations (like political parties, trades unions and the church), entrenched ways of thinking and the memory of old battles long ago won or lost. Collective intelligence, on the other hand, is shaped by individuals' flashes of awareness and intuitions as they meet, interact and, with the help of empathy, somehow coalesce. It can foster real innovation.

3) A growing number of leaders and innovators able to imagine and bring about sociosystemic innovations and guide social processes

The organisational culture of many old-style public sector organisations and large companies is still imbued with the monolithic, hierarchical character of the societies that they were born into. Old mental models prevent their leaders and innovators from adopting systems thinking. They are not socially aware, they cannot sense the latent potential in the people around them, nor the deficits that might be made up, nor the dynamics that cry out to be embraced. This blindness serves only to shore up the persistent failures, obstructiveness, paralysis and conservatism of the past.

But women and new generations of men are assuming influential positions. In society as a whole, but also in the heart of big business, institutions and politics, socially-aware leaders and innovators are now taking their place.

---

1   Title of a 1989 book by Pierre Bourdieu, the term *Noblesse d'Etat* describes the governing and administrative elite, suggesting a new sort of technocratic aristocracy.

They are change agents. They have realised that this is an age that welcomes sociological innovations that improve people's lives, that facilitate the running and self-governance of society and that feed back into, and strengthen, themselves. Theirs is an acute intuition in matters of societal dynamics and latent trends; they can make out still emergent patterns and major social currents; they naturally grasp reality in a systemic way, understanding its chains of action and interaction; and they are always one step ahead. Because of this, the innovations that they develop have a good chance of meeting a latent demand and of generating even further demand. These innovations serve to encourage the emergence of new social forms. We could call them sociogenic or sociostructuring.

Some of these innovations underpin Web 2.0. Relying on the extraordinary possibilities offered by the Web, ordinary people are creating **blogs, forums and social networks.** Sparked off by one individual or by a small group of like-minded people, each tends to focus on the intimate thoughts or feelings of one individual, or to promote a political stance or interest group, or to provide information on a particular disease or illness, or to bring together players of a computer game, and so on. Some of these sites flourish and are able to create networks of connections and discussion and to generate self-sustaining content. Each is the seed of its own social network. Even when they are successful, they often remain small in scale but, together, combine to create a sociological phenomenon of enormous proportions.

At the same time, other innovators have created **search engines, web portals** or websites that are in themselves complex sociological systems. In a few short years some of them, such as Google, Yahoo, Wikipedia or Facebook, have become giants, contributing to the self-organisation and vitality of society.

Other innovations depend less directly on new computer and communication technologies. In business, for instance, change agents launch managerial and organisational learning approaches and systems as a way of escaping bureaucratic constraints and fostering participation, creativity and collective intelligence. Other companies develop completely new business plans centred on the strengths and weaknesses of developing countries or on the demand for truly sustainable growth. But today most large companies are profoundly divided. Alongside these change agents, and at times in conflict with them, other senior executives are centralising and reasserting their authority.

Here and there, a few senior military officers are asking themselves what the army would look like if its central goal was no longer to win wars but to work intimately with the surrounding social environment and help to create a viable society.

In Vienna, Lyons, Paris and elsewhere, the city authorities are setting up sophisticated free bicycle-hire schemes that are improving people's day-to-day lives.

The range of examples that I have just given underlines the breadth of the phenomenon. These innovations are welcomed because they facilitate governance and self-governance in today's complex societies. They address the new sensibilities, sufferings and problems that accompany the civilising process. They make life easier, enable us to find moments of happiness and ease our pain. They bring with them greater personal freedom, new possibilities for informed choice and widen the range of connections that we can make. They help people to free themselves from convention and authority and to influence events directly. There are opportunities for growth, to enrich one's personality, to discover its unsuspected facets, to learn new skills and to become more creative and innovative. These innovations also allow us to cooperate, share, adapt in real time and participate in vibrant groups and collectives that, in turn, contribute to social fluidity, self-regulation and harmony. They allow us to find new sources of meaning in that they are good for the environment, people, children, health, and so on. Participation in these social networks has a considerable effect on society as a whole. It changes the way we communicate and behave, opens up new horizons, connects us to new mental and social worlds and saps hierarchy and convention of their residual influence.

This new wave of innovation will probably continue to strengthen over the coming years and, at the same time, wiser innovators will grow in number and the science of skilful life-navigation – made possible by an understanding of underlying processes – will improve.

4) Achieving a peaceful, multipolar world calls for a 'politics of civilisation'

A sort of diffuse anxiety impregnates our collective intelligence. Today we find ourselves trapped on a planet that we have entirely colonised and we are faced with two mutually reinforcing, life or death challenges: these are the threats to the environment and the threat from weapons of mass destruction, which I discussed in Chapter 10.

These threats require an urgent response, which must be both global and wise. It would be unreasonable to wait for a world government to deliver it. Short of a massive catastrophe or an unlikely extraterrestrial threat, the next few decades will not see the emergence of a planet-wide government with a monopoly of violence.

Nor are we seeing 'the end of history' under American rule. After the collapse of the Soviet Bloc, it did not seem impossible that the future held in store a unipolar planet dominated by the USA, which would act as the world's policeman and impose its values everywhere. Today, this scenario is scarcely credible. Indeed, by banking on its power, America has lost some of its actual influence. It remains by far the strongest economic, technological and military power, but its inability to capture Osama bin Laden, to re-establish order in Afghanistan and to extract itself from Iraq shows the world how impotent power can be. People, including the American people, are aware that in the complexities of the 21st century, even an overwhelmingly dominant power cannot lay down the law.

At the same time, others are gaining or regaining power and influence. Amongst them China and India are witnessing astonishing economic development. At the start of the 20th century China, with a quarter of the world's population, accounted for less than 1% of world GDP and 0.5% of international trade. Today, it accounts for 8-9% of GDP and international trade. If the trend continues, it will account for 20-25% in another twenty years. Chinese and Indian businesses compete with our own: not only because of lower wages, but also because of their excellence in certain fields of research and cutting-edge technology and because of the quality of their management.

So it seems that we are destined to live on a planet that is no longer bipolar (as in the Cold War), nor unipolar, but multipolar. A multipolar and warring world, one ruled by alliances and power struggles and awash with terrorism, would be catastrophic. We have to avoid such a scenario at all costs.

Our collective intelligence and some of the forces active in the civilising process favour the **self-organisation of a cooperative and multipolar world centred around the search for, and application of, creative compromise**. Such an outcome will become more likely if governments adopt a 'politics of civilisation'.

After the disasters of the Bush era, the USA will probably have more socially aware, and therefore wiser, governance.

Europe once stood for bellicose and authoritarian national governance, but is now on the verge of inventing a post-national form of governance: one that is both peaceful and participative. It is not trying to create a sovereign European state, but it is bringing into being a new political entity. This is not a government as such, but a system of governance in which states, regions, trades unions, organisations, companies and civil society itself participate in ways that are still unclear. In following this path, Europe walks in step with the civilising process and is creating a model for other continents to follow.

It is leading the way in green governance and is in a position to hasten the emergence of a new social contract (adapting to a society composed of people and networks rather than masses, a society that consists of shifting and particular cases rather than uniform and unchanging rules) and to work hand-in-hand with the emergence of a new form of capitalism (one that allies itself with sustainable growth and the socio-human dimension of life).

Face-to-face and mutually empathetic interactions between European political leaders and the personal involvement of those of them who feel they have a historic mission have played a decisive role in this novel socio-political construction. What works for Europe could serve as a model for other world leaders and should remain the hallmark of the 'European way of doing things'.

Religious fanaticism is a serious threat to world peace. The civilising process has reawakened the search for meaning. It brings with it a new and emotional spirituality and a resurgence in religious feeling. This feeds into the growing number of individualist, syncretic and mutually tolerant neo-spiritual practices that flourish everywhere. But in some situations it also encourages some of the followers of the three great monotheistic religions to find ways of sharing strong collective emotions and to adopt aggressive, fundamentalist positions that pose a serious threat to world peace.

Christian and Jewish fundamentalism are important influences on the American leadership. The American war on terror and on the so-called axis of evil has fostered the growth of violent Islamic fundamentalism around the world, rather than discouraging it.

The civilising process in Europe has led to the resurgence of a gentle and tolerant neo-spirituality that can have a pacificatory role in discouraging religious fundamentalism at home and abroad. Europe should be well placed to contribute to a modernisation of Islam, if it can learn to do so skillfully. But, over the last two decades, it has tended rather to fan the flames by allowing levels of alienation and hopelessness to grow among the young immigrant populations in Germany, England and France.

Indeed, across the modern world as a whole, those who have no hope of ever being able to carve out a life that suits them, a life that offers them some of the meaning that their education led them to expect, are a fertile seedbed for disaffection and violence.

Despite this failure, Europe remains one of the places where a 'politics of civilisation' could be explored and tested – a politics that would allow Islamic life to flourish, support young, second-generation immigrants and prepare the ground for Westerners and those of Arabic or Muslim origin to coexist fruitfully.

While the civilising process was, at the outset, a strictly Western phenomenon, Sociovision has observed that, since the early years of the new century, it is increasingly being co-created worldwide. Recent studies in China, South Korea, India, Russia, Saudi Arabia, Iran and elsewhere confirm this. This allows opportunities for dialogue and mutual understanding. For example, there are signs that synchronous developments in China and Europe could be drawing the two closer together. Over the last 50 years, Europe has broken with one of the old mainstays of its culture: its aggressive and predatory tendencies are giving way to a culture that seeks harmony and a new alliance between mankind and nature. A similar change, which bodes well for the future, is emerging in China. Discussions at one recent forum[2] show that there is a new awareness of the depth of the environmental problems facing us among society at large and the authorities in Europe and China. There is a growing willingness to put an end to the environmental destruction that has characterised Chinese economic growth over recent decades. A tendency to seek to work with nature and the environment, traditionally a feature of Chinese culture, seems to be re-emerging. If this pattern is confirmed, it could form the basis for a new level of cooperation between the two regions.

Three great civilisations in flux now meet one another. The civilisations of China and India are much older than ours (indeed, they are as old as the Pharaonic civilisation of Egypt) and they are still alive and vibrant. They interest us, attract us and have much to teach us.

---

2   With the support of the *Fondation pour le Progrès de l'Homme*, the China-Europa Forum brought together, over four days in October 2007, a thousand Chinese and European participants in several dozen European cities.

At the same time, it seems to me that a wave of collective intelligence is emerging in Europe and North America which tends to make us, collectively, more humble. It leads us to doubt whether we can continue to impose our values and ways of thinking on the rest of the world. It helps us realise that the products, business models and scientific and technological advances that will shape our future won't only be invented by us, but by us, by them and by us all in collaboration.

A dialogue between these great civilisations could begin. For this to work, it will be essential to understand the different dynamics that could draw the West, India and China together or drive them apart and the different characteristics that could serve to build bridges and nourish fruitful and harmonious relations between us.

It is possible that our heads of state, encouraged by a wave of collective intelligence and by numerous change agents, will come to realise that they have a civilising mission. And it is possible that we will see a growing number of governments, networks and organisms start to take care of our civilisation, our species and our planet in a non-ideological but informed and wiser way.

5) The Third Modernity could lay the groundwork for a new era of human development

While the 18th and 19th centuries were illuminated by the idea of Progress, the notion that we were at the onset of a new era emerged in the West in the 20th century. Teilhard de Chardin foresaw the Omega Point. Science fiction writers talked of, among much else, astral man. The Age of Aquarius was much heralded. And our contemporaries at the start of the 21st century sense the arrival of a kind of society profoundly different from those of recent millennia: a humanist, heterarchical and cooperative society that seeks to work with nature. And they sense that it may even be possible to speed its arrival.

If the trends that we have sketched out continue, and particularly if wiser governance is put in place sooner rather than later, the 21st century will see humanity reuniting and returning to certain characteristics of the hunter-gatherer era.

Women today are once again finding a place in society similar to the one they held in hunter-gatherer societies. Among the hunter-gatherers, the respective status of men and of women was probably not clearly defined. Men were stronger but women gave birth; the cult of the Mother Goddess was a feature of many primitive societies. Then, with the onset of sedentarisation, property ownership and hierarchy, women tended to become inferior to men and God became a male figure. But today the tables are being turned.

For over 50,000 years, our hunter-gatherer ancestors simultaneously improved their chances of survival and populated the earth by learning to cooperate with one another and to live in harmony with nature. Their successors, first farmers and pastoralists then merchants and industrialists, began to appropriate, exploit and subjugate nature, all the while laying the emphasis on competition. Perhaps we are at the dawn of a new entente between the human race and nature, unless we are forced to taste its vengeful wrath.

Empathy flourished in these small bands of hunter-gatherers whose members all knew, and were able to adapt to, one another. They probably lived a life characterised by informality, spontaneity and heterarchy. Then the invention, 12,000 years ago, of agriculture and pastoralism increased the size and complexity of these collectives. In a few thousand years, we invented hierarchical organisations that became increasingly large, structured and stratified, and that allowed us to simplify complexity in the process. However, an explosion of complexity in the 20th century outweighed the capacity of hierarchy to simplify things. Now a new form of regulation and governance is emerging from the transformation that individuals and society are undergoing and from the revolution in communication technology, which puts everything instantly in touch with everything else and promotes complexity, self-organisation and self-regulation.

Among the hunter-gatherers, as in the most advanced 21st century societies, power is dispersed. It resides with ordinary people and those who know how to influence them. Leaders and innovators working in cooperation or competition will make use of advances in nanotechnology, molecular and cellular biology, neuroscience and social sciences and technologies, which open up enormous opportunities for us to navigate matter, energy, life and society with a steady and wiser hand.

Alain de Vulpian
9th February, 2008

Glossary

Adaptive Navigation

See *Navigation.*

Anomie

In 1897, Emile Durkheim used the word anomie in his book on suicide. He was describing the sense of meaninglessness found in a society where the norms, values and reference points that govern people's behaviour and maintain social order have disintegrated. Anomie is accompanied by a feeling of dissatisfaction and malaise.

Affective

Associated with feelings and emotions, rather than with the rational and logical or with the strictly physical. As the Second Modernity (q.v.) emerged, ordinary people became more and more affective as they deepened their connection with their own physicality and rationality.

Biodegradable

When the author uses this term to describe couples or relationships, he means more than simply 'temporary' or 'short-term'. When life no longer nourishes the relationship, the relationship ends. There is also the sense that the experience of one biodegradable relationship is not simply discarded but feeds our awareness and skills in handling future relationships, as compost feeds the garden.

Civilising Process

The German sociologist, Norbert Elias, suggested this idea when describing the fundamental transformation undergone by European societies from the Middle Ages to the 19th century. The transition from feudalism to the modern age was characterised, according to Elias, by the assertion of the power of the sovereign state, which had a monopoly on the use of legitimate violence within its borders, and by the spread of shame, self-restraint and the repression of our instinctual desires. This process came about through a complex web of interactions that involved, amongst others, peasants, the middle classes, courtiers, guilds and other organisations, princes, knights, priests, scholars, inventions and technical advances, social and economic structures, and so on.

The civilising process in which we are involved today is of a similar nature, but its principal actors and dynamics are radically different and it is leading us in a quite different direction. As before, no-one is steering the process; it self-organises; and its future course cannot be exactly foreseen. But it is not impossible, if we are able to grasp the main strands and interconnections that make up the process, to anticipate the most likely future scenarios and, therefore, to influence the direction that they take.

[Also referred to by the author as the 'modernising process'.]

Collectives

A general term encompassing more or less formal groups, societies, networks, associations, clubs, interest groups and discussion groups.

Entreprenautes

Entrepreneurs who are comfortable with, and operate primarily through the medium of, the Internet. (The French word *internaute* was early coined to denote a user of the Internet and *entreprenaute* is a play on that term.)

Erotico-affective

A term applied to relationships that value, and are characterised by, strong emotional ties and erotic attraction (more common in couples that have married for love than for social convenience). The modern couple lasts for as long as it continues to generate a relationship that is both erotic and affective.

Ethology

The science and study of behaviour and patterns of behaviour in man and other animals. It tends to focus on specific behaviours and patterns (like aggression or submission).

Governance

Used by the author to mean the whole system of interactions that lead an organism to move in a particular direction (rather than simply to take a decision, which may not be accompanied by the movement that was anticipated). The organism may be a family, a business, a nation, a political party or even the entire planet.

Governance is called 'smarter' or 'wiser' if it leads the organism to move in a direction that maintains or increases its vitality (self-actualisation) and that of the ecosystems of which it forms an integral part.

Halo of Emotion

One of the four types of quasi-community identified by the author. Modern people are sometimes swept up by waves of emotion or surges of compassion which draw them into a short-lived community of sentiment, be it at the level of their city, their country, their continent or the entire planet. Such a wave is termed a halo of emotion because of the blurred boundary and the luminescence that it shares with an astronomical halo.

Hedonists

The Hedonist current was one of the first to be identified and described by the author early in the 1950s. Hedonists clearly break with the old morality based on duty, sacrifice and acceptance. For them, happiness, pleasure and desire are no longer seen as illicit. They try to free themselves from the tendency to repress the desire for sensory pleasure and seek to escape the most irksome constraints.

Although fascinated in the decade before the war and in the 1950s and '60s by the search for 'perfect happiness', they would later come to focus more and more on sustaining those moments of pleasure, affection and well-being that make one's life happy.

Heterarchy

James A. Ogilvy describes the heterarchy paradigm in his book, *Creating Better Futures: scenario planning as a tool for better tomorrow*. Heterarchy is a characteristic of humanity. It is not about anarchy (i.e. the absence of hierarchy), but about there being a multiplicity of hierarchies. Different orders can overlap in such a way that A commands B, who commands C, who commands A or that X can inspire Y in some situations, whilst in others the reverse will be true. Gerard Fairtlough includes heterarchy with hierarchy and responsible autonomy as one of the three ways of getting things done that characterise Triarchy Theory.

Interconnections and Inter-reactions

The author uses the term *enchaînements d'enchaînements* to describe the interconnections (in Systems Thinking terms) that link sociosystems (q.v.) at different levels. Micro-sociosystems are linked to, and integrated into, sociosystems at a higher level; these, in turn, are integrated into those at a still higher level. All these sociosystems affect one another via a series of feedback loops. At the level of the civilising process itself, where the lives of ordinary people, the social fabric, technology or the behaviour of the authorities are transformed, these sociosystems interact in a series of interconnections and inter-reactions.

Intraception

Intraception is the name given by Cofremca to a socio-cultural current that it identified and described in the 1960s. It describes the capacity (primarily an 'intuitive' one rather than a cognitive one) to be aware of one's own situation vis-à-vis the rest of the world and to interpret and decode one's own state of mind and that of others. Linked to empathy, intraception can be seen as an aspect of being what is often called 'psychologically minded'. It brings with it a tendency to try to understand rather to judge others. The term was developed and used by US psychologist and statistician Alan L. Edwards (1914–94) in a purely psychological dimension, while it is used here in a socio-psychological dimension.

Introception

A term coined by developmental psychologist William Stern to describe the ability to be aware of one's own stance and position vis-a-vis the rest of the world. For Stern, introception was one of the three modalities of life and was related to the notion of the superego. The others being vitality and experience, related respectively to the id and the ego.

Isolates

One of the four types of quasi-community identified by the author. Modern people (q.v.) - amongst them the very poor and the very rich - may withdraw, more or less deliberately, into closed, fortress-like communities, including ghettoes, gated residential communities and religious sects.

Kindred spirits

One of the four types of quasi-community identified by the author. Kindred spirits – those we like – are relatively long-term groups of people brought together by similarities or by shared lifestyles, philosophical or spiritual positions, ethnic origins, cultural background, the sense of sharing material or cultural interests, or pastimes. This sense comforts them and allows them to feel they have a place in society and to identify with others.

Modern people

The author's observations of changing social structures and patterns and of changing attitudes and behaviour, characterised here as the First, Second and Third Modernity (q.v.), inevitably revealed that some people were 'ahead' of others in terms of this modernising process. Often it was possible to see that young people were ahead of their parents, or that the educated, urban middle classes were ahead of the working classes and those living and working in the countryside, or that Europe was ahead of America (or vice versa) in terms of any given trend. Again, some people were precursors (q.v.) or pioneers in this respect, while others joined in more or less willingly as the changes became increasingly widespread or fashionable.

In any 'Modernity' and for any of the trends discussed in this book, the term modern people (in French, *moderne*) describes those who are actively participating in, or who identify themselves with, that trend or current.

Modernity

First Modernity – the first phase of the modernising process (from the end of the Second World War into the age of mass consumption).

Second Modernity – the next stage, whose first signs were visible in the late 1960s and which we are still immersed in.

Third Modernity – the coming phase whose weak signals are just being detected and about whose shape and characteristics the author speculates towards the end of this book.

Motivation Research

A type of market research that is used to investigate and understand the psychosociological reasons why individuals buy specific goods, respond to specific advertising appeals and make specific brand choices.

Mouvances

One of the four types of quasi-community identified by the author. Mouvances unite people with shared goals or aims. They differ from 'Kindred Spirits' (q.v.) in that those who take part in Mouvances tend to feel that they are trying together to bring about a significant change, for example, in seeking to return to the 'religion of our fathers' or to support human rights in Third World countries. However, in many other ways, they are similar to groups of kindred spirits. They are bottom-up rather than top-down. Most of them are one-dimensional and do not insist on exclusivity – i.e. they do not ask people to renounce their other interests and they do not seek to bind them in forcibly. They are flexible, open, overlapping, biodegradable (q.v.), and can take on many different forms and operate at different levels of intensity. They feed off waves of emotion that may briefly intensify their members' sense of belonging or draw new members in.

Navigation

The author uses the term '*pilotage*' in the original. He talks of ordinary people 'navigating their lives' to convey the sense that living is a two-way process. We may choose a destination or set a course, but life's equivalents of bad weather, shoals, tides, reefs, doldrums and pirates require us to alter course and adapt constantly.

Strategic Opportunism (also called *Adaptive Navigation* by US sociological observers) is a term used by the author from the mid-1980s to describe an increasing trend for (mainly younger) people to accept that they could not predict or determine with any certainty the precise course that their lives would take. This new approach was more accepting of change and permitted more flexible and reactive ways of navigating life.

The term 'navigate more wisely' (*pilotage avisé*) is used to suggest the skilled navigator who can anticipate tides, currents and changes in the weather and bring the ship safely to harbour.

Polysensuality

So long as people's physical and emotional sensations had been inhibited, repressed and channelled, their relationship with the world had been primarily a visual one. But, starting in the 1950s, the author observed that little by little, and sometimes without realising it, they began to be aware of the variety of their emotions and sensory experiences. They stopped describing and representing and started to feel and experience. They developed a somatic awareness of their emotions and their feelings and began to lean more towards their emotions than their intellect. The author described this new awareness as polysensuality.

Precursor

Individuals, groups, societies and cultures where the characteristics, currents and tropisms (q.v.) of modernity were first identified are here called precursors. This term retains the biochemical sense of the word, suggesting that the precursor is not just an early example of something, but that it helps to shape and change subsequent instantiations. For example, emotions felt by a large number of people could be the precursors of new values that might eventually emerge at a subsequent stage of the civilising process (q.v.).

Self-Organisation(s)

Self-organisation is a spontaneous phenomenon of increasing order that runs counter to the much-discussed tendency for systems, when left to themselves, to descend into chaos (entropy). Self-organisations (the author's term *auto-organisations* means a self-organising organisation) often have emergent properties. Self-organisation is the inverse of top-down organisation. At the heart of the civilising process (q.v.), that part of social life and the social structure which self-organises spontaneously is increasing at the expense of that part which is organised by tradition, custom, the authorities, legislation or bureaucratic planning.

Shaping Trends

Social and societal trends repeatedly seen and noted by observers and deemed to be of unusual importance in that they both symbolise and promote large-scale change in the beliefs, values and behaviour of individuals and of society as a whole. Trends are deemed to be shaping trends if they meet the following three criteria: they are described by observers in several countries; the process out of which they emerge appears to remain a vigorous one; they embody and herald significant changes.

Single-storey Sociosystems

Non-hierarchical sociosystems (q.v.) that effectively operate with all their members working on an equal footing.

Social Radar

The capacity to navigate (q.v.) social situations skilfully that is born of empathy, improved social skills and greater awareness of oneself and one's emotional and physical feelings and sensations; a more acute awareness of what others are experiencing in a given social situation.

Socio-cultural Currents

Lasting changes in ways of thinking and mental models which lead people to act differently and lead whole populations to change their behaviour. These are not fluctuations or fashions but slow and steady currents, representing the diffusion of a particular tropism (q.v.) through a population.

Sociogenic

Tending to encourage the emergence of new social or societal forms and structures.

Sociological Microscope

The combination of research, interview and observation expertise, techniques and practices developed and used by the author and his colleagues at Cofremca/Sociovision. It allows its users to analyse society at the level of the individual and also at the level of systems.

Sociostructuring

See *Sociogenic*.

Sociosystem

Sociosystems are not just groups of people, nor are they organisations. They are self-organising, normally informal, interactive 'ensembles' that bring together individuals, collectives (q.v.) and even, sometimes institutions. They are not usually closed; rather they are open to other sociosystems. The civilising process (q.v.) strengthens their role at the expense of formal organisations and institutions and established authorities.

See Chapter 6 for more detail and see also *Interconnections and Inter-reactions*.

Spirals of conflict and violence

The feedback loops that characterise the 'Interconnections and Inter-reactions' (q.v.) that occur in and between sociosystems can be both 'positive' and 'negative'. In the latter case, this can lead to spirals of increasing violence and disorder or social alienation (which the author calls *effets pervers* or *processus pervers*). Such spirals can result both from inaction by the authorities (for example, a failure to intervene to improve education in poor areas) and from actions intended to have the opposite effect (for example, violent police intervention may provoke further unrest rather than restoring order).

Strategic Opportunism

See *Navigation*.

Tropism

A term that is generally applied to those forces that govern the movement of plants: that which tends to encourage a living organism to move in a certain direction. Used here to indicate the whole range of impulses (conscious or not) that lead someone to act in a certain way or move in a particular direction.

Vitalists

As polysensuality (q.v.) spread in the last three decades of the 20th century, more and more people explored their emotions and physical sensations and got in touch with their inner and somatic worlds and with those parts of themselves they had once dismissed as bestial: their instincts, drives, physicality, emotions and intuition. In so doing, people experienced a renewed vitality. In 1984, Cofremca decided to call those people most affected by the trend (about half the population at this time) Vitalists.

Weak Signals

Evidence of a change or trend that will affect how we live, behave, do business, etc. The weak signals are usually new and surprising to the signal receiver and are often difficult to track down amid other noise and signals. There is also, usually, a substantial lag time before the trend will mature and become mainstream – this represents an opportunity to learn, grow and evolve.

The author concentrates on socio-cultural, socio-economic, socio-technological, socio-political and socio-historical weak signals. Society speaks to those who take the trouble to listen. The weak signals (and sometimes strong ones) that it gives out help to support the hypotheses that we make about new currents, the strengthening or weakening of existing ones, changes of direction and possible future scenarios.

Acknowledgements

Thank you to sociologist Henri Mendras who read an earlier version of this book and whose advice and encouragement helped me a great deal.

This book would not have been possible without 50 years of work by the people at Cofremca and Sociovision who dedicated themselves to the study of the socio-cultural changes that were taking place over that period. But this book is a personal interpretation of the observations gathered by those teams and responsibility for it rests with the author.

I would like particularly to mention with gratitude the contributions of the following:

- Anne Catherine Lombroso, Yves Rickebusch and Michelle de Vulpian, at the end of the 1960s and early 1970s when the idea of 3SC was being conceived (Système Cofremca de Suivi des Courants Socio-Culturels).

- Yvan Corbeil (Montreal), the people at Data (Madrid), Gérard Demuth (Paris), Giampaolo Fabris (Milan), Carmen Lakajus (Frankfurt), Elizabeth Nelson (London), Jay Ogilvy and Peter Schwartz (San Francisco), Florence Skelly (New York), Pierre Wack (London) and Hans Zetterberg (Stockholm), for their contribution to observing and understanding the changes taking place in the 1970s and '80s.

- The people at Cofremca Sociovision (Paris), Sinus Sociovision (Heidelberg), Sociovision UK (London), CROP (Canada) and Environics (Canada and USA) and particularly Anne Chanon, Patrick Degrave, Jean Pierre Fourcat and Daniel Weber for observing and understanding the changes taking place in the 1990s.

Thank you also to Matthew Carey, Napier Collyns, Rosie Beckham and Andrew Carey for their help in publishing this English translation of the book.

About Triarchy Press

Triarchy Press is an independent publishing house that looks at how organisations work and how to make them work better. We present challenging perspectives on organisations in short and pithy, but rigorously argued, books.

We have published a number of books by authors who come from a Systems Thinking background. These include: *The Three Ways Of Getting Things Done* by Gerard Fairtlough; *Management F-Laws* by Russell Ackoff, Herb Addison and Sally Bibb; *Systems Thinking in the Public Sector* by John Seddon and *Erasing Excellence* (published in the USA as *Liberating the Schoolhouse*) by Wellford Wilms.

Through our books, viewpoints, e-publications and discussion area, we aim to stimulate ideas by encouraging real debate about organisations in partnership with people who work in them, research them or just like to think about them.

Please tell us what you think about the ideas in this book. Join the discussion at:

www.triarchypress.com/telluswhatyouthink

If you feel inspired to write - or have already written - an article, a viewpoint or a book on any aspect of organisational theory or practice, we'd like to hear from you. Submit a proposal at:

www.triarchypress.com/writeforus

For more information about Triarchy Press and Systems Thinking, or to order any of our publications, please visit our website or drop us a line:

www.triarchypress.com
info@triarchypress.com

Printed in the United Kingdom
by Lightning Source UK Ltd.
129736UK00001B/91-138/P